The United States Lifesaving Association Manual of Open Water Lifesaving

The United States Lifesaving Association Manual of Open Water Lifesaving

B. Chris Brewster

Editor

BRADY/Prentice Hall, Upper Saddle River, New Jersey 07458

Library of Congress Cataloging-in-Publication Data

The United States Lifesaving Association manual of open water
  lifesaving/B. Chris Brewster, editor.
      p. cm.
    Includes bibliographical references and index.
    ISBN 0-8359-4919-2
    1. Life-saving—Study and teaching—Handbooks, manuals, etc.
    2. Lifeguards—Training of—Handbooks, manuals, etc. I. Brewster,
  B. Chris, (date). II. United States Lifesaving Association.
GV838.68.U55 1995
797.2'0028'g—dc20   95-11842
                                                              CIP

Brady Production Manager: *Patrick Walsh*
Director of Production/Manufacturing: *Bruce Johnson*
Prepress/Manufacturing Buyer: *Ilene Sanford*
Production/Design: *Page Two Associates, Inc.*
Publisher: *Susan Katz*
Editorial Assistant: *Carol Sobel*
Cover Image: Allstock, ©*Marty Loken*
Cover Design: *Miguel Ortiz*
Printer/Binder: *Banta Printers*

©1995 by Prentice-Hall, Inc.
Upper Saddle River, New Jersey 07458

Printed in the United States of America

10 9 8 7 6 5 4

ISBN 0-8359-4919-2

PRENTICE-HALL INTERNATIONAL (UK) LIMITED, *LONDON*
PRENTICE-HALL OF AUSTRALIA PTY. LIMITED, *SYDNEY*
PRENTICE-HALL CANADA INC., *TORONTO*
PRENTICE-HALL HISPANOAMERICANA, S.A., *MEXICO*
PRENTICE-HALL OF INDIA PRIVATE LIMITED, *NEW DELHI*
PRENTICE-HALL OF JAPAN, INC., *TOKYO*
PRENTICE-HALL ASIA PTE. LTD., *SINGAPORE*
EDITORA PRENTICE-HALL DO BRASIL, LTDA., *RIO DE JANEIRO*

We gratefully dedicate this text
to the men and women who have
risked their lives in the water
for the lives of others
and to those who gave their lives in the effort.

CONTENTS

PREFACE

This manual is meant to be used as a guide in the instruction and training of open water lifeguards, a reference for professional lifeguards, and a yardstick against which beach lifeguard agencies can measure their performance. It is the product of the combined knowledge of the members of the United States Lifesaving Association (USLA), the only national association of beach lifeguards at both surf and inland beaches. While there have been many texts written for instruction of pool lifeguards, some of which also reference inland beaches, we know of no other text which has focused on the role of lifesaving at ocean and inland beaches in a comprehensive manner.

In many countries of the world, lifesaving evolved under the umbrella of a national organization which set standards from the beginning. This resulted in universally consistent operating procedures and training levels. In America, however, each beach lifeguard agency has historically developed unique training programs and standards.

For many years, agencies charged with protecting visitors at open water beaches in the United States have called for the establishment of clear, objective training programs for professional lifeguards. Organizations with interests in water safety have struggled with the concept and the procedures for providing that training.

One of the most significant events in the development of lifeguard training programs occurred in 1980, when leaders from water safety organizations across the country gathered at Texas A&M University in Galveston for a "Conference to Develop Guidelines for Establishing Open-Water Recreational Beach Standards." This conference was conducted in an effort to address the extraordinary challenge of creating nationwide standards for the diversity of conditions found at beaches throughout the United States.

Armed with the findings of the conference, and with hundreds of aggregate years of open water lifeguard management experience, members of the USLA National Certification Committee began meetings to develop a national lifeguard training program. Problems with a project of this scope surfaced immediately. How could one training program meet the needs of every lifeguard agency in the United States? Could one program be applicable at both a large, urban, year-round beach operation in Southern California and at a small, seasonal beach operation in the Northeast? How should local variances in water conditions, climate, aquatic life, beach attendance, and other aspects of beach management be handled?

USLA moved ahead in 1981 with the publication of our first manual, *Lifesaving and Marine Safety*, and the USLA National Certification Committee began to assemble a list of standards to accompany it. The most immediate product of their labors was the 1983 publication of a booklet entitled *Guidelines for Open Water Lifeguard Training*. The contents of this booklet immediately served as a model for beach lifeguard agencies throughout the United States, but there remained a desire on the part of USLA and open water lifeguard agencies for more — a program to certify beach lifeguards and the standards of beach lifeguard agencies.

In 1992 a newly composed National Certification Committee amended and added to the 1983 guidelines to create *Guidelines for Open Water Lifeguard Training and Standards,* along with the national USLA Lifeguard Agency Certification Program. This program creates a set of clearly defined guidelines and minimum recommended standards for beach lifeguard agencies and allows agencies in compliance to become nationally certified. These agencies are then empowered to certify the lifeguards they train as having successfully completed a USLA certified training course.

During the many years of work by the National Certification Committee, another committee was formed to revise the textbook. Dr. James McCloy, then Director of the Center for Marine Training and Safety, Texas A&M University at Galveston and a member of the Gulf Coast Region of USLA, initially headed this committee. Later, it was chaired by Charles Hartl of the Mid-Atlantic Region. The task of rewriting the text was given to Tim Hall of New England, who did a yeoman's job in beginning a compilation of the aggregate experience of lifeguards from throughout the United States into a single, authoritative text. Mr. Hall completed a draft update in 1991, but several obstacles to publication remained and the effort was delayed until development of the Lifeguard Agency Certification Program in 1992 created a major impetus to finally bring about publication of a USLA manual.

When the National Certification Committee updated the guidelines in 1992, the committee chair was B. Chris Brewster, Lifeguard Chief for the City of San Diego. He was asked by USLA President William J. Richardson to chair the USLA National Textbook Committee with a goal of updating the text a final time and bringing about publication.

A publisher was found and a newly composed National Textbook Committee, made up of representatives from across the United States, convened in Chicago in February of 1994. At this final meeting, extensive work was done to update the manuscript over which Tim Hall had toiled. Subsequently, hundreds of hours of research and editing coalesced the many recommendations of the committee.

The extraordinary efforts required to compile this manual were not the work of paid USLA staff members, for none were available. Rather, it was a labor of love and dedication to the lifesaving profession. The lifeguards involved gave of their free time unselfishly and with a common purpose.

MISSION OF THE UNITED STATES LIFESAVING ASSOCIATION

The mission of the United States Lifesaving Association is to establish and maintain high standards for open water (beach) lifeguards, to educate the public, and to promote actions intended to result in the saving of human life in and around the aquatic environment.

ABOUT THE UNITED STATES LIFESAVING ASSOCIATION

The United States Lifesaving Association (USLA) is a nonprofit membership organization. Membership is critical to support USLA's mission and is open to anyone.

To qualify for *Regular Membership* an individual must be a current member of an ocean, bay, river, or other open water lifesaving or rescue service. Our regular membership includes seasonal lifeguards, full time lifeguards, lifeguard supervisors, and lifeguard chiefs from virtually every major ocean lifeguard service in the U.S., along with those of the Great Lakes and many inland open water areas.

Associate Membership is available to those who do not qualify for regular membership.

Junior Lifeguard Membership is available to youths who are active participants in a junior lifeguard program affiliated with a local USLA Chapter.

Corporate Membership, Honorary Membership, and the position of *Chief Patron* may be designated by the Board of Directors.

For further information, write:

> USLA Secretary
> PO Box 366
> Huntington Beach, California 92648

EDITOR'S NOTE

- This text represents the collective knowledge of lifeguards associated with the most highly regarded lifeguard agencies in the United States. It is intended to be a comprehensive text essential to the effective training and retraining of open water lifeguards. Each beach lifeguard agency in America faces unique challenges posed by the local environment and the particular assignments of its personnel. Therefore, this text will only be fully effective when used in conjunction with a training program in compliance with the USLA Lifeguard Agency Certification Program and supplemented by appropriate specialized training addressing local conditions.

- This text does not and cannot stand alone as a lifeguard training manual. It has been deliberately written to be used in conjunction with an agency's lifeguard manual, which must contain the specific policies and procedures pertaining to the information provided in this text.

- THE MATERIAL CONTAINED IN THIS TEXT CONSTITUTES THE CONSIDERED AND EXPERT OPINION OF THE AUTHORS AND USLA. THE AUTHORS AND USLA MAKE NO EXPRESS OR IMPLIED WARRANTY OR GUARANTEE AS TO THE MATERIAL, OPINIONS, OR METHODS CONTAINED IN THIS TEXT.

- The procedures, techniques, and equipment used in open water lifeguarding are constantly changing and improving. It has only been through experimentation over the years by more forward thinking lifeguards and lifeguard agencies that innovative lifesaving techniques have been developed. This process must continue if we are to face the challenge of the future.

ACKNOWLEDGMENTS

It is difficult, if not impossible, to acknowledge the contributions of every person connected to the production of this manual. It was created, revised, written, and reviewed by committees of the United States Lifesaving Association on the national, regional, and chapter level. Literally hundreds of professional lifeguards and lifeguard administrators added their knowledge and expertise to the text. Special appreciation, however, should be expressed to key contributors.

Tim Hall of Maine started the process moving by completing extensive work during the initial update of the manuscript.

The entire 1994 Textbook Committee, who met in Chicago in an unprecedented editorial effort, must be thanked extensively. They are:

- Dan McCormick, Aquatic Administrative Analyst, East Bay Regional Park District, San Francisco Bay Area, who also worked tirelessly to coordinate the photographs.
- David M. Shotwell, Sr., Beachfront Supervisor, Ocean Grove, New Jersey, who also worked to expand upon the Glossary and Emergency Planning and Management chapter, and provided far more information on dories than was requested.

- Peter Wernicki, MD, Medical Advisor to USLA, who, though a computer illiterate, chaired a sub-committee which compiled the Medical Care chapter and conveyed the information on a diskette.
- Mike L. Hensler, Sr., Lifeguard Lieutenant, Volusia County, Florida, who also provided a wealth of valuable photographs.
- Don C. Rohrer, Lifeguard Chief, County of Los Angeles
- Jerome Gavin, Lifeguard Captain, Beach and Pool Unit, Chicago Park District
- William McNeely, Jr., Chief of Marine Safety, St. Lucie County, Florida
- Kim W. Tyson, Aquatic Coordinator, University of Texas at Austin
- Carl Martinez, Water Safety Coordinator, Gateway National Recreation Area, National Park Service

Members of the Los Angeles County Lifeguard Service made extensive recommendations to the 1994 Textbook Committee and did further work to assist in creation of the generic report forms.

Dr. John Fletemeyer, Chief of Ocean Rescue, Town of Palm Beach, Florida, contributed information on marine life.

Kenna Kay, with the able assistance of George Bates, contributed her artistic expertise in producing the line drawings.

Douglas G. D'Arnall, former Director of Community Services, Huntington Beach, California; Don C. Rohrer, Lifeguard Chief, Los Angeles County; Bob Shea, former Lifeguard Captain, City of San Diego; and Richard Mark deserve recognition for the tremendous work they contributed to the forerunner of this text, *Lifesaving and Marine Safety*.

William J. Richardson, President of USLA and Joseph A. Pecoraro, Past President of USLA must be recognized for their leadership in encouraging the production of quality training materials for America's lifeguards.

This text is a testament to the memory of Bruce Baird, Lifeguard Chief, City of Laguna Beach, California, and past Vice-President, United States Lifesaving Association, who dedicated his life to the furtherance of lifesaving.

Special thanks are extended to the lifeguard agencies of the United States, which have shared the expertise of their lifeguards and administrators in the completion of this manual.

B. Chris Brewster, Editor

LIFESAVING HISTORY

Chapter Highlights

The First American Lifesavers

Roots of Modern Lifeguarding

Modern Lifeguarding

In This Chapter

One of the most gallant and skillful crews in the [U.S. Lifesaving] service was lost at Point aux Barques, Lake Huron, in October, 1880, and the heart-rending details of the calamity are known to the world through its sole survivor. These loyal men went out in the surf-boat in prompt response to a signal of distress displayed upon a vessel three miles away. The boat was capsized and righted several times, but finally remained capsized, the men clinging to it; but the cold was such that one after another perished, until six were gone... These heroic men had during the same year saved nearly a hundred lives.[1]

THE FIRST AMERICAN LIFESAVERS

The first lifesavers in America rarely worked during summer. Most of their work came during fall, winter, and spring and much of it was accomplished in the dead of night. There were cold and lonely vigils, sometimes in snowstorms, as lifesavers met each other on foot patrols along desolate beaches. Consider the following passage from the 1884 Annual Report of the U.S. Lifesaving Service describing one of the scores of dramatic rescues by lifesavers that year. This one took place April 3 in Wellfleet, Massachusetts, on the outer shore of Cape Cod. It involved the schooner Viking, "on her way from George's Bank with a fare of fish, for Boston."

> "At a few minutes after 2 in the morning, the weather being rainy and dark, with a strong northeast wind blowing and a rough sea, Surfman F.H. Daniels, of the Cahoon's Hollow [Lifesaving] Station... saw a bright light ahead which he at

first supposed to be the station on fire, but which after a moment's reflection he concluded from its bearing must be the distress signal of a stranded vessel. He at once started on a run and in a short time arrived abreast of a schooner aground in the breakers about 50 yards from the beach… two miles north of the station [and any assistance from other surfmen].

His first thought was to keep on and alarm his comrades, but upon considering the time it would take to get to the station he determined on a bold effort to save the vessel's crew single handed. The bright light that had attracted his attention was still burning when he arrived, and proved to be some clothing saturated with kerosene oil which the crew had ignited as a signal for aid.

The whole scene was brilliantly illuminated by it, and the sailors, seeing Daniels arrive, watched their opportunity and threw him the end of a lead line. This he managed to secure by rushing down into the surf, and in a few minutes the end of a larger line was bent to it and drawn ashore. One of the men then secured the bight of the rope around his body, and, with a shout to Daniels to haul away, plunged into the boiling surf. The gallant surfman was equal to the task, and, with the water waist deep around him, he pulled on the rope and succeeded in landing the man all right, the latter exclaiming, as he staggered to his feet upon reaching the beach, "For God's sake, who are you?" The reply of Daniels was brief and to the point: "I am a life-saving man, and you must lend me a hand to save the rest."

At a signal from Daniels the line was quickly hauled back, and in a short time the entire crew, twelve in all, were safely landed… It was about 3 o'clock when the last man was drawn ashore and then Daniels, after turning the water out of his hip boots, started with the wrecked crew for the station…."[2]

After this rescue, the schooner's owner wrote, "The circumstances under which this crew was saved were those of the most extreme peril, not only to themselves but also to the gallant man who, single-handed, attempted and providentially achieved their rescue. His name is not known to us, but we think his deed one worthy to be widely known and well rewarded."[3]

During the late 1700s, much of the American coastline was totally uninhabited. Life was hard and recreational swimming was of little interest. Yet loss of life due to drowning was a serious problem. Shipwrecks were the reason.

With today's modern navigational aids and high powered vessels, shipwrecks are relatively uncommon, but prior to these advancements, sailing ships were navigated by compass, sextant, and educated guess. They were always at the mercy of nature. Storms and inclement weather, particularly in winter, brought tragedy time and time again as ships foundered along the American coastline. In the mid-1800s on Massachusetts' Cape Cod alone, shipwrecks occurred at an estimated frequency of once every two or three weeks.[4] Few people could swim and the sometimes frigid waters were unmerciful to even the most hardy swimmer. Passengers were often left to drown as their ships broke up a short distance from shore.

The first organized efforts at lifesaving began with the founding of the Massachusetts Humane Society in 1786.[5] The Humane Society built houses of refuge along the Massachusetts coast for shipwreck survivors and in 1807 the Society set up the nation's first lifeboat station on Cape Cod. By the mid-1800s, the Massachusetts Humane Society operated 18 stations with lifeboats and line-throwing equipment.[6]

In 1839 William A. Newell, a New Jersey physician witnessed a shipwreck near Long Beach, New Jersey, and watched as 13 people drowned trying to swim 300 yards to safety. The doctor remembered this tragedy and later, as a New Jersey Congressman, helped to persuade the U.S. government to become involved in lifesaving. In 1848, Congress appropriated $10,000 which was spent to build and equip eight small lifeboat stations along the New Jersey coast between Sandy Hook and Little Egg Harbor. The Massachusetts Humane Society provided assistance in the endeavor.[7] The next year, $20,000 was appropriated and provided to the Life-Saving Benevolent Association of New York for the purpose of building lifesaving stations along Long Island.

At first, lifesaving stations were simple unstaffed houses of refuge containing basic lifesaving equipment. Keys to the stations were left with local townspeople who, by following a list of printed instructions, were expected to rig and use the equipment to save those stranded aboard foundering ships. While this system resulted in some success and occasionally heroic rescues, without a posted watch many shipwrecks went undetected along uninhabited stretches of the coast. In these cases the occupants perished before any lifesaving efforts could be mounted. In addition, volunteer lifesavers from local towns were sometimes simply unable to effectively employ the lifesaving equipment due to lack of skill and training. Occasionally, lifeboat stations were vandalized and lifesaving equipment stolen. They eventually became run down and of little use.

By 1854 the magnitude of the problem could no longer be ignored. Congress appropriated additional funds to hire a superintendent for the Long Island and New Jersey coasts and a keeper for each station.[8] The keepers were initially paid an annual salary of $200.[9] Patrols were organized and station keepers were expected to walk the coastline at night, regardless of the weather, to detect shipwrecks. Despite these advances, however, there were no funds for maintenance, no regular lifesaving staff to depend on in emergencies, and no regulations to follow. Without a paid lifesaving staff, regular drills could not be organized to effectively prepare the volunteers for rescues.

During the Civil War the system deteriorated, but once the war was over, Congress again turned its attention to lifesaving. In 1869 the Revenue Marine Division was established to combine administration of lifesaving stations, the Revenue Cutter Service, steamboat inspection, and marine hospitals. The Revenue Cutter Service had initially been established in 1790 as an arm of the Treasury Department with a goal of revenue protection—enforcing payment of customs and tonnage duties—but beginning in 1832, vessels of this service had been assigned to cruise the coast during winter months to assist ships in distress.[10] Sumner Increase Kimball was appointed to administrate the Revenue Marine Division in 1871, and was to be the single most important influence in early lifesaving.

Congress appropriated additional funds to staff lifesaving stations on a seasonal basis, but as Kimball toured the stations shortly after his appointment, he was disappointed to find many in deplorable condition. Some keepers were not even living at the stations. Kimball embarked upon a crusade to improve the quality of the service. He enacted regulations, inspected the stations on a regular basis, and discharged those who failed to measure up.

Despite advances, funding continued to be a serious problem. The appropriation for 1877–78 was so low that the lifesaving stations could not open until December. Unfortunately, in late November of that year the steamer Huron grounded along the North Carolina Coast and, in the absence of lifesavers, 98 persons were lost. In the wake of this disaster, in 1878 Congress appropriated funds to create a separate organization, the U.S. Lifesaving Service, with Kimball to be its first and only leader.

During Kimball's tenure, crews were employed to staff each station and the stations' size and comfort facilities were expanded. Most stations were staffed with six surfmen and an Officer in Charge (the keeper). Professionalism in the system grew as strict regulations were set for competence, performance, routine beach patrols, and physical conditioning. The system eventually grew to comprise 189 lifesaving stations—139 on the Atlantic coast from Maine to Florida, 37 on the Great Lakes, seven on the Pacific coast, and one in Ohio.[11]

Like other emergency responders, lifesavers worked long and often tedious shifts, with daily drills and monotonous foot patrols throughout the night. But once the cry, "Ship ashore" was sounded, the boredom was replaced by heroism in harrowing and exhausting struggles with the sea to save lives. When this happened, the primary tools of the early lifesavers were the breeches buoy and lifeboats.

Lifeboats used on the Great Lakes and most of the Pacific coast were self-righting and self-bailing with air chambers to prevent capsizing. They weighed about four thousand pounds and were generally launched from safe harbors. In some cases, tugs would pull them to the mouth of a harbor, where the lifesavers aboard would take over using eight oars for propulsion. According to an 1880 article in *Scribner's Monthly,* "It is a common occurrence for the life-boats to go under sail and oars ten or twelve miles from their stations to the assistance of vessels in distress."[12]

The lifeboats most commonly associated with early lifesavers were those used along the Atlantic coast. These wooden boats weighed 700 to 1,000 pounds and were about twenty-five to thirty feet in length. Some had air chambers at either end to help prevent swamping, but they were not self-righting or self-bailing. The Atlantic lifeboats were generally rowed by a crew of six surfmen, with the station keeper at a sweep oar.

Atlantic lifeboats were stored inside the lifesaving stations. When duty called, they were rowed by lifesavers wearing primitive lifejackets and oilskins, to repel water. Since lifesaving stations were miles apart, Atlantic coast lifeboats had to be moved along the beach in wagons drawn through the soft sand. This effort alone could sap the strength of lifesavers, so some stations eventually acquired horses to draw the wagons.[13]

Most Atlantic coast rescues involved boats aground on bars near the beach, having been driven there by storm surf. Since the Atlantic coast lifeboats were vulnerable to capsizing, when seas were high and the wrecked vessel near shore, lifesavers turned instead to the breeches buoy apparatus.

The breeches buoy itself was actually a large life ring. Canvas was slung loosely across the center with two holes for the legs of a victim, forming a sort of trousers. The victim could hang securely in the breeches buoy with legs through the holes and the life ring under the armpits. The device used to deploy the breeches buoy was more complex.

When a grounded vessel could not be safely reached by use of a lifeboat due to surf or other weather conditions, the lifesavers brought out the breeches buoy apparatus on a beach cart. The apparatus consisted primarily of a wooden crotch, extensive amounts of line on large reels, lighter lead line in a faking box, and apparatus to throw the lead line to the vessel in distress. The wooden faking box had upturned, gently pointed pegs inside, around which strong linen thread was neatly laid, ready to easily play out when one end of the line was thrown or shot.

Beach cart with the full breeches buoy apparatus aboard. Lifesavers would pull this cart through the sand to the point of the rescue. [Photographic Credit: Brian Feeney, National Park Service]

The first step was to get a line to the foundering vessel. If the ship was close enough, a heaving stick was used. With light lead line attached to this weighted stick, it could reportedly be thrown up to 50 yards.[14] When the ship was out of reach of a heaving stick, the Lyle gun was employed.

The Lyle gun was a small 163 pound canon, developed by Captain David A. Lyle of the U.S. Army in 1877. The lifesavers would fire a projectile from the Lyle gun toward the rigging of the foundering ship. Attached to the projectile was one end of the linen thread from the faking box. With this thread attached, the projectile could be shot up to 400 yards.[15] If the shot was a good one, the line became entangled in the rigging of the foundering ship. If not, the line was retrieved and another attempt made. Sometimes, repeated attempts were required.

One hazard of the Lyle gun was its violent recoil. In the interest of keeping the gun light and portable, Lyle eliminated much of the weight normally used to minimize recoil. Modern tests suggest that in some cases recoil of the gun may have been as much as 16 feet.[16]

Once a connection was made to those aboard the ship, heavier line would be attached to the lead line by the lifesavers ashore and persons aboard the ship would draw it aboard. Directions were provided to the shipwrecked victims on a wooden

Lyle gun. [Photographic Credit: Brian Feeney, National Park Service]

The Lyle gun is fired during a drill toward a practice target intended to simulate ships rigging. Note heavy projectile with line attached and faking box in the foreground with upturned pegs. [Photographic Credit: Brian Feeney, National Park Service]

pallet attached to the heavier line. These explained how to make the line fast to a high point in the rigging. Meanwhile, the lifesavers erected the wooden crotch on the beach, to provide a high point for the shore end of the line, and anchored it in the sand. Eventually, both ends of the heavy line were made fast and the line was drawn taught.

The breeches buoy was hung from the line on a pulley and drawn back and forth by use of a separate line. When it worked properly, victims on board the ship could be pulled ashore one at a time, sitting in the breeches buoy without even touching the water.

During a drill, a victim sits in the breeches buoy while being pulled toward the wooden crotch, which would be erected on the beach. [Photographic Credit: Dave Foxwell (photo of a National Park Service display)]

Lifecar [Photographic Credit: Dave Foxwell]

Lifecars were also used in some cases. Like the breeches buoy, these devices were hung from the hawser and pulled back and forth. They were made of copper or iron and enclosed with bolts. Three or four adults could be squeezed inside.

An example of use of the Lyle gun and breeches buoy occurred one snowy December night in 1879, and is recorded in the Annual Report of the U.S. Lifesaving Service for that year:

"At 2:30 a.m. the patrol of Station No. 14, Second District, Massachusetts, discovered a vessel at anchor about a mile and a half east-northeast of the station, burning a torch as a signal of distress. He answered the signal and returned to the station for help. The lifesaving crew on reaching the shore found it impossible to launch the boat through the breakers. The keeper then sent to Station No. 13 for assistance, and in the meantime went north abreast of the distressed vessel and showed signals to her and caused fires to be built to show her the deepest water in case her chains should part. The wind was blowing a strong gale with blinding snow squalls, and a heavy sea was running.

When the crew of No. 13 arrived it was evident that the vessel was dragging toward shore. The lifesaving men now brought the mortar cart with the Lyle gun and equipment abreast of the vessel, which was now near the breakers. The first shot took the line across the headstays, but the crew were so exhausted and benumbed that they were unable to get to it. The second shot laid the line over the fore-yard and was happily made fast.

The breeches buoy was then taken aboard, and in thirty minutes the entire crew, eight men, were landed in safety, though five of them were in such a helpless condition that they had to be assisted to the station, where they were furnished with hot drinks, dry clothing, and comfortable beds."[17]

Lifesavers patrolled the beaches on foot throughout the night, awakened in turn for their watch. They would walk to a halfway point to the next station, exchange a brass "check" with a lifesaver from the neighboring station, and return to wake up the next lifesaver whose turn it was to patrol. The check proved that the patrol had been completed. If a ship was sighted near shore, the lifesavers would burn a red coston signal (a flare) as a warning to turn away.

Although the work was sometimes tedious, the rescues were often harrowing and sometimes lethal. Regulations stated, "You have to go out."[18] Discretion in the face of adversity was not an option. J. H. Merryman, writing in *Scribner's Monthly,* quoted a lifesaver as saying, "When I see a man clinging to a wreck, I see nothing else in the world, and I never think of family and friends until I have saved him."[19]

Heroism of the lifesavers became legendary, particularly considering the fear of open water that many people of the day harbored. *Harper's Monthly* reported the following incident, "One of the most gallant and skillful crews in the service was lost at Point aux Barques, Lake Huron, in October, 1880, and the heart-rending details of the calamity are known to the world through its sole survivor. These loyal men went out in the surf-boat in prompt response to a signal of distress displayed upon a vessel three miles away. The boat was capsized and righted several times, but finally remained capsized, the men clinging to it; but the cold was such that one after another perished, until six were gone. The keeper drifted upon the beach, insensible, and was found steadying himself by the trunk of a tree... These heroic men had during the same year saved nearly a hundred lives."[20]

Another famous incident was known as the Monomoy disaster. On March 17, 1902 a lifeboat crewed by eight lifesavers had picked up five victims from the Wadena, a distressed vessel off Monomoy Point on Cape Cod, Massachusetts. As the lifesavers were making their way back to shore, the victims panicked and the lifeboat was overcome in high seas. All but one of the lifesavers perished, as did all of the victims.

According to the report of the U.S. Life Saving Service for 1902, "The loss of the 7 lifesaving men who so nobly perished created everywhere a sense of profound sorrow. There was no more skillful or fearless crew on the whole coast, and since it appeared that the Wadena remained safe for days after the disaster, there was a general conviction that the men were practically a sacrifice, on the one hand to the needless apprehensions and senseless panic of the men from the [Wadena], and on the other to their own high sense of duty, which would not permit them to turn their backs upon a signal of distress. 'We must go' said the keeper, 'there is a distress flag in the rigging.'" Over $45,000 was raised to help the widows and orphans of the drowned men and a monument was placed ashore in memory of the victims. It can be found today at the Coast Guard Station in Chatham, Massachusetts.[21]

In its short lifetime, the U.S. Lifesaving Service amassed a truly extraordinary record—28,121 vessels aided and 178,741 people saved. In 1915, the Lifesaving Service was again merged with the Revenue Cutter Service, this time to form the United States Coast Guard. Sumner Kimball retired after 43 years of service, but the lifesavers continued on in their duties as part of the Coast Guard for many years thereafter. As navigational aids improved and powered vessels became the norm, shipwrecks occurred with diminishing frequency. The need for skilled persons to go out through the surf in lifeboats slowly dwindled. The last known use of the breeches buoy was in 1962.[22]

Memorial to the Monomoy lifesavers, Chatham, Massachusetts. [Photographic Credit: Kenna Kay]

ROOTS OF MODERN LIFEGUARDING

During the late 1800s, life in America began to change as the country grew. Americans became more prosperous and less dependent on constant work for survival. Recreation time was on the rise and Americans discovered that recreational swimming, once widely thought to be a sure cause of death, was an enjoyable pastime. Beach resorts sprang up along the coastline and on lakes. Governments began to acquire beachfront property and guarantee public access specifically for the purpose of recreation. By the 1890s, open water swimming was all the rage, but it was not without risk.

Newspapers buzzed with reports of drownings, particularly when several lives were lost in a storm surf or rip current. In many areas, lifeboats and swimming lines, to which swimmers could cling, were standard equipment, but as was found in earlier efforts to save shipwreck victims, provision of equipment alone was inadequate without the presence of trained lifesavers to employ it. In reaction, beach resorts began to hire especially good swimmers to "guard" the beach. Local governments, spurred on by public pressure, also began to hire what became known as lifeguards for publicly owned or controlled beaches.

Still there were drownings. The Young Men's Christian Association (YMCA) was very concerned about recreational drownings and became active in developing the concept of "lifesaving"—which they defined as preparing lay people with the skills necessary to rescue fellow swimmers in trouble. The YMCA entered into the lifesaving field in the late 1880s and established the United Volunteer Lifesaving

Corps in 1890 to provide rescue services at beaches and pools not staffed with lifeguards. In 1911, lifesaving work and research was established at the YMCA's national college in Springfield, Massachusetts. The national YMCA Lifesaving Service was organized in 1912. The first published American book on lifesaving was written as a thesis at Springfield College by George Goss in 1913, and was eventually published as a lifesaving textbook in 1916. This book was first promoted as *Water First Aid*.

In 1914, Commodore Wilbert E. Longfellow formed the Life Saving Service of the American Red Cross, a corps of volunteers recruited and trained to provide rescues at beaches not regularly patrolled by lifeguards. Not being satisfied that this adequately addressed the drowning problem, Commodore Longfellow recruited the strongest swimmers from the Corps to teach swimming to beach visitors. He began a program to "waterproof America" by teaching people to swim, and by training lay people in the skills necessary to rescue a drowning person. His slogan, "Everyone a swimmer, every swimmer a lifesaver," became the motto of early Red Cross programs that taught swimming, water safety, and lifesaving to many children and adults.

At the same time that these efforts took hold, professional beach lifeguard services were being created across the United States. There was little consistency among these services, largely due to the lack of a national organization charged with setting standards for the new profession. This was unusual compared to other countries, such as those of the British Commonwealth, where lifesaving societies were chartered and mandated to set standards for lifeguard operations.

In some countries, lifesaving societies actually supervised and ran lifeguard operations, regardless of who owned or had responsibility for the open water recreation site. The U.S. government failed to charter or mandate such an organization, and lifeguard professionals did not start one themselves. In fact, the pioneering American lifesaving organizations declined to become involved in professional lifeguarding, contending that their programs were intended to promote safe swimming and provide training in personal rescue techniques for lay people, not professional lifeguards.

As in the case of the first lifesavers, great tragedies often precipitated the creation of public lifeguard services. In Atlantic City, New Jersey, seasonal lifeguards were first hired in 1872 in the wake of 13 drownings. Their salaries were initially paid in part by the railroads, whose owners wished to encourage trips to the beaches. Later, the Atlantic City Council took over paying the lifeguard's salaries.[23]

Lifeguards were not hired by the City of San Diego until 1918 when 13 people drowned on a single day in flash rip currents. Gradually, beach lifeguard services were created by local governments as the need became evident. They used techniques that had evolved from the U.S. Lifesaving Service, along with the growing body of knowledge being developed by the lifesaving programs of the American Red Cross and the YMCA. Many agencies utilized the expertise of other professional emergency services, including police and fire departments. By the end of the 1930s, publicly employed lifeguards had become a common site at many beaches across the United States.

At the same time that open water recreation became established as a major national pastime, acquisition of park systems and provision of recreational opportunities came to be seen as an important role of government. Recreation programs and departments were created on a national and local level. During the Great Depression, numerous federal public works projects involved construction of recreation facilities. After the Depression, many of these facilities were turned over to local and state recreation agencies, and lifeguards were added to operation staffs.

During World War II, the male dominated profession of lifeguarding was impacted by recruitment of men into the armed forces. As was the case in other professions, women sometimes filled the vacancies that were created. In some areas of the country, where beach lifeguards were seen as essential public safety providers, waivers were provided so that trained and experienced lifeguards could stay on the beach.

Lifeguard equipment also evolved significantly during this period. Line reels and dories had been adapted from use in shipwreck incidents to use in swimming rescues. When the famous Duke Paoa Kanhanamoku, father of Hawaiian surfing, visited the west coast in 1913, he introduced his redwood surfboard to Long Beach, California lifeguards. Eventually, surfboards came to be used as rescue devices and an important tool for beach lifeguards.

The first rescue floatation device (RFD) was developed in 1897 by Captain Harry Sheffield for a lifesaving club in South Africa. It was four feet long, pointed at both ends, and quite heavy. The design was modified in the United States where the heavy sheet metal was replaced with copper, then aluminum.

Some original rescue buoys. They were often known as "can" buoys because of their metal construction. [Photographic Credit: Mike Hensler]

Shortly after World War II, Pete Peterson, a rescue boat operator for the City of Santa Monica lifeguard service, came to believe there was a need for an RFD which could somehow be wrapped around the victim. Unable to find a foam rubber product compatible with water use, he created an inflatable, bright yellow RFD with a snap hook molded onto one end and a 14" strap on the other. A line and harness were then attached to the strap for use. This highly visible, reasonably durable RFD was used by many lifeguard services into the early 1960s. The inflatable rescue floatation device had one significant draw-back—if used around piers or rocks, the RFD could be punctured and deflated.

In response to the problem of punctures, Peterson redesigned the inflatable RFD, constructing it of flexible, open cell foam with an orange skin to keep water out of the foam. While this was an improvement, the skin was still subject to piercing and the open cell foam eventually became waterlogged. By the late 1960s however, closed cell synthetic foam was invented and the tube was perfected to a form which today is used around the world. This RFD is widely known as the Peterson tube.[24]

The next major breakthrough in RFD design occurred in the mid-1960s. Steve Morgan, a seasonal lifeguard in Los Angeles County, designed an RFD to be constructed of hard plastic. His design was based on the original torpedo buoy, but with a more streamlined shape and inset handles for easy gripping by both victims and lifeguards. A University of California at Los Angeles professor, Ron Rezek, had developed a manufacturing process called rotational molding, ideally suited to production of a plastic RFD. Rezek added a rear handle to Morgan's design and won first place in an industrial design contest. When Morgan encountered difficulty in funding production of the device, he shared his ideas with Lt. Bob Burnside of Los Angeles County and asked for assistance in bringing the project to fruition. Burnside funded the project and the first "Burnside buoys" were on the beach in 1972. Buoys of this design are now a basic tool of open water lifeguards.[25]

As lifesaving equipment evolved, so did lifeguard agencies. Unlike police and fire services with centuries of history, professional lifeguards were relatively new providers of public safety, and their place in governmental structures varied greatly. In areas where lifeguards were on duty year round, some lifeguard services became divisions of other safety services or were organized into separate departments. These organizational structures gave the lifeguards a stature equivalent to that of police officers or firefighters. In other areas, beach lifeguard services were administered as part of recreation programs or park systems, and lifeguards were sometimes titled as "recreation assistants" or "program aides." This perception of lifeguards persisted in many areas of the United States well into the 1960s until two events changed the course of professional lifeguarding.

MODERN LIFEGUARDING

In 1966, the National Academy of Sciences published a document entitled *Accidental Death and Disability: The Neglected Disease of Modern Society.* This document outlined a poor state of training and service standards for emergency medical care providers in the United States, where many ambulance attendants had little or no training beyond basic first aid. It helped to spur passage of the nation's Highway Safety Act of 1966, which charged the U.S. Department of Transportation with the development and establishment of an Emergency Medical Service Standard. Thus began the development of training standards leading to the establishment of the certification known as "Emergency Medical Technician" and the standards in emergency medical care now taken for granted in the United States.

Recognizing the problems in the nation's emergency medical services also motivated citizen groups and government organizations to carefully evaluate training and service standards for other emergency services, including police, fire, and beach lifeguard services. It became evident that many lifeguard agencies worked with little or no formal training. Others required training aimed at "drown proofing" the general public, rather than preparing professional rescuers. Many had wrongly considered pool lifesaving training adequate for beach lifeguards, even those assigned to the most treacherous surf beaches.

It became clear that pool and open water environments are incomparable for purposes of training or standards. As a result, beach lifeguards began to seek specialized training for their unique environment. None being available, more progressive lifeguard agencies developed their own standards, networking with each other for consistency and validation of their practices. Nonetheless, the beach lifeguard profession suffered greatly for lack of state or national standards.

The second major development to impact open water lifeguarding took place in 1964. In that year, professional lifeguard agencies along the coast of California, encouraged by the success of similar groups in other countries, formed the National Surf Life Saving Association of America. By 1979, this organization had expanded its membership to include all inland open water and surf lifeguards across the country, and became known as the United States Lifesaving Association (USLA). For the first time, American lifeguard agencies and professional lifeguards had a national organization they could use to exchange information on professional techniques, lifesaving equipment, lifeguard agency organization, and other items of concern. Two main goals have been maintained by the USLA since its inception: 1) to establish and maintain high standards of professional open water lifesaving, and 2) to educate the public in water safety and the role of lifeguards.

In 1980, a conference held at the University of Texas A & M brought together all of the major American organizations concerned with promoting public safety in and around the aquatic environment. The intent of the conference was to discuss ways to develop standards for open water lifeguards. The result was a Sea Grant funded publication entitled *Guidelines for Establishing Open-Water Recreational Beach Standards.*[26]

The following year, the first USLA textbook, *Lifesaving and Marine Safety,* was published. In 1983, USLA published a booklet entitled *Guidelines for Open Water Lifeguard Training* that set the first nationwide recommended standards for open water lifeguards at both inland and surf beaches. Ten years later in 1993, the USLA revised the original guidelines and published *Guidelines for Open Water Lifeguard Training and Standards,* which was designed as the basis for the first national certification program for both inland and surf beach lifeguards. In that same year, the USLA launched the Lifeguard Agency Certification Program to provide an independent review of beach lifeguard programs, and to encourage lifeguard agencies across the country to meet minimum standards for open water lifeguarding.

These publications, along with the ongoing work of USLA training committees, have greatly added to the body of knowledge used by beach lifeguard agencies, and enhanced development of an image of the lifeguard as a professional emergency provider. Today, the USLA is known nationally and internationally as an authoritative body in the field of open water lifeguarding and marine safety. USLA guidelines are required by law in some areas for training newly hired lifeguards.

The profession of lifeguarding will always be unique among emergency services due largely to its highly seasonal nature. In Florida, California, and Hawaii hundreds of lifeguards work year round on a career basis; while lifeguards in most other states work seasonally. Whether year round or seasonal, professional

Chicago Park District lifeguard staff. [Photographic Credit: Bob Burtog]

lifeguard services have perhaps the most direct and profound impact on public safety per employee of any emergency service providers. Beach lifeguards consistently and continually make the difference between the life and death of otherwise healthy people through timely preventive acts. While other emergency services are largely reactive, responding once an emergency has manifested itself, alert lifeguards can often prevent the emergencies from developing in the first place and pluck unsuspecting people from harm's way.

In the warmer states, lifeguards have particularly broad responsibilities. Some American lifeguards are armed police officers serving a dual role of rescuer and law enforcer. Others are called upon to perform duties such as marine firefighting, coastal cliff rescue, paramedic services, swiftwater rescue during flooding, and scuba search and recovery. Several American lifeguard agencies keep their personnel on duty 24 hours a day to provide response to nighttime aquatic emergencies. In some areas, such as the City of San Diego, when a citizen calls 9-1-1 to report an aquatic emergency, the reporting party is connected directly to a lifeguard dispatcher.

Lifesaving equipment continues to evolve as lifeguards experiment and innovate. The inshore rescue boat (IRB), pioneered in Australia and New Zealand, has become standard equipment in many areas, replacing the traditional dory. Hard hull rescue boats up to 32 feet in length, some with firefighting equipment, are also employed. The Baywatch vessels of the Los Angeles County lifeguards represent perhaps the best prepared fleet of open water rescue vessels maintained by a local government in the United States. Many lifeguard agencies have begun to successfully employ personal watercraft as an inexpensive alternative method of providing motorized vessel response.

Increasing expectations by the general public for emergency medical care have resulted in dramatic improvements in the quality of emergency medical training. USLA minimum recommended standards require that all lifeguards have emergency medical aid training, well beyond the basic levels available to the general public. More advanced beach lifeguard agencies now require their personnel to be certified at the level of Emergency Medical Technician or the equivalent of Department of Transportation First Responder. Medical equipment such as spineboards, cervical collars, and oxygen have become a must for beach lifeguard agencies. It is no longer acceptable to wait precious minutes for an ambulance to deliver such essential pieces of equipment.

Facilities have improved, also. Properly designed lifeguard facilities minimize stress and fatigue by providing refuge from the elements. Most larger lifeguard stations include areas which allow the provision of private, sterile treatment to persons requiring medical attention.

The period from the 1960s through the 1990s has brought a great change to the role of the professional lifeguard. Lifeguarding has emerged as a true emergency service with the same charge as that of other emergency services—the protection of lives and property. In a typical year in this country, well over 100,000 lives are saved by beach lifeguards and many millions of dollars in property protected.

Despite these advances, not all of today's beach lifeguard agencies can boast of having modern equipment and facilities. Many seasonal agencies still operate following years of tradition based on equipment developed for lifesaving more than 100 years ago. Other lifeguard services employ the most basic equipment and training. At some parks and beaches, solitary lifeguards work long hours without assistance, while at others administrators struggle over how, or even if, lifeguards should be employed.

The lessons of the past are hard learned and oft forgotten. On Memorial Day in 1994, five people drowned at American Beach in northern Florida. No lifeguards were present because they had been eliminated in a cost saving measure. Shortly after the drownings, and ensuing nationwide attention, lifeguard protection was restored. Unfortunately, as in many other cases in American history, lifeguard staffing was provided only after an avoidable tragedy dramatically punctuated the need for prevention.

At treacherous Ocean Beach in San Francisco, lifeguards are not provided. Instead, the National Park Service chooses to simply accept the fact that "drownings occur annually." [Photographic Credit: B. Chris Brewster]

There was a time that common public perception of lifeguards was that of sun worshipers with little more to offer than directions and sun tan lotion. It has changed through the efforts of beach lifeguards who understand that recognition of their essential public safety role is directly tied to the professionalism of lifeguards themselves. Lifeguards who willingly accept the old stereotypes directly contribute to their perpetuation, irreparably harming not only their own image, but that of their fellow lifeguards. On the other hand, lifeguards who demonstrate respect for their occupation through preparedness, maturity, and dedication help ensure that lifeguards will be recognized, trained, equipped, and compensated at appropriate levels.

The first lifesavers who walked the beaches of America in search of ship-wrecked victims were not fully respected or funded until they adopted regulations, drilled regularly, and demonstrated an ability to handle the most complex rescues with the ease of professionals. It was through their own actions that their profession became recognized as essential to the safety and well-being of the public. The same is true today. Every beach lifeguard is directly responsible for the professional image of all beach lifeguards.

1   *Harper's Monthly, February 1882,* as reprinted by Vistabooks, 1989.

2   Annual Report of the U.S. Life-Saving Service, 1884.

3   Ibid.

4   Quinn, William P., *Shipwrecks Around Cape Cod,* Farmington, Maine: The Knowlton and McLeary Co., 1973.

5   Johnson, Robert Erwin, *Guardians of the Sea, History of the United States Coast Guard,* Anapolis, Md.: Naval Institute Press, 1987.

6   Ibid.

7   Ibid.

8   Ibid.

9   Quinn, William P., *Shipwrecks Around Cape Cod.*

10 Johnson, Robert Erwin, *Guardians of the Sea, History of the United States Coast Guard.*

11 Ibid.

12 Merryman, J.H., *The United States Life-Saving Service—1880, Scribner's Monthly,* 1880.

13 Ryder, Richard G., *Old Harbor Station,* Norwich, Ct.: Ram Island Press, 1990.

14 Dlaton J.W., *The Life Savers of Cape Cod,* Orleans, Mass.: Parnassus Imprints, 1902.

15 Ryder, Richard G., *Old Harbor Station.*

16 Barnett, J.P., *The Lifesaving Guns of David Lyle,* South Bend, Ind.: Town and Country Press, 1974.

17 Ibid.

18 Quinn, William P., *Shipwrecks Around Cape Cod.*

19 Merryman, J.H., *The United States Life-Saving Service—1880, Scribner's Monthly,* 1880.

20 *Harper's Monthly, February 1882,* as reprinted by Vistabooks, 1989.

21 Quinn, William P., *Shipwrecks Around Cape Cod.*

22 Ryder, Richard G., *Old Harbor Station.*

23 Le Vine, Jess, Lifesavers of the Past, *American Lifeguard Magazine,* 1994.

24 Don Rohrer, Los Angeles County Lifeguards.

25 Ibid.

26 Texas A & M University, *Establishing Open-Water Recreational Beach Standards,* Marine Information Services, 1980.

CHAPTER TWO

BEACH USE IN AMERICA

CHAPTER HIGHLIGHTS

Beach Popularity

Protecting the Beach Environment

Lifeguard Challenges and Rewards

IN THIS CHAPTER

The stress of a lifeguard's responsibilities can sometimes be immense. The challenges, however, make lifeguarding one of the most diverse and rewarding jobs available. How many people are able to go home after work with the satisfaction of knowing that they have performed the most important act of all in our society—the saving of human life?

BEACH POPULARITY

The beach is a major focus of American recreational activity. While baseball may be known as the American pastime and football is also a popular sport, swimming is regularly ranked in public opinion polls as America's number one recreational activity. Each year, millions of families travel to their local beach to enjoy the sun, sand, and water.

The beach has become more than a strip of sand from which we swim. The sociology of the beach has changed as Americans and their activities have evolved. Today, the beach attracts rich and poor, young and old, and people from all races, cultures, and creeds. It draws sun worshipers, game players, girl and boy watchers, and people who surf, water-ski, sail, eat, swim, run, sell, relax, work-out, read, preach, walk, skin and scuba dive, parasail… the list goes on almost indefinitely.

Swimming, while still a primary activity, is not a prerequisite for a fun day at the beach. Indeed, many people with no swimming skills whatsoever visit the beach regularly. It has become a place to be with family, friends, strangers, or simply alone. In addition to providing an ideal area for recreational activities, the aquatic environment has an intense attraction for simple relaxation and contemplation. For many people, it has a calming, almost therapeutic effect. For these and other reasons, the beach has become an integral part of American culture.

Oak Street Beach, Chicago. [Photographic Credit: Joe Pecoraro]

PROTECTING THE BEACH ENVIRONMENT

Just as the beach draws visitors, it also attracts people for long-term habitation. A home with a view of the water, any open body of water, is typically the most sought after in a community. This development pressure, added to the increasing popularity of beaches and water activities, has caused problems for the fragile beach environment. In some areas of the United States, public access to sandy beaches has been challenged by private ownership rights. Other beach areas suffer pollution from sewers, illegal dumping, and the effects of crowded human residence nearby.

Beaches are also threatened by development as shorelines are reinforced to protect buildings and other improvements constructed at the water's edge, resulting far too often in significant loss of sandy beach frontage. Most sandy beaches are created and regenerated by erosion of the adjacent coastline. When coastline erosion is stanched by development, beaches suffer. In many communities, this problem is so severe and the beach so valuable that sand is trucked or pumped in at great cost to replace that which is no longer replenished naturally.

People once saw the beach as just a sandy amusement park; but they have come to recognize it as a precious resource which must be preserved for present and future generations. Watchdog groups monitor the discharge of wastes to ensure water quality. Concerned citizens encourage government acquisition of shorefront property to forestall commerical development. People work to enact environmental and zoning laws to preserve not only the beach, but all aspects of life surrounding it, from views to public access. Americans now jealously guard their cherished and limited beach resources.

LIFEGUARD CHALLENGES AND REWARDS

While the increased popularity of beaches creates a sense of protectionism, it also creates more intensive use. Beaches have become afflicted with social problems such as vandalism, litter, drug and alcohol abuse, thefts, assaults, confrontations, and even more serious crimes. As more users arrive, conflicts among those same users increase. Today, a major aspect of beach management is people management. This means protecting people from themselves and each other, in addition to protecting them from the hazards of the aquatic environment.

Professional lifeguards have become an integral part of today's beach society, and are expected to help solve some of the growing beach problems. The following are some important considerations in dealing with these challenges:

A busy day at the beach in Los Angeles County. [Photographic Credit: Los Angeles Times]

- Water is not a natural environment for humans. With proper skills, people can safely recreate in water, but they are ill-equipped for surviving in all water conditions.
- People sometimes behave differently in groups and some may push themselves beyond their capability just to impress others.
- Lifeguards should never assume that beach visitors are familiar with a beach's particular hazards or energy conditions. Emergency situations often develop when people incorrectly presume that water conditions will be similar to those near their home.
- Lifeguards should be advocates for the beach environment. It is important to encourage people to recognize the beach as an irreplaceable natural resource of inestimable value—one that must be protected. By helping people to see the beach as more than a sandy amusement park, lifeguards can help to protect not only their jobs, but also the future enjoyment of generations of beach visitors.
- Beach activities frequently conflict with one another. Therefore, lifeguarding can involve mediating among differing uses. Lifeguards sometimes find themselves in the position of social referees in a game where the rules are not always clear and sometimes simply ignored. In a recreational setting, people do not always feel obligated to adhere to established law or societal ethics. The use of alcohol can exaggerate these problems.
- Lifeguards are sometimes drawn away from the water to handle emergencies involving medical aid, law enforcement contacts, and so on. Unless adequate backup is available to maintain watch over the water, a lifeguard should conclude any contact which diverts attention from the water as soon as possible. Attention directed away from the water, even for short periods of time, can result in a drowning.
- There are many hazards in the modern beach environment beyond those that are obvious. Discarded hypodermic needles and broken glass pose serious dangers, particularly considering that lifeguards are usually barefoot. Unlike police and firefighters, lifeguards often lack attire and immediate access to barrier devices that would help to provide protection from exposure to communicable diseases. Lifeguards may be forced to enter contaminated water areas to effect a rescue. Skin cancer from overexposure to the sun has killed lifeguards and seriously injured others. These and other hazards must be guarded against every day.

Experienced lifeguards know that the job includes more than just watching the water and responding to emergencies. High levels of coordination with other emergency service providers are needed to help protect people from themselves and their fellow beach users. One day the lifeguard may be expected to mediate a dispute among beach patrons as tempers rise to the boiling point over a seemingly minor conflict. Another day, the lifeguard must allay the terror of a mother whose child is lost in a sea of beachgoers. A beach patron collapses, the victim of a heart attack, and everyone turns to the lifeguard to perform lifesaving CPR. Each day of work, the pressure is on, the public is watching, and lifeguards hold the lives of the people they watch over in their hands. A momentary distraction may mean that a person in a lifeguard's care will die, so constant vigilance is imperative.

The stress of a lifeguard's responsibilities can sometimes be immense. The challenges, however, make lifeguarding one of the most diverse and rewarding jobs available. How many people are able to go home after work with the satisfaction of knowing that they have performed the most important act of all in our society—the saving of human life? Lifeguards have many opportunities to experience that very feeling, as long as they are prepared to respond professionally when the need arises.

Rescue from an inshore hole. [Photographic Credit: Mike Hensler]

CHAPTER THREE

THE ROLE OF THE PROFESSIONAL LIFEGUARD

CHAPTER HIGHLIGHTS

Responsibilities and Expectations

USLA Code of Ethics

IN THIS CHAPTER

Unlike other emergency services, which are able to rely heavily on mechanized support, lifeguarding in its purest form comes down to a simple struggle against the forces of nature by one human being endeavoring to save the life of another.

RESPONSIBILITIES AND EXPECTATIONS

The United States Lifesaving Association is an organization largely composed of professional lifeguards. Why then are we not known as the United States Lifeguard Association? The answer is that all lifeguards are dedicated to a key goal—lifesaving. Our organization is named for that goal. In truth, anyone can be a lifesaver. Heroic acts are not the sole province of lifeguards or other emergency responders. In fact, many of the most impressive and selfless acts of heroism are performed by persons with little or no training in lifesaving. Unfortunately, so are many of the most tragic acts.

Unlike untrained citizens who may bravely or impulsively respond to an unexpected emergency, lifeguards are specially prepared to prevent, anticipate, and respond to emergencies in and around the aquatic environment. Most lifeguards who spend any significant time in the profession will perform countless lifesaving acts with little recognition or expectation thereof. This is as it should be, since a lifeguard who is properly trained and prepared will prevent loss of life as a daily routine. It is, after all, the basic job of a lifeguard to help ensure that those who visit the nation's beaches, waterways, and adjacent parks return home alive and uninjured. Not all accidents can be prevented, but well trained professional beach lifeguards rescue tens of thousands of people from drowning in America each year, and perform many times that number of preventive actions to intervene before emergencies develop.

In the United States, beach lifeguards have worked hard to be recognized as equals to other emergency services professionals. This has been accomplished through a steady process of improving the quality of the services provided and a constant dedication to public safety. As a result, Americans have come to expect professional lifeguards on their beaches just as they have come to expect professional police, fire, and emergency medical services in their communities.

San Diego lifeguards assist one of five victims of a boat fire. Lifeguards extinguished the fire, but the boat was a total loss. [Photographic Credit: *San Diego Union-Tribune*—John Gibbins]

Lifeguarding is viewed by many as the most physically demanding job among the various emergency services. This is because, unlike other emergency services which are able to rely heavily on mechanized support, lifeguarding in its purest form comes down to a simple struggle against the forces of nature by one human being endeavoring to save the life of another. Even with new developments in motorized rescue equipment, many rescue situations depend on the sheer strength, physical endurance, and swimming skills of the lifeguard.

While the basic role of the professional open water lifeguard in the United States is well defined, job descriptions can vary dramatically from one locale to the next. This is particularly true as local employers seeking to stretch thin budgets ask their lifeguards to perform increasingly diverse public safety functions. At one agency a lifeguard may find that the job is a diverse blend of several aquatic related public safety responsibilities. At another, the job may be defined more narrowly, emphasizing traditional aspects of lifeguarding.

The intimate familiarity of lifeguards with the aquatic environment is not confined to managing swimming safety alone. Persons hired as lifeguards are typically very knowledgeable about all facets of the aquatic environment and adjacent land areas. This familiarity leaves lifeguards uniquely prepared to handle a variety of functions such as coastal cliff rescue, boat rescue, marine firefighting, emergency medical services, swiftwater rescue, and scuba search and recovery. Many lifeguards have law enforcement responsibility in order to help maintain public safety on their beaches. It is critical, however, that lifeguards not be assigned duties beyond those directly related to their public safety role. Such assignments only serve to diminish attention to safety, and can result in serious consequences.

The first professional beach lifesavers rescued victims stranded aboard foundering boats, not recreational swimmers. The diverse responsibilities of beach lifeguards which have evolved since then make it clear that beach lifeguards have the ability to adapt to providing the aquatic oriented emergency services needed by the American public, whatever they may be.

USLA CODE OF ETHICS

In recognition of the fundamental responsibilities of a professional beach lifeguard, the trust and confidence placed in the lifeguard, the unwavering devotion to duty required of the lifeguard, and the dignity commensurate with the lifeguard's position, the United States Lifesaving Association recognizes certain ethical principles. Lifeguards will:

- Maintain an unwavering dedication to the safety of those they are assigned to protect.
- Recognize and accept that heightened personal dangers are an unavoidable aspect of the job.

Competitors in the annual All Women Lifeguard Tournament carry victims from the water. [Photographic Credit: Chris Gierlich]

- Maintain high standards of fitness, recognizing that their strength, stamina, and physical skill may mean the difference between life and death.
- Make every reasonable effort to prevent accidents before they occur.
- Avoid any undue distraction which may deter them from their primary responsibility.
- Proudly carry out the duties they are assigned, providing the highest possible levels of courtesy, respect, and assistance to those whom they watch over.
- Take proactive steps to educate the public about the hazards of the aquatic environment and ways to safely enjoy aquatic recreation.
- Promote their profession through personal actions which serve to demonstrate that lifeguards everywhere are deserving of the trust placed in them by the public they serve.

CHAPTER FOUR

LIFEGUARD QUALIFICATIONS AND TRAINING

CHAPTER HIGHLIGHTS

Types of Lifeguard Training

Minimum Recommended Standards

IN THIS CHAPTER

USLA has developed minimum recommended standards to be met and maintained by open water lifeguards. In order to be certified, the training program and lifeguards must meet these qualifications. Some standards must not only be met initially but also maintained throughout the course of employment.

There are many different aquatic environments requiring lifeguard protection. USLA believes that they fall into two general categories: (1) the controlled environment of pools and water parks, and (2) the natural environment of open water beaches. Because of the fundamental differences of these environments, there are two corresponding categories of lifeguards—pool/waterpark lifeguards and open water (beach) lifeguards. The table on the following page provides some examples of the different challenges faced by these two groups. It is presented in part to explain the reason why open water lifeguards require higher skill levels and training.

Beach lifeguards are sometimes stationed at remote locations where advanced medical support can be greatly delayed, so they must be prepared to support victims with medical problems for long periods. They are frequently responsible for aiding boaters in distress. Many communities expect their beach lifeguards to perform other responsibilities such as law enforcement, cliff rescue, flood rescue, marine firefighting, and scuba search and rescue. Beach lifeguards are often

COMPARISON OF AQUATIC ENVIRONMENTS

Condition	Pool/Waterpark	Open Water (Beach)
Water Temperature	May be controlled	Subject to natural conditions
Water Clarity	Controlled	Subject to natural conditions
Difficulty of Rescue	Handled by jumping into pool or swimming a very short distance	May require long distance swimming in adverse conditions
Natural Hazards	None	May be extensive and may not be readily apparent
Wave Action and Currents	None or predictable and fully controllable	Surf and related currents are often present—may present the most significant source of swimmer distress
Attendance Levels and Hours	Can be controlled	Generally not controllable
Weather Conditions	Little effect	Possible severe effect

expected to operate emergency vehicles with lights and siren, rescue boats, and other technical equipment. In short, the beach environment is a particularly challenging environment for lifeguards, requiring markedly differing physical conditioning, training, and skills from the controlled environment of pools and water parks.

While beach lifeguard operations share many similarities, they can differ in a variety of ways. A surf beach in Maine, for example, has a different climate, water conditions, and even a different type of visitor than a similar surf beach in Florida or Texas. A surf beach on the urban Chicago lakeshore has conditions and needs distinctly dissimilar to a lake beach in rural Kentucky. Beaches employing lifeguards will also have different organizational structures, authority, pay levels and available equipment.

Beach lifeguards may work for town or city recreation departments, county beach or harbor departments, police or other public safety agencies, state or national park systems to name a few possibilities. In developing this training text and training guidelines for open water lifeguards, USLA has taken into account many of the unique aspects inherent in open water lifeguard operations across the country. The USLA publication entitled *Guidelines for Open Water Lifeguard Training and Standards,* which is the basis for the USLA Lifeguard Agency Certification Program, was designed to provide a training curriculum and recommended minimum standards flexible enough to meet the training needs of all agencies employing beach lifeguards, while recognizing the myriad differences among them.

Pool lifeguards usually receive their training from instructors working under the auspices of one of several national organizations. The course completion certificates they receive, which are generally honored by pool managers across the country, are based on training programs that are essentially identical in content regardless of the geographic location where they are given. Under these systems, if a candidate successfully completes training as a pool lifeguard in Michigan, for example, the training is likely to be accepted by a pool manager in Arizona as adequate for employment. This is possible because of the inherent similarity in the pool environment regardless of where the pool is located.

Since the open water environment lacks such consistency, USLA developed a certification system which allows flexibility and specialization in beach lifeguard training to address local conditions. For example, under the USLA Lifeguard Agency Certification Program, beach lifeguard training in Colorado need not provide information on effecting surf rescues. Similarly, a lifeguard training program for surf lifeguards in California need not discuss issues particular to rescues in reservoirs. With the time available for lifeguard training limited, this allows beach lifeguard training programs to go into greater depth on handling tasks specific to each local agency's geography and mission. Because of this specialization, however, beach lifeguard training conducted under the USLA system is not interchangeable. Retraining is necessary if the lifeguard moves to a different agency with different conditions.

Despite the flexibility offered by the USLA system, fundamental responsibilities of beach lifeguards differ little from place to place. Therefore, core aspects of the USLA system involve a curriculum and minimum standards which do not vary

First day at the lifeguard academy in Chicago. [Photographic Credit: Al Shorey]

from place to place. This manual is designed to provide information on core aspects of open water lifeguarding in which all beach lifeguards should be skilled, as well as specialized information to assist in training that is unique to particular geographic locations. It is the responsibility of agency training officers to select portions of the text for trainees which are pertinent to the local area.

This text will be most effective when used to train lifeguards in a manner consistent with USLA's recommended curriculum for beach lifeguards. Lifeguard agencies which have been certified under the USLA Lifeguard Agency Certification Program have demonstrated their adherence to these guidelines and standards.

TYPES OF LIFEGUARD TRAINING

In developing guidelines for open water lifeguard training, the USLA recognized three major types of training used by lifeguard agencies in selecting and preparing lifeguards for work on the beach. The manner in which the various types of training are used by an agency will impact on the local training program.

PREREQUISITE TRAINING

For years, many organizations employing beach lifeguards used prerequisite training without any supplemental training. This included national certification programs with titles such as Lifesaving, First Aid, and CPR. By using prerequisite training, some lifeguard agency administrators erroneously believed they could hire individuals pre-trained as lifeguards, with "licenses" in the form of certification cards. In some areas, prerequisite training is still the only training required by law for beach lifeguards.

Some forms of prerequisite training can constitute a valuable component of a comprehensive training program. Particularly for seasonal operations, prerequisite training can cut down on the training time required to prepare a lifeguard for service. This training can help pre-select qualified candidates by attracting applicants who have demonstrated a willingness and ability to acquire pertinent knowledge and skills prior to the actual hiring process. Prerequisite training is not, however, adequate in and of itself to prepare lifeguards for work in the open water environment.

Most national organizations offering pre-employment certification programs in lifesaving and lifeguarding stress that the programs offer generic or general training only, and that local training is absolutely necessary to prepare a lifeguard for duty at a particular agency. Other certification programs are designed to teach skills to assist in an emergency situation, but are not designed for professionals who will have ultimate responsibility. Most importantly, it is the belief of USLA that currently available national lifeguard training programs with a combined emphasis on the pool and inland beach environment lack the depth of training appropriate for beach lifeguards. Furthermore, there is currently no national program for certification of lifeguards at surf beaches other than that provided by employing agencies under the USLA Lifeguard Agency Certification Program.

In training programs which adhere to USLA recommended minimum guidelines and standards, prerequisite training and certification are acceptable and may be required. For example, current certification in one person adult, two person adult, child and infant cardiopulmonary resuscitation (CPR), including obstructed airway training, is a must for all beach lifeguards. CPR may be a prerequisite or part of an agency's formal pre-service training. USLA training guidelines do, however, require that any prerequisite training be objectively tested by each agency to ensure that the skills of a new employee meet the standards of the certification program. If, for example, CPR training is required by an agency as a qualification for employment, the agency is expected to independently validate the skills of the lifeguard so trained.

PRE-SERVICE TRAINING

Pre-service training is that which is provided by an employing agency to prepare lifeguards before they begin work on the beach. In some agencies, this training is actually part of the recruitment and qualification procedure and is used to help the agency determine if a lifeguard candidate will actually be offered a position. In other agencies, pre-service training is provided after hire, but before the lifeguard is assigned to work on the beach.

Lifeguards practice CPR during pre-service training. [Photographic Credit: Al Shorey]

Pre-service training is the essence of USLA training guidelines and is required to some extent in all USLA training programs. It is a fundamental principle of USLA guidelines that no one should be assigned to perform the duties of a beach lifeguard prior to receiving the minimum training needed to perform the function. Pre-service training may be integrated into the first weeks of actual beach work as long as trainees are not permitted to work outside the immediate supervision of an experienced lifeguard with at least 1,000 hours of beach lifeguard experience, until basic training is concluded. Furthermore, the ratio of experienced lifeguards to such trainees should be no greater than one to one. Minimum recommended pre-service training is detailed in the USLA *Guidelines for Open Water Lifeguard Training and Standards.*

IN-SERVICE TRAINING

The third major type of training recognized by USLA is in-service training. This is used by many lifeguard agencies to develop and maintain the skills and knowledge of lifeguards working for them. Required in-service training may include daily physical conditioning or regular reviews of rescue procedures. Lifeguards may be encouraged or required to pursue higher levels of training in areas such as special equipment operation, emergency medical treatment, or law enforcement. Some agencies may require lifeguards to acquire Emergency Medical Technician training after hire, for example.

Lifeguards gather for in-service training. [Photographic Credit: Mike Hensler]

USLA recognizes the value of in-service training and encourages agencies to set aside training time as a part of every lifeguard's work week. USLA also encourages lifeguard agencies to develop their own in-service programs to train and certify lifeguards in the operation of special rescue equipment, supervision, management, and other operational areas that lie outside the scope of basic lifeguard operations.

MINIMUM RECOMMENDED STANDARDS

USLA has developed minimum recommended standards to be met and maintained by open water lifeguards. In order to be certified, the training program and lifeguards must meet these qualifications. Some standards must not only be met initially but also maintained throughout the course of employment. These standards are detailed in the USLA booklet, *Guidelines for Open Water Lifeguard Training and Standards.*

The following is a brief synopsis of USLA standards available at the time of publishing this manual. Acquisition of the most current USLA booklet is necessary for updated information and essential to development of an effective training course which meets USLA minimum recommended standards. USLA currently recognizes three classes of open water lifeguards: (1) Open Water Lifeguard Trainee, (2) Seasonal Open Water Lifeguard, and (3) Full Time Open Water Lifeguard. USLA also sets minimum recommended standards for Open Water Lifeguard Instructor. All USLA standards are subject to revision.

1 *Open water lifeguards should be at least 16 years of age.* USLA recognizes that a lifeguard must be physically and mentally mature to handle the responsibilities of professional lifeguarding. Although age alone is not a perfect measure of maturity and competence, the consensus of opinion is that age 16 is an acceptable minimum age for an open water lifeguard. Many professional beach lifeguard agencies have established higher minimum ages commensurate with more complex responsibilities.

2 *Open water lifeguards must have training in first aid and emergency medical care.* USLA believes that all lifeguards should be trained in first aid at a level appropriate for professional providers of medical aid—that is, beyond training designed for the general public. At a minimum, such training (not including CPR training) should be 21 hours in length. Courses equivalent to U.S. Department of Transportation First Responder are strongly recommended and agencies which employ full time lifeguard personnel with regular medical aid responsibilities should consider a requirement of Emergency Medical Technician.

3 *Open water lifeguards must have training in cardio-pulmonary resuscitation.* Prolonged submersion results in respiratory distress and ultimate respiratory and cardiac failure. Therefore, CPR training is absolutely essential. USLA minimum recommended standards call for up-to-date successful completion of a course in providing one person adult, two person adult, child and infant CPR, including obstructed airway training, accepted by the Federal Government or by the government in the state of employment.

4 *Open water lifeguards must successfully complete all training course requirements of the hiring agency.* USLA minimum recommended standards call for a course of not less than 40 hours in open water lifesaving which meets the current recommended curriculum requirements of USLA. This is *in addition to* training in first aid and CPR. More advanced agencies are expected to provide a minimum 65 hours of training.

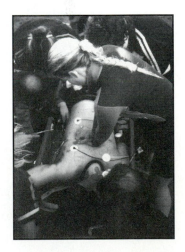

A lifeguard performs CPR on a drowning victim with the assistance of paramedics and flight nurses.

[Photographic Credit: B. Chris Brewster]

5 *Open water lifeguards must be able to swim at least 500 meters over a measured course in ten minutes or less.* Strong swimming skills are critical in open water lifesaving. While few rescues occur 250 meters offshore, the 500 meter timed swim is a well established minimum standard which should be met and maintained at all times by all open water lifeguards. It ensures that open water lifeguards will have adequate stamina to swim themselves and the victims they rescue to shore in adverse conditions, such as strong currents or surf. It also helps to ensure the stamina necessary to perform multiple rescues when necessary. Agencies are encouraged to set higher standards for swimming proficiency to address local needs and conditions as long as the minimum guideline is met.

6 *Health and fitness must be adequate for the stresses of lifesaving.* Open water lifeguards must possess adequate vision, hearing acuity, physical ability, and stamina to perform the duties of an open water lifeguard as documented by a medical or osteopathic physician.

7 *Scuba training is necessary in some circumstances.* Any open water lifeguard who will be required to utilize scuba equipment in the course of employment must, at a minimum, be certified as a scuba diver at the basic level by a nationally recognized certifying organization. Scuba certification also provides valuable information to lifeguards regarding the physiology of scuba diving which can be invaluable in treating victims of scuba related injuries.

NOTE: USLA guidelines establish *minimum* recommended qualifications only. Individual agencies are encouraged to establish minimum qualifications that exceed these requirements to address local needs and conditions.

CHAPTER FIVE

THE SURF BEACH

CHAPTER HIGHLIGHTS

Waves

Rip Currents

Backwash

Shorebreak

Lateral Currents

Sandbars

Inshore Holes

Beach Topography

IN THIS CHAPTER

The United States Lifesaving Association estimates that rip currents are the primary source of distress in over 80% of swimmer rescues at surf beaches. Rip currents are sometimes referred to as *the drowning machine* because of their almost mechanical ability to tire swimmers to the point of fatigue and, ultimately, death.

At sea, powerful forces generated by water movements are continuously at work. The surf, calm at one moment, can quickly become rough and dangerous. Seemingly gently sloping beaches can hide deep channels that produce strong currents. While calmer surf conditions may appear to allow lower lifeguard staffing levels than when surf is high, the lack of predictability of surf conditions necessitate consistent staffing levels aimed at reasonably expected conditions.

The unpredictable nature of the surf is of vital concern to every lifeguard assigned to a surf beach. Surf provides a unique environment for aquatic sports and recreation. Surfing, whether through use of a surfboard, a bodyboard, or bodysurfing, attracts millions of people each year. Even people who do not surf enjoy playing in the surf and feeling the power of waves crashing around them.

Nonetheless, surf can be a powerful force capable of killing or injuring even experienced swimmers and surfers. Surf beach lifeguards must therefore be prepared at all times to intervene when the power of the surf overwhelms swimmers, surfers, or boaters.

WAVES

Many people understandably believe that waves are composed of water moving on a lateral plane at the speed of the wave, ultimately crashing on the shoreline. This is a fallacy. In reality the most common type of open water waves— *surface waves* — are cyclical forces of energy in the surface of the water. When offshore, these waves of energy simply cause the water surface to move up and down on a vertical plane, hardly causing it to move forward at all, except in the most tempestuous conditions.

[Photographic Credit: Mike Hensler]

Perhaps what confuses logic in understanding wave energy is observation of the way it is dispersed upon reaching shore. At this point, the energy results in breakers that push water up the beach in a strong uprush, moving it quickly forward. Offshore though, wave energy can be compared to a mouse running under a rug—the rug rises as the mouse runs along, but then falls back to the floor when the mouse has passed, moving forward little if at all.

With few exceptions, such as seismic activity and tides, waves are formed by the force of wind against the water. Even the casual observer has seen ripples form on calm water as a breeze blows across it. Stronger, more continual winds create progressively larger ripples and ultimately form disturbances in the water surface commonly called waves. Large waves can be created by strong local winds very near a beach, but most large waves are formed by storms well offshore. These wind-generated waves frequently travel across thousands of miles of open sea before the energy from the wind is diffused as the waves break upon shore. Three major factors contribute to the size and power of wind-generated waves: (1) wind velocity or speed, (2) distance traveled over open water (fetch), and (3) duration of the blow.

Waves can be measured in a number of ways, such as the following:
- *Wave period*—the time it takes two consecutive wave crests to pass a given point
- *Wave length*—the horizontal distance between two wave crests (or troughs)
- *Wave height*—the vertical distance between the crest and trough of a wave
- *Wave velocity*—the speed at which the incoming set of waves advances

As waves form, moving out and away from the wind that creates them, their crests become more rounded and take on a similar period and height. Thus waves begin their journey toward shore. A succession of waves from a single source, with a consistent direction, is known as a *wave train.*

If all waves arriving at a beach came from a single source, the waves would tend to be quite regular in appearance and therefore of a fairly consistent period, length, height, and velocity. This is rarely if ever the case because many different storms can contribute to the wave energy that ultimately arrives at a beach at any given point in time. As two or more wave trains collide and intermingle, the appearance of the water surface also changes.

When waves from two or more wave trains meet trough to crest, they tend to cancel each other out and disperse the energy they carried, reducing wave height. Conversely, when two waves from different wave trains match each other trough to trough, crest to crest, the ultimate height of the combined wave may be greatly increased over the individual height of the two waves. This phenomenon is believed to be responsible for what are known as *rogue waves* — sudden waves in open water that are far higher than any other waves in the area. Some shipping and sailing disasters have been attributed to rogue waves.[1]

Usually, the intermingling of wave trains as they arrive at a beach results in *set waves*. These are occasional groups of larger waves interspersed among a greater number of smaller waves. As the wave trains come into phase, matching each other's pattern, the waves increase in size. At other times when they are out of phase, the waves are smaller and irregular. Surfers will sometimes wait for long periods of time, well outside the majority of breaking waves, for the larger sets to form.

Set waves can be dangerous. They are unpredictable in regularity, except in a general sense over time. Inexperienced swimmers may go out during the lull between sets and then unexpectedly be caught in surf beyond their capabilities. Pedestrians are sometimes pulled into the water and killed or injured when unexpectedly large sets suddenly break onshore. An important phenomenon associated with set waves is that currents typically pull most strongly during the lull just after a set of larger waves has come through (see the description of rip currents later in this chapter).

Swells, on almost any beach, come from a predictable direction that, unless altered by storm activity, changes with the seasons. For example, on the western shores of the United States, predominant swell direction from late April to early October comes from storms as far south as 40 degrees latitude in the southern

Pacific (off the southern portion of South America). From late October to mid-April, the swell direction changes and waves along the western coast originate most often in the Gulf of Alaska near the Aleutian Islands.

The changing source of coastal swells causes clearly visible changes in the beaches themselves. For example, during the wintry northern drift, sand is lost from West Coast beaches, but in most cases it is promptly replaced from its off-shore depository when summer swells from the southern Pacific take over again. These changes of underlying sand can have profound effects on the formation and strength of rip currents. As swell direction changes, bottom conditions along the beach become unsettled, creating the undulations that facilitate the formation of rip currents.

When waves approach a beach, they refract. That is, they bend to conform to the coastline. Even waves that originate at a sharp angle to the beach tend to wrap around nearly parallel to the beach before breaking. This is particularly true on long sandy beaches. Refraction makes it difficult to judge the initial direction of the waves when observing them from shore.

Refraction is an important concept for surfers, because generally, the more diagonal the approach of the breaking wave the better. When waves strike a beach at a fully refracted, perpendicular angle, they are difficult to surf and produce short rides. On the other hand, when waves strike a beach at a sharp angle, the break moves laterally along the shoreline allowing long rides. Breaks caused by irregular offshore reefs and peninsulas are also prized because the effects of refraction are minimized and the break tends to peel off these geographic barriers.

Swells are called *surface waves* if they are moving in water deeper than one-half of their wave length. Surface waves move at speeds equal to three and a half times their wave period in seconds. For example, a wave with a period of ten seconds is traveling about thirty-five miles per hour. This ten-second period is the average time between storm swells reaching the shores of the mainland United States.

Velocity slows as a wave approaches shallower water. When this occurs, a surface wave becomes a *shallow water wave.* The length decreases, wave height increases, and velocity is reduced, but the period remains unchanged. As water depth continues to decrease, the wave steepens, becoming higher and higher. Finally, upon reaching a depth approximately 1.3 times its height, the wave can no longer support itself and the crest falls forward, forming surf. The remaining shore-ward moving water—or uprush—runs onto the beach until its final energy is spent. Then the force of gravity pulls the water back into the sea.

Bottom contour has a decisive influence on the manner in which a wave breaks. When a large swell is forced to expend its energy rapidly upon colliding with a steep underwater slope or reef, the crest of the wave tends to plunge or peak quickly, causing the water to mix with air and form foam or "white water." A bottom that slopes gradually upward into shallows forms a wave that spills more gently, with the small froth of white water being pushed ahead of the broken wave on its journey to the beach. These gentle waves create less sound than plunging waves that spray into the sky as air and water are compressed together.

The experienced lifeguard knows how important the sound of waves in the darkness or in a fog can be to rescue work. Wave sounds can indicate to the lifeguard four vital conditions:
- The *type* of wave that is breaking
- The *power* of the surf

- The *location* of the main break in the surf
- The approximate *width* of the surf zone

Anyone who has sat by the shore and surveyed the sea understands that no two waves are ever alike—similar, but never identical. Waves can, however, be classified into three primary forms:

- *Spilling waves*—formed by swells as they move over a sea floor that ascends gradually beneath them, with the crest of the wave spilling onto the wave face until the wave itself is engulfed by foam
- *Plunging waves* (also known as shorebreak)—formed when a swell suddenly strikes a shallow bottom, reef, or other obstacle and breaks with flying spray, expending most of its energy and transforming it into a spilling wave for its remaining distance to shore
- *Surging waves*—created where water is deep adjacent to shoreline cliffs, reef, or steep beaches, with the waves keeping their trochoidal form until they crash against the shoreline barrier

Waves are measured in different ways for different purposes. The space from trough to peak just before breaking differs from the front to the back of a given wave. The heights of incoming waves are of vital interest to lifeguards, who use this information to assess the turbulence of the surf and its potential effect on those in, on, or near the water. Unless waves can be measured against a nearby structure of known size, wave height is estimated by comparison to the body of a surfer standing erect on the surfboard or in relation to swimmers.

Waves cause problems for beach visitors because of their tremendous power and energy—both forward toward the beach and downward, as they break. Many people underestimate the sheer power contained in a breaking wave and may be injured by the forward motion of the wave. As an example, one may think of filling a gallon container with water and tossing that container across the room to a friend. Most people would be concerned with such a weight being thrown to them. A single wave may represent the equivalent of thousands of such containers approaching at a similar velocity.

The forward motion of waves may knock visitors down, injure them, or put them at the mercy of water that quickly recedes after breaking onto a beach. The downward motion of waves can violently thrust swimmers and surfers to the bottom, causing serious trauma to the head, neck, back, and other parts of the body. Plunging waves on steep beaches are particularly likely to cause neck and back injuries because the energy is expended so suddenly and in shallow water.

Very heavy surf is sometimes beneficial to lifeguards as it may keep swimmers close to shore, if not completely out of the water. During lulls (calm periods between successive sets), however, beach patrons often venture further into the surf than they should, only to suffer the consequences when larger sets return. This situation can be exacerbated by the fact that it is during such lulls, immediately following larger sets, that rip currents and lateral drifts are strongest.

Lifeguards who have charge of surf beaches must be intimately familiar and experienced with waves and wave action. Waves produce extraordinary energy which can injure, but these forces can also be used to the benefit of the astute lifeguard. It is strongly recommended that all surf beach lifeguards spend extensive periods in activities such as board surfing, body surfing, paddling rescue boards, and rowing surf dories. In doing so, lifeguards learn to read waves and know exactly when they will break. Similarly, lifeguards can learn to use the same rip currents which endanger swimmers as a tool to quickly get out through strong surf to victims in distress. It is only through a thorough familiarity with wave action that lifeguards can successfully effect rescues with necessary confidence and safety.

RIP CURRENTS

USLA estimates that rip currents are the primary source of distress in over 80% of swimmer rescues at surf beaches. Rip currents are sometimes referred to as *the drowning machine* because of their almost mechanical ability to tire swimmers to the point of fatigue, and, ultimately, death. The danger of rip currents is increased by the fact that, to the untrained observer, a rip current may be invisible or even appear to be an attractive area for swimming.

In some areas of the country, the rip current is referred to as a runout. The term rip tide is a misnomer, and demonstrates a lack of understanding of the cause of rip currents. While tides can cause strong currents, particularly as water rushes through the entrance to a bay or estuary, tidal action has only a peripheral effect on currents along most open water beaches. The main cause of rip currents is surf.

Rip currents vary in size, width, depth, shape, speed, and power. They are most commonly created in the following sequence: As waves break, they push water up the beach above the mean level of the sea. Once the energy of the wave is

A lifeguard comes to the assistance of several swimmers caught in a rip current. Note outgoing current in the upper left of the photo. [Photographic Credit: Mike Hensler]

expended, the water that has been pushed up the slope of the beach is pulled back down the slope by gravity. As it is pulled back, however, more waves may continue to push additional water up the beach, creating a transient damming effect. The returning water continues to be pulled by gravity and seeks the path of least resistance. This may be an underwater trough in the sand or the protected area beside a groin or jetty, for example. As the returning water rushes to a concentrated channel, it becomes a current moving away from the beach. Depending on a number of factors, this current may be very strong. Some rip currents dissipate very close to shore, while others can continue for hundreds of yards.

As mentioned in the previous section, waves break in a water depth of approximately 1.3 times their height. Therefore, waves will not break as readily over an underwater channel. In addition, the force of a rip current moving away from the beach in a channel tends to diminish the power of incoming waves. The resulting lack of surf often attracts unsuspecting beachgoers who may see relatively flat water over a rip current channel and believe they are choosing the most calm area for swimming.[2] This can be a deadly error.

Even expert swimmers can be almost helpless in a rip current. The speed of water in a rip current and the panic caused by being pulled away from the beach can be overwhelming. On the other hand if a swimmer is knowledgeable about rip currents, they pose little danger except in their most extreme form.

A lifeguard (right) tows a scuba diver toward shore against a strong rip current. The scuba diver holds a rescue buoy. [Photographic Credit: B. Chris Brewster]

TYPES OF RIP CURRENTS

There are four types of rip currents:
- Fixed Rip Currents
- Permanent Rip Currents
- Flash Rip Currents
- Traveling Rip Currents

Fixed rip currents—These are found only on sand beaches. They pull offshore in one location because the depth directly underneath is greater than surrounding depths. These rips remain fixed in the same location as long as sand conditions remain stable. When surf conditions change, fixed rips may change if wave action subtracts or adds more sand to the hole. Therefore, a fixed rip may lie in a given spot one day, then change characteristics, or simply disappear on the next day, or on the next tide.

Permanent rip currents—These rip currents are stationary year round, though they may vary in intensity. They are usually found on rocky coastlines and exist due to undulations in the bottom that do not change. The speed and power of these rips depend predominately on the size of the surf. Large surf feeds these rips a great volume of water, whereas small surf may hardly feed them at all. While larger surf increases the power of all rip currents, it is much more noticeable in the permanent type. Rock beach rip currents usually pull harder than sand beach rips because water moves more forcefully over solid, stationary obstacles, and the excess flow of water is concentrated in the more pronounced rock channels.

Piers, rock jetties, drain pipes, projecting points of land, and some beach contours may force currents running parallel to the beach (lateral currents) to turn seaward, creating permanent rip currents. Tidal outflows from bays, along with places where rivers and streams flow into the sea are considered to be permanent rip currents. In many areas, permanent or fixed rips are given names that relate to nearby landmarks or streets. Such identification can be invaluable when lifeguard teams answer emergency calls because they pinpoint the location where assistance is needed.

Flash rip currents—Temporary rips generated by increased volumes of water brought to shore from concentrated sets of waves are called flash rip currents. Flash rips do not typically accompany depressions in the bottom. They usually occur during periods of irregular and stormy surf conditions or when the surf is heavy, with long lulls between sets of waves. They can also result as a result of sudden changes in the composition of offshore sandbars. Flash rips, like flash floods on land, occur unexpectedly and without warning. When they suddenly strike an otherwise safe swimming area, part of the crowd can be quickly swept from shallow water. Since flash rips usually subside rapidly, many people caught in them can return to shore without assistance, but those who are non-swimmers or have panicked require expeditious rescue. It is not easy to determine from the beach who may be endangered due to lack of swimming ability, so rescue operations must begin immediately and usually several lifeguards are needed.

In some cases, crowds of waders actually create an effect similar to that of a jetty or pier, obstructing the flow of a lateral current and causing it to turn seaward, forming a flash rip. In these cases, part of the group may be drawn seaward with the rip current.

Traveling rip currents—Like other types of rip currents, traveling rip currents pull away from the beach, but these rip currents do not accompany depressions in sand or reef formations. They move along the beach pushed by the prevailing direction of the waves. Traveling rips usually occur in a strong, one-direction swell movement with long, well-defined periods. The wave action moves the rip away from the set of waves that feeds it. A traveling rip usually continues moving and pulling well into the lull period until the excess water has dissipated. The next set of waves starts the process all over again.

Traveling rips can be pushed 200 or 300 yards and further along the beach, depending on the size of the surf and/or the number of waves in a set. They are similar in all respects to flash rips except that their movement is predictable once their sequence has begun and the established pattern repeats itself. Like flash rip currents, traveling rips can wreak havoc on a swimming crowd as they move along the beach, pulling large numbers of people offshore.

CHARACTERISTICS OF RIP CURRENTS

Although rip currents can vary greatly in appearance, as a general rule they look somewhat different from the surrounding surf. A rip may seem especially rough or choppy, may have the dark color of deeper water, and may or may not have foam. Rips sometimes pick up debris, kelp particles, or sand, giving the water a dirty or muddy quality. At other times the seaward current shows clear evidence that the water at the surface is running in the opposite direction from incoming waves—either flowing perpendicular to them or at another angle from the shore. Rips moving through calm, level surf are easily detected, but rips are harder to spot when the sea is rough and conditions are windy. Under most conditions, rips can be readily identified by a trained lifeguard from a high elevation overlooking the surf line.

Fixed and permanent rips typically pull the hardest when tides are low. At this point the rip channels are deeper and more defined compared to the surrounding areas, which are at their shallowest. Consequently, the excess water is considerably more concentrated into the channels while returning seaward. Rip currents also pull hardest during the lull immediately following a set of waves. With the absence of incoming waves, the beached water has complete freedom on its return. Certain rips characteristically stop pulling at high tide, only to begin again at low tide, although the reverse situation is also possible. Because of all these changing rip conditions, lifeguards must constantly read the surf in order to safeguard the assigned area.

Although there are constant problems with rip currents at surf beaches in the United States, some areas report seasons when rips are particularly hazardous. For example, spring and early summer are the most hazardous times on the West Coast as the prevailing swell direction swings from its northerly origin to a southerly origin. This change of swell direction causes holes and channels in the sand that foster rip current formation. Other areas report more serious problems with rip currents in the late summer, or at other particular times of the year.

COMPONENTS OF RIP CURRENTS

"Rip Currents Form in Different Ways"

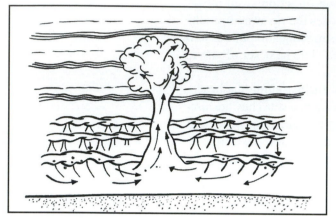

Multi-feeder

One Feeder

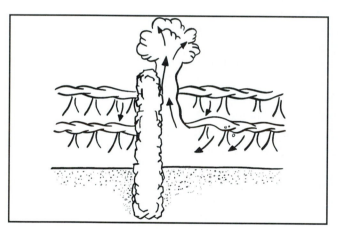

Jetties and Groins

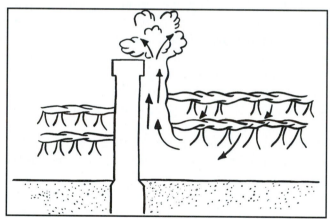

Piers

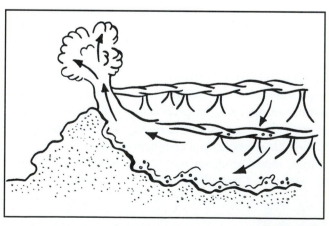

Rocky Points

Rip currents have three major components:
- The *feeder*—This is the main source of supply for the rip. Water that has been pushed up the beach and is being pulled back by gravity seeks out the path of least resistance—the rip current channel. To get there, the water may have to travel laterally along the beach some distance. Once the water finds a channel or an obstacle in its lateral drift, it will turn seaward.

  A rip current may have one or two feeders. For example, waves breaking on both sides of a deep water channel would create two feeders. Single feeder rip currents are however, much more common.
- The *neck*—This is the river of water running away from the beach. The neck can vary in width from a few yards to many tens of yards. The majority of both rescues and drownings occur in the neck. This is where the rip current has its strongest effect.
- The *head*—This is the area where the offshore current from the neck ends, dispersing broadly. The current's momentum, which was initially caused by waves pushing water up the slope of the beach and then by gravity pulling the water back from whence it came, is now exhausted.

Rip currents affect people differently, depending upon their level of swimming skill. The obvious effect of a rip current is to pull those in its path away from the shore, which for non-swimmers can quickly be lethal. Even persons with a basic ability to tread water are likely to be quickly overcome by panic when suddenly pulled offshore by a rip.

The effect of a rip current on persons with moderate to strong swimming skills is different. These people may at first be completely unconcerned about being in water over their head and oblivious to any danger. Then they may attempt to swim directly to shore, but notice that they are making no progress or even going backwards. At this point, even good swimmers can panic. Once swimmers panic, their stroke becomes less effective and their energy is quickly expended. There is a marked desperation on the part of those caught in rip currents which is fed by their loss of control.

The simplest way for a swimmer to escape from the seaward pull of the neck is to swim perpendicular to the pull of the current. Since rip currents normally pull directly away from the beach or slightly diagonally, the best direction to swim is parallel to the beach. This will allow the swimmer to move across the current instead of against it. Once the force of the rip current has been left behind, the swimmer can turn and swim to shore, often aided by the wave action which typically borders a rip current. This maneuver is easy if the rip current is a stationary one, but if it is a traveling rip moving in the same direction as the swimmer, then an attempt to escape the force by swimming to the side can be futile. Another danger is that swimmers may escape the neck of a rip current and swim toward shore only to enter the broader feeder zone and be sucked back into the neck. Lifeguards sometimes refer to this as being recirculated.

Another way to escape from a rip current is to relax and allow oneself to be carried to its outermost limit—the head—which is usually not far beyond the breaking surf. After judging the width of the rip current, the swimmer then can swim parallel to the beach in relatively calm water, re-enter the surf, and swim safely to shore. This strategy is perhaps easier said than done. Even good swimmers with surf experience can become panicked when pulled away from the beach, and some rip currents pull hundreds of yards offshore before expending their energy. It is best, therefore, to attempt to swim sideways to the rip current a significant distance and then to swim in.

BACKWASH

Backwash, also known as a runback, is most noticeable on steeply inclined beaches around the time of high tide. Backwash occurs when water pushed up the beach by waves is pulled back by the force of gravity, gaining momentum on the steep incline. The returning water can knock people's feet from beneath them and pull them forcefully into deeper water. When the surf is rough, a second uprush can meet the returning backwash, creating extensive turbulence that is particularly dangerous to young children and older people who may lack the strength to maintain their footing. Rip currents are less prevalent on steeper beaches and tend to pull only a short distance offshore, but when they are present, the combination of backwash and a rip current can both knock a beachgoer down and pull the person offshore.

For many years, the term *undertow* has been used, perhaps to describe the phenomenon caused by backwash. This term is a misnomer and should be used by lifeguards only to correct others. It suggests a condition which can actually suck a person under the water. Backwash can knock a person down and may pull a person offshore, but it does not pull the victim underwater. Of course, if a non-swimmer or poor swimmer is carried into deep water, the person may submerge, but this is due to gravity and the loss of buoyancy, not a downward sucking action of current.

SHOREBREAK

In addition to backwash, steep beaches are also subject to shorebreak—plunging waves that break in shallow water. On such beaches, waves five to eight feet high or higher have been known to break in knee deep water during heavy surf conditions. When this occurs, a vigorous suction is caused both by the breaking wave and by the backwash from previous waves. As a result of this seaward flow, a person can be knocked down and caught up in the next wave.

If unfamiliar with the sea, beachgoers can be injured and non-swimmers may drown under the weight of the oncoming waves. People caught off balance in such situations should push themselves under and toward the oncoming shorebreak, curl their bodies to withstand its force, and break out of this position on the other side of the wave. A tense, extended body, if hit by the full force of these waves, can suffer serious injury to the back and neck and receive abrasions to the skin (important signs in evaluating the need to treat for spinal injury).

LATERAL CURRENTS

A lateral current, also known as a longshore current or lateral drift, runs roughly parallel to the beach. These currents are often caused by waves coming from an angle diagonal to the beach, thus pushing water along the beach as the waves break. They can sweep swimmers along at a fairly rapid rate and feed into rip currents.

Lateral currents are less dangerous than rip currents, however, because the natural tendency of a swimmer in a current is to swim toward shore. A person in a lateral current swimming toward shore will be swimming perpendicular to the direction of the current and should be able to reach the shore relatively easily.

SANDBARS

Sandbars and troughs (also known as sloughs) are found where a persistent lateral current has cut a channel into the bottom near the beach. The shapes of these channels vary, but they are sometimes as much as eight or ten feet deep and run hundreds of feet parallel to the shore before turning seaward. Rip currents occur when waves spilling over the sandbar and into the trough on the shoreward side pile up, then exit quickly through any break in the wall of sand that traps them. These troughs range from only a few feet to perhaps 150 feet wide. Water rushing along such a trough seeking a seaward outlet may move faster than a beach patron can swim. Even a wader may not be able to regain the safety of the shore against its pull.

Sandbars can be attractive deceptions to poor swimmers. Seeing others standing in shallow water far offshore, poor swimmers may try to wade out, not realizing that deep water lies between them and their goal, and may quickly find themselves beyond their capacity to swim or cope with the current. Another common scenario occurs when a poor swimmer wades successfully to the sandbar at a low tide, becomes entrapped by a rising tide, and is forced to attempt to swim ashore through deep water and a strong outgoing current. Many rescues on the outer shore of Massachusetts' Cape Cod, for example, are caused by complications related to sand bars and longshore currents.

INSHORE HOLES

Inshore holes are depressions up to several yards in diameter dug into the sand by wave action. Small children can step easily from ankle deep water into depths over their heads. These holes are also a serious hazard to lifeguards who can sprain or fracture an ankle while running to make a rescue. A more serious problem with inshore holes is that lifeguards at surf beaches tend to focus their attention on known current areas and other problems away from the immediate shoreline. Inshore holes can be killers and lifeguards must remember to scan the entire water area, both inshore and offshore.

BEACH TOPOGRAPHY

In addition to inshore holes, beach topography can cause problems for walkers and swimmers alike. As previously mentioned, the angle of the beach (or berm) leading to the water can affect how waves break on the beach. If the berm angle is steep, it is more likely that there will be a shorebreak. Steep berm angles will also increase the effect of backwash.

Rock outcroppings, piers, groins, and cliffs cause other problems. Obviously, a person forced onto such structures by incoming waves and currents can suffer serious injury. But there can be problems, also, with people who venture out onto these rocks to be close to the water with no intention of swimming. Waves may sweep them into the water, which is usually deeper than water just off the beach, and often full of currents. Rescuing such victims can be arduous and dangerous because the lifeguard may be forced upon the rocks during the rescue attempt.

Cliffs and rock promontories often seem to invite people to dive, unaware of dangerously shallow water adjacent to the outcropping. Wave surges and tides alter water depth from one moment to the next and improper timing of a dive can then leave the diver in water shallow enough to cause serious injury.

Underwater rocks, reefs, and other obstacles also cause problems. Since these obstacles are hidden from beach visitors, they sometimes cause serious injury to unsuspecting swimmers who are suddenly thrown against them by incoming surf. Other obstacles exposed at low tides cause problems when tides rise, hiding them from the uninformed swimmer. Submerged objects in shallow water are particularly dangerous to surfers, body surfers, and bodyboarders, who are moving quickly through the surfline.

It is not unusual for flotsam to appear at surf beaches, pushed ashore by waves and surf action. Where feasible, dangerous pieces of flotsam should be removed immediately. One of the reasons for regular patrols by lifeguards is to check for the presence of beach and water hazards.

1 Bascom, Willard; *Waves and Beaches,* Doubleday, (1980)
2 Ibid.

CHAPTER SIX

THE FLAT WATER BEACH

CHAPTER HIGHLIGHTS

Lack of Surf

Currents

Beach Topography

Weeds and Plant Life

Turbidity

IN THIS CHAPTER

At flat water beaches, distress can develop immediately and unpredictably, requiring and instant reaction prior to disappearance of the distressed person. A high level of vigilance on the part of the lifeguard and constant readiness for immediate response are essential.

In comparison to surf beaches, flat water swimming areas may seem tranquil. The very nature of flat water, however, presents a significant challenge to lifeguards.

LACK OF SURF

Many people who are given a choice, choose flat water over surf because they consider this condition safer, particularly for family members or friends with weak swimming ability. This is not necessarily a sound assumption. Lifeguard agencies with a dual responsibility for both types of beaches report that lack of surf seems to lessen fear of drowning. While there may be less incidence of distress at flat water beaches, the danger of drowning is no less severe.

At surf beaches, most rescues develop as a result of observable surf and rip current conditions. Those venturing into the surf often have moderate or even strong swimming abilities, enabling them to maintain buoyancy until the lifeguard arrives if a problem arises. These factors allow surf lifeguards to concentrate their attention on known hazard areas. They also provide the opportunity to anticipate problems and time to react.

At flat water beaches, conversely, distress often develops immediately and unpredictably, requiring instant action to prevent submersion of the distressed person. This presents a major challenge to the flat water lifeguard. A person standing in water up to the neck playing with a ball, for example, may appear

[Photographic Credit: Lucy Woolshlager]

quite comfortable, but may be a complete non-swimmer. One step in the wrong direction can instantaneously leave this person submerged and out of sight. A high level of vigilance on the part of the lifeguard and constant readiness for immediate response are essential.

Reliance on floatation devices at flat water beaches is also a serious problem. Surf generally prevents poor swimmers with floatation devices from venturing into deep water, but no such impediment is present at flat water beaches. Many people visiting flat water areas use inflatable rafts and similar devices to move offshore. These devices make it difficult or impossible for the lifeguard to assess swimming ability. When poor swimmers fall from a raft, they may quickly disappear while a significant distance from shore, making effective rescue extremely difficult. For all of these reasons, the lack of surf at a flat water beach can change the entire approach to lifeguarding, from observation techniques to response procedures.

CURRENTS

Although the water may appear calm, many flat water areas experience significant currents. In salt water bays, tides can create inflow and outflow currents which are much stronger than rip currents. These are true rip tides. People caught in such currents can be drawn rapidly into deep water, where serious problems can develop.

The currents of rivers can be far more dangerous than the rip currents caused by surf action, because river currents are relentless. There is no occasional lull as is typical in the case of rip currents. A person caught in a strong river current can be caught and pinned against a stationary object, quickly drowning. Currents are also prevalent at some lakes and reservoirs, particularly at areas close to inflows or out-flows.

Many people caught in a current react by swimming against the current. Little if any progress can be made with such a response and the effort usually drains the energy and strength of the victim. Swimmers caught in currents should be instructed to swim with and diagonally across the current toward the safety of the shoreline.

BEACH TOPOGRAPHY

Currents, tides, natural configuration, and even human engineering can effect the topography of the beach at flat water areas. Where water is moving swiftly, the topography of the land under the water can change suddenly and often. Drop-offs where the bottom suddenly dips to cause deep water very close to relatively shallow water are the greatest concern. The calm and even surface of the water can hide these drop-offs from the unsuspecting wader, who may suddenly be in deep water without the skills necessary to deal with it. At tidal areas, drop-offs can be further hidden at high tide, when the water close to the drop-off is also deep. When the water level drops at low tide, the drop-off can appear unexpectedly.

Rock outcroppings, cliffs, and rocky shores present safety hazards at flat water beaches. In many areas, the water just off a rocky shore can be quite deep. The unsuspecting person who jumps or falls into the water from the shore can suddenly need immediate assistance. Outcroppings and cliffs also invite people to dive, even though the water may not be deep enough for that purpose. Submerged obstacles are a related problem, especially where water bodies and beaches have been created by planned flooding. Tree stumps, rocks, and other objects can lie hidden below the water's surface. Other submerged objects can be washed in with currents and deposited beneath swimming areas. Changing water conditions, reservoir heights, and tides may effect the water depth at these popular diving spots.

The greatest hazard posed by submerged objects involves diving. Serious injury can result from diving into unknown waters. The unexpected striking of an underwater hazard or shallow bottom is a prime cause of the most tragic of non-lethal injuries—paralysis from permanent spinal cord damage.

Where feasible, extraordinary hazards which are not normal features of the area should be removed or marked. This is not to suggest that every stump or out-cropping of rock must be signed or eliminated, but such action is appropriate for those hazards which are of an unusual nature or easily removed. The most obvious examples are logs and other floating debris that wash up on a beach. Regular patrols to check for beach hazards are appropriate, particularly during and after storms.

WEEDS AND PLANT LIFE

Calm water areas can experience problems with weeds and other plant life that flourish in the absence of currents. While the obvious problem may appear to be that people will become entangled in weeds, experience has shown that this is a rarity in the flat water environment. Instead, the fear of becoming entangled in weeds may cause a panic that is more dangerous. When some swimmers come in contact with an unseen substance, they panic and require assistance, even though they may not actually be in danger. Most swimmers who react calmly to contact with marine plants can free themselves easily using slow shaking motions.

TURBIDITY

Water clarity can cause problems at flat water beaches. With a lack of movement and flushing by currents or tides, sediment can build up on the bottom. Clay and other soils may predominate. When people enter the water at areas with these types of bottoms, the water can become cloudy, blocking a clear view of the swimming area by the lifeguard. This becomes a particular problem during lost person incidents or an underwater search procedure. Turbidity can also help mask drop-offs and other hazards from beach visitors. When the water is opaque, depth perception is eliminated and underwater obstacles, such as rocks, are hidden.

CHAPTER SEVEN

THE AQUATIC ENVIRONMENT

CHAPTER HIGHLIGHTS

Marine Life

Sharks
Rays
Schooling Fish
Venomous Fish
Portuguese Man-of-War
Jellyfish
Marine Mammals
Other Marine Life

Fresh Water Life

Leeches
Snapping Turtles
Mussels
Fish
Snakes
Other Reptiles and Lizards
Semi-Aquatic Animals

People

IN THIS CHAPTER

Shark attack is viewed by most beach users as the ultimate risk associated with swimming in the ocean. Although a concern and the subject of a great deal of fear and overreaction, the actual danger of shark attacks has been grossly exaggerated. It is estimated that worldwide there are 75 or fewer shark attacks each year and 10 or fewer deaths.

Aquatic life includes all organisms (plants and animals) that live totally or partially in water. Since aquatic life differs widely in the salt water (marine) and fresh water environments, it will be discussed separately.

MARINE LIFE

One of the keys to understanding the dynamics of ocean beaches lies in the fact that they represent components of large and complex marine ecosystems. Living within these ecosystems is a host of highly adapted organisms, some of which are capable of inflicting injury on humans. Most aquatic injuries associated with marine life are in the form of lacerations, abrasions, and punctures; however, sometimes injuries can involve bites and stings.

Usually when one thinks of dangerous marine life, such notorious animals as sharks, barracuda, and Portuguese man-of-war come to mind, but even seemingly benign organisms such as barnacles and kelp can be very dangerous. Conducting a complete inventory of all dangerous marine life inhabiting American coastal waters is beyond the scope of this text. Therefore, only the most common will be discussed.

From a lifeguard's perspective, the initial consideration when dealing with any form of potentially dangerous marine life is early, accurate identification. Identification can be complicated by glare off the water, turbidity, and distance from shore. Another complicating factor in identification is the innate behavior and deceptiveness of some aquatic organisms. This includes camouflage, cryptic coloration, mimicry, and stealth behavior.

In addition to these factors, many dangerous marine animals can be confused with those not generally considered dangerous. For example, in Florida waters, several kinds of large fish and mammals have a tendency to swim just below the surface. Only certain sharks, however, are considered to present serious danger. Proper identification is essential, because clearing the water for a non-dangerous animal may cause panic and later non-compliance when a real danger exists. To prevent this, some agencies use a key—a small sheet with pictures—to help inexperienced lifeguards make correct identifications.

SHARKS

Shark attack is viewed by most beach users as the ultimate risk associated with swimming in the ocean. Although a major concern and the subject of a great deal of fear and overreaction, the actual danger of shark attacks has been grossly exaggerated. It is estimated that worldwide there are 75 or fewer shark attacks each year and 10 or fewer deaths. In the United States, the risk of death from lightning is 30 times greater than from shark attack.[1] While the most common site in the United States for shark attack appears to be Florida, this is probably due to high annual water attendance, rather than unusual concentrations of sharks.

Experts recognize over 250 species of sharks, but only a few of these are considered a threat to people. Three shark species are the most frequent attackers of humans. These are the tiger shark, bull shark, and white shark (known as the great white shark).[2]

Most shark attacks occur in nearshore areas. This includes the area between sandbars, where sharks are sometimes trapped at low tide, and areas with steep dropoffs. Sharks are drawn to such areas because their natural prey can be found there. Attacks occur more commonly when waters are murky. This condition increases the chance of a shark making a prey identification mistake, accidentally attacking a human.

In Florida, the predominant food items of sharks are small fish. In this area, shark bites seem to occur when sharks confuse the splashing of surfers and swimmers in murky nearshore waters as being from schooling fish. Injuries are seldom life-threatening and, as of mid-1994, no surfer had ever died in Florida as the result of shark attack. Most attacks in Florida result in a single bite or slash, with no repeat passes at the victim.[3]

Along the middle and northern California coast, the threat to humans engaged in aquatic recreation is essentially confined to one species, white sharks. Surfers are the most common victims in recent years and injuries can be quite severe, occasionally resulting in death. Attacks in this area are believed to occur when the shark confuses the size, shape, and actions of a person with a seal or sea lion—a major indigenous food item.[4]

In Hawaii, attacks largely involve the tiger shark. Like the white shark, this species is known to attack humans and life threatening injuries can result. Surfers are the most likely victims. A favorite haunt of the tiger shark is the area where the surf breaks over reefs, which is also a favorite area for surfers.[5]

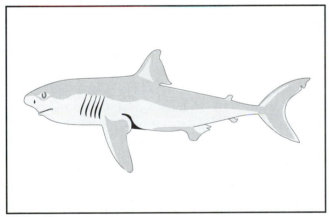

This drawing of a shark shows the vertical tail fin.

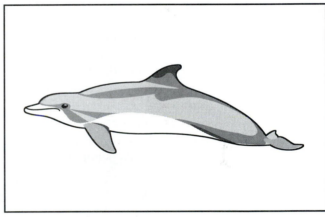

Porpoises have a horizontal tail fin.

In regard to lifeguard practices, the data on sharks suggest that their behavior must always be regarded as *unpredictable*. In some areas, swimming crowds are cleared immediately upon any observation (direct or indirect) of a shark. When clearing the water, lifeguards should make every effort to avoid panicking swimmers because thrashing is an activity that can attract sharks.

Porpoises are often mistaken for sharks, but they are harmless to swimmers. Porpoises have a horizontal tail fin, so they usually expose only their dorsal fin when swimming near the surface. They regularly swim in groups, continually surfacing and submerging in forward arcs. Sharks, on the other hand, have a vertical tail fin. When swimming along the surface, the dorsal fin cuts through the water, while the tail fin moves back and forth. Sharks do not swim in an arcing motion. Instead, when swimming along the surface, they cruise at a fairly consistent depth, with their fins exposed for longer periods than porpoises. Such observations are extremely rare on the West Coast, but occasionally seen on the East Coast, particularly in Florida.

Periods when shark attack is more likely along the West Coast include times of heavy seal and sea lion activity, especially during the annual birthing period. Under these conditions, white sharks are more likely to move into the surf zone. Along the East Coast, where shark bites are sometimes sustained near schooling fish, it may be prudent to warn swimmers away from heavy concentrations of fish —often indicated by sea bird diving. In addition, periods of onshore winds along the east coast of Florida can result in concentrations of fish and sharks in poor visibility water—a bad combination when humans are added to the mix. In Hawaii, surfers and swimmers should avoid dawn and dusk periods when tiger sharks are particularly active, and the areas around the mouths of rivers, especially after heavy rains, where tiger sharks may scavenge.[7]

The result of shark attacks on humans can involve serious lacerations, puncture wounds, avulsions and even eviscerations. Treatment for these biting wounds includes immediate removal from the water followed by standard procedures for preventing blood loss and mitigating shock.

Following a shark attack, the water is usually cleared of all swimmers immediately and kept clear until it can be determined that the immediate threat is over. That decision depends on factors which include water conditions, behavior of the shark (aggressive or non-aggressive), and policy of the agency. Some studies have found that unusual noise may aggravate sharks. Therefore, calling in a helicopter to cruise at low altitude and check a swimming area for sharks should be carefully considered.

The International Shark Attack File, a compendium of worldwide shark attack data, is kept at the Florida Museum of Natural History, University of Florida, Gainesville. Lifeguards are strongly encouraged to report attacks so that information can be gathered for future reference. A shark attack report form can be found in Appendix B.

RAYS

Only a few members of the ray family are considered dangerous. The most common is the stingray, which is equipped with a barb and a venom gland in the tail. Stingrays are not aggressive animals and are easily frightened, but they often bury themselves in the sand in shallow water for protection against their predators. This is when they are most hazardous. If accidentally stepped on by a hapless wader, stingrays flip their tail, which has a barb at the end. If the barb comes into contact with a foot, ankle, or other part of the body, the barb can penetrate the skin and venom enters the wound.

When stung, the victim typically experiences intense, sharp, and shooting pain in the affected area. Usually the pain will intensify for the first 90 minutes. Besides pain, the victim's blood pressure may fall significantly. Also, the victim may experience vomiting, diarrhea, sweating, arrhythmia, and muscular paralysis. Death can result in the most severe cases.

Treatment protocols for stingray wounds vary from agency to agency, but some procedures are used extensively with great success by many lifeguard agencies and are worthy of consideration. The wound should be checked to make sure that the sheath and barb is completely removed. Otherwise, envenomation will continue. After the wound has been cleansed, the injury should be soaked in water as hot as the patient can tolerate without producing further injury to the tissue. In most cases, hot water reduces the pain dramatically. The affected extremity (usually a foot) is then left in the hot water until it can be removed without the pain returning. This sometimes takes an hour or more.

As with any other type of envenomation, allergic reaction is a potentially serious result. Persons with heart problems or similar maladies may need immediate hospitalization. Treatment should include procedures to protect against shock.

In some areas, stingray envenomation is a regular occurrence. Lifeguards in these areas routinely treat and release persons who have been stung. This approach should be considered, depending upon the medical qualifications of lifeguard personnel involved, with input from local medical authorities. Some local medical authorities prohibit primary providers of medical aid from treating and releasing victims of envenomation.

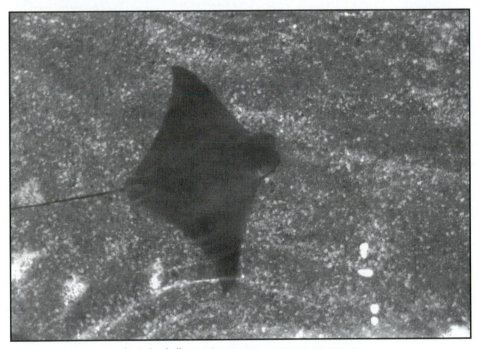

A ray in shallow water. [Photographic Credit: Dave Foxwell]

SCHOOLING FISH

Most schooling fish do not represent a problem because they are not equipped with the physical anatomy to injure a swimmer. A few species under certain circumstances can inflict injury. Some of these include jacks, tarpon, mackerel, and bluefish.

During migrations and feeding frenzies, these species have been known to brush against a swimmer causing lacerations and abrasions. Schools of bluefish have been reported nipping at swimmers' hands and feet, causing numerous, nasty bites. Schooling fish can also attract larger predatory fish.

Whenever schools of large fish are observed, they should be carefully monitored. Some lifeguard agencies clear the water of swimmers immediately. This is an agency by agency decision based on past experience.

If a swimmer is bitten by a predatory fish, it is crucial to get the victim out of the water. This will help prevent blood from entering the water and provoking additional bites. Minor wounds should be cleansed and disinfected. Major wounds require immediate transport to a medical facility.

BARRACUDA

Barracuda are large, streamlined predatory fish usually found in tropical and subtropical waters. Biologists classify at least 20 species of barracuda. Only one of these species, the Great Barracuda, is considered dangerous to people.

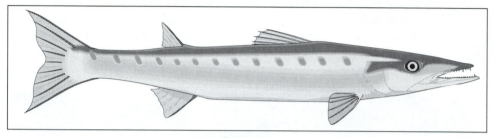

Barracuda

Although attacks are rare, there have been authenticated reports. Most of these attacks are associated with blood in the water, either from an injured fish or a human. There are also reports which suggest that attacks may result from swimmers wearing bright and shiny objects during times of poor water visibility. When a barracuda, especially a large one, is observed near a swimming area, it should be monitored carefully. Some agencies will establish a barracuda sighting as criteria for the water to be cleared of swimmers, especially if it appears that there are also baitfish in the area.

VENOMOUS FISH

Venomous fish are classified in the family Scorpaenidae. There are hundreds of species in the family which are widely distributed along both coasts of the United States. Most biologists divide these fish into two groups: scorpionfish and stonefish. Some of the common names for members of the two groups include: stonefish, lionfish, rockfish, turkeyfish, and sculpin.

Lionfish [Photographic Credit: Dave Foxwell]

These fish are usually bottom feeders. Many are found in or around coral reefs or kelp beds, into which they blend quite well due to their protective coloration. Some species prefer sandy bottom habitats and enjoy lying motionless on the bottom for long periods of time.

The venom of the scorpionfish is stored in special sacs located in hypodermic-like dorsal spines. When a swimmer steps on these fish, venom is injected into the wound. The result is intense, sharp, and shooting pain. Besides pain, the victim may suffer convulsions, nervous disturbances and even cardiac failure. In some cases death may ensue.

Treatment should be directed toward alleviating pain, reducing the effects of the venom, and preventing secondary infection. Immediate treatment includes encouraging bleeding of the affected area and irrigating the wound in hot water. Sometimes, applying a constricting band directly above the puncture site is indicated. All cases require transportation to a medical facility.

PORTUGUESE MAN-OF-WAR

The man-of-war is sometimes confused with the jellyfish, to which it is related. It is a colony of animals called hydroids, which appear to be a single animal. Portuguese man-of-war are found in many warm water areas, but also drift north with warm currents to cooler zones. In marine waters of the United States they are found most often in the Gulf Stream of the northern Atlantic Ocean.

The Portuguese man-of-war is most readily identified in water by a brilliant blue, pink, or violet float which is gas filled and bladder-like. The float is usually about two to eight inches in length. Atop the float is a crest which functions somewhat like a sail, allowing the man-of-war to move with the wind. Hanging below are clusters of polyps, which form tentacles. Some of the tentacles serve to capture prey for the man-of-war by use of nematocysts—stingers that paralyze small fish and other organisms.

Portuguese Man-of-War.

Humans are stung when they come into contact with the man-of-war tentacles. Usually intense pain accompanies this contact. In most cases this pain will last a couple of hours. However, some victims complain of pain for many days. In addition to pain, paralysis or shock may occur in severe cases, making medical attention imperative.

Once a lifeguard identifies a victim who has been stung by a man-of-war, treatment should be directed toward accomplishment of three primary objectives: relieving pain, alleviating the neurotoxic effects of the venom, and controlling shock. The first recommended step in providing first aid is to remove any tentacles adhering to the skin of the victim. This can be accomplished by using some gauze, a towel, seaweed, or any other available material. Next, a solution should be applied to the victim's skin to inhibit further activity of the nematocysts.

Numerous solutions have been advocated by various agencies throughout the country. These include solutions of vinegar, lemon juice, papaya, ammonia, meat tenderizer, sodium bicarbonate, and boric acid. Empirical data gathered by lifeguards indicates that vinegar is the most effective treatment. Ammonia, fresh water, or vigorous rubbing should be avoided as these treatments have been found to worsen the pain.

Even if a victim appears to be recovering from a man-of-war sting, the patient's condition should be monitored closely. Special precautions, which may include transport to a medical facility, should be taken with victims who have a history of reactions to insect bites and stings. Any person with extensive stings or stings to the face, particularly in the case of children, should be transported or referred to a hospital.

JELLYFISH

The jellyfish is a form of hydroid. Most jellyfish are free swimming, colorless, and range in size from a few inches to three feet in diameter. Their appearance on surf beaches tends to be seasonal—spring and summer is the time they are most common. Like the Portuguese man-of-war, most jellyfish feed on small animals they catch in their tentacles by use of nematocysts. Humans can be stung when they come into contact with the tentacles. Although there are hundreds of species of jellyfish, only a few are considered to pose a serious danger. Perhaps the best known is the sea wasp. One Australian species of sea wasp can cause death to a human within a few minutes after contact.

Treatment of a jellyfish sting is the same as for the man-of-war. It is important to carefully monitor the victim's condition to evaluate the possibility of serious medical complications.

MARINE MAMMALS

Killer Whale

Marine mammals are common visitors to nearshore waters, usually on a seasonal basis. Marine mammals which inhabit coastal waters of the United States include whales, manatees, dolphins, porpoises, seals, sea lions, and sea otters, among others. Under normal conditions, these mammals are not dangerous. However, when sick, injured, or stressed they can represent a considerable danger. Consequently, whenever a marine mammal is observed behaving abnormally or is hauled out on a beach, people should be kept at a distance. Many areas have local marine mammal stranding networks capable of responding to a sick or injured animal. Various Federal and state laws protect marine mammals from harm or harassment. Lifeguards are often called upon to help enforce these laws.

OTHER MARINE LIFE

There is a host of other marine organisms capable of inflicting injury to humans. Some of these include barnacles, crabs, marine worms, coral, sea urchins, marine shells, eels, catfish, and sea turtles. Due to the limited distribution of many of these animals and the limited danger they represent, only a few are considered here.

Coral

Coral can cause cuts, abrasions, welts, pain, and itching. Severe reactions are not usual. Coral cuts can be rinsed with baking soda solutions, weak ammonia, or even plain water.

Sea Urchins

Sea urchins are spiny marine invertebrates, found in rocky crevices in the intertidal area. Urchin wounds are usually sustained when people step on urchin spines. The spines from these creatures are equipped with multiple venom organs. They can penetrate the skin, even through protective clothing, to cause a wound with intense burning sensations followed by redness, swelling, and aching. More severe reactions to urchin wounds include weakness, loss of body sensation, facial swelling, and irregular pulse. Rare cases involving paralysis, respiratory distress, and even death have occurred.

Treatment for urchin wounds differs from agency to agency, but often includes the application of hot compresses or soaking the affected area in hot water. Follow-up with a doctor should be recommended, particularly if infection develops.

Cone Shells

The Cone Shell is actually a snail with an apparatus for injecting paralyzing toxin by means of a dart. Most are under five inches in length and found in the Indio-Pacific region. Medical symptoms of envenomation include numbness and tingling around the victim's nose and mouth, along with paralysis. Fatalities are very rare. Treatment includes soaking the wound area in hot water, careful monitoring of symptoms, and transport to a medical facility if necessary.

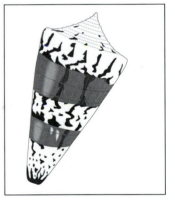

Cone Shell

Other Mollusks

Barnacles, mussels, oysters, and other mollusks can cause lacerations that are easily infected. The wound should be cleansed and a sterile dressing applied. Serious cases may require transport to a medical facility. In cases where the patient is treated and released, the patient should be advised to seek further medical care if infection develops.

Sea Snakes

Certain species of sea snakes can bite. Toxic signs, appearing within twenty minutes, can include malaise, anxiety, euphoria, muscle spasm, respiratory problems, convulsions, unconsciousness, as well as all the signs and symptons of shock. Immediate transport to a medical facility is generally appropriate.

Mussels

FRESH WATER LIFE

Although the number of animal species capable of inflicting harm on swimmers is much larger in salt water than in fresh water, lifeguards at lake, river, and pond beaches must take the time during their training to become familiar with local species and assess the possible risks to visitors. Some of the types of potentially dangerous fresh water aquatic life are listed here.

LEECHES

Leeches are bloodsucking worms. They typically have a flattened, segmented body with a sucker at both ends, used to bore into flesh and draw out blood. Leeches are found in many fresh water bodies throughout the United States.

Although leeches are not life threatening, the presence of a leech on a person usually evokes a strong emotional response and requests for assistance. Because of this, many agencies on beaches with leech problems provide lifeguards with equipment to help detach and dispose of leeches. A common practice is to place salt directly on the leech to cause it to detach from the visitor.

SNAPPING TURTLES

Several species of turtles frequent the fresh water bodies of the United States. Most pose no danger whatsoever. One type of turtle that may present limited concern is the snapping turtle. These turtles have a rough shell and powerful jaws. Although most are not particularly dangerous, some species have been known to deliver painful bites to people who knowingly or unintentionally corner or trap them. Lifeguards should become familiar with the turtles specific to their area and which, if any, display aggressive behavior. Lifeguards can then work to minimize possible confrontations between these turtles and humans. With this knowledge, lifeguards can also reassure those who may become needlessly concerned.

MUSSELS

Fresh water mussels are bivalve mollusks found in many areas of the United States. These mussels usually have a dark, elongated shell and dwell on the bottom in the mud. The edges of their shells can be very sharp and lacerate the feet of beach visitors. This is particularly likely in the case of half-shells from dead mussels.

A particularly serious problem in some areas of the country is posed by zebra mussels. Zebra mussels look like small clams with a yellowish and/or brownish D-shaped, striped shell. These barnacle-like mussels are the only fresh water mollusks that attach themselves to solid objects. They can grow up to two inches long, but most are under an inch in length. Zebra mussels propagate at a high rate and are said to pose a multi-billion dollar threat to drinking supplies and shipping. In some areas, public agencies such as fish and game departments ask that any sighting be reported to help aid in eradication.[8]

FISH

Although many species of fish are found throughout fresh water bodies of the

United States, few pose any threat to swimmers. Some areas report problems with different species of catfish due to their tactile barbs, but injuries involving fish usually occur when people fishing remove them from the hook.

SNAKES

Some types of water snakes or snakes that travel on water can indeed be dangerous or poisonous, particularly in warmer climates. Snake problems are regional in nature and should be addressed through local training programs. Immediate treatment and transport to a medical facility is needed if the type of snake is unknown or known to be poisonous.

OTHER REPTILES AND LIZARDS

Some species of reptiles and lizards can prove dangerous to beach visitors, particularly in the south. Alligators, for example, can be extremely dangerous in a fresh water body that also includes a swimming beach.

SEMI-AQUATIC ANIMALS

Semi-aquatic animals are those that, while not adapted to living underwater, spend a great portion of their time in the water environment. Examples of semi-aquatic animals include beavers, otters, muskrats, and various species of waterfowl.

Most of these animals will pose no threat to swimmers at fresh water beaches, as they actively avoid contact with humans under most conditions. There may be situations, however, when a semi-aquatic animal approaches or even enters a swim area unsuspectingly. Waterfowl may be drawn into a swim area when visitors attempt to feed them and while they are not usually dangerous, they may be hosts to various parasites that can cause conditions similar to swimmer's itch syndrome.

Cars are permitted on Daytona Beach in Florida
[Photographic Credit: Mike Hensler]

PEOPLE

In closing this overview of the aquatic environment, some mention must be included on the impact of people. While people are visitors to the beach environment rather than part of it, their presence can create or intensify environmental problems. People may litter or even bury refuse in the beach sand, discharge wastes into the water, leave fires burning on the beach, or bury hot coals in the sand. They may underestimate environmental conditions and place themselves or other people in danger through actions such as erecting a beach umbrella in the sand on a windy day.

Lifeguards are seen by many as aquatic park rangers, whether or not they have actual enforcement authority. This image should be used to help educate beachgoers about the aquatic environment, and to encourage them to leave it as they have found it so that others may enjoy it. Some beach areas employ a maxim worth repeating to beach users throughout the world: "Leave only footprints."

1 Burgess, George H., "Shark Attack and the International Shark Attack File," in *Discovering Sharks,* ed. S.H. Gruber, Sandy Hook, N.J.: American Littoral Society, 1990

2 Burgess, George H., "Shark Aggression in Nearshore Waters: A Florida Perspective," in *Proceedings of a Sea Symposium 89,* ed. J. Fletemeyer: Florida Sea Grant Press, 1989

3 Burgess, George H., International Shark Attack File, 1994, Letter to the Editor

4 Ibid.

5 Ibid.

6 *Lifeguard Training Manual,* Volusia County Beach Department

7 Burgess, George H., International Shark Attack File, 1994, Letter to the Editor

8 University of Wisconsin Sea Grant Institute

CHAPTER EIGHT

WEATHER AND OTHER HAZARDS

CHAPTER HIGHLIGHTS

IN THIS CHAPTER

People in a recreational setting sometimes ignore obvious signs of threatening weather until it is too late. At that point, panic and injury may occur when people run for cover or are injured by lightning, high winds, and the like. Prudent lifeguards monitor atmospheric conditions and take reasonable steps to warn beachgoers of looming weather problems.

While drowning prevention is a critical task of lifeguards, hazards other than the water can cause injury in the beach environment. Professional lifeguards make it their business to understand these hazards, take steps to reduce their effects, and make preparations to respond as needed. This chapter covers some of these hazards, and the actions lifeguards can take to help beach users avoid injury.

WEATHER

Effective lifeguarding requires a basic understanding of both weather and climatic conditions. There is a difference between the two. Weather is the temporary or present state of atmospheric conditions, while climate is the long-term trend or average weather for a particular geographic region. While weather can influence beach use on a particular day, the climate of a region can dictate beach use trends for the entire season or year.

People in a recreational setting sometimes ignore obvious signs of threatening weather until it is too late. At that point, panic and injury may occur when people run for cover or are injured by lightning, high winds, and the like. Prudent lifeguards monitor atmospheric conditions and take reasonable steps to warn beachgoers of looming weather problems.

Simple weather monitoring can be accomplished with visual observation and the use of a barometer. Many lifeguard services keep inexpensive radios on hand which receive continual broadcasts from the National Weather Service. Better models of such radios can be set to broadcast only in the case of severe weather advisories. They are widely available for under $20. Even with such devices, however, an understanding of what creates adverse weather conditions is helpful.

To help beach visitors avoid injury from storms lifeguards should:
- Monitor weather conditions to help anticipate storms
- Warn beach visitors of impending storms
- Advise and assist visitors regarding appropriate reaction to approaching storms

FRONTAL STORMS

When atmospheric conditions push bodies of warm air into bodies of cold air (or vice-versa) these masses of air clash. The edge of two such conflicting masses of air is known as a front. As fronts advance across land or water, many factors can combine to create weather phenomena that are potentially dangerous to beachgoers and lifeguards alike. Lightning storms, tornadoes, waterspouts, and squall lines are examples. The dangers of these storms is obvious to anyone who has experienced them. In many cases, frontal storms appear unexpectedly, taking beach visitors by surprise.

OTHER STORMS

While frontal storms may appear suddenly (and can dissipate just as quickly), storms caused by lingering low pressure cells and other factors can settle in for a longer period. These types of weather conditions are usually predicted and will affect beach operations mostly by keeping people away. Such weather patterns can cause high surf, water turbidity, strong currents, high water, and floods.

A hurricane hundreds of miles away from an ocean beach may cause no change in the local weather, but may result in tremendously powerful surf for days after the storm. These conditions cause problems for beach visitors who wrongly expect water conditions to reflect the immediate weather, not a storm that has passed or completely missed the beach area. Some people are attracted to an area after a storm to view the post-storm effects. Surfers and swimmers are often drawn by the challenge of large surf conditions, with which they may well lack experience. Pedestrians may be swept into the water, while surfers and swimmers may be overcome by the unexpected power of the waves.

LIGHTNING

It is estimated that 40 million lightning strokes hit the ground each year in the United States. Lightning is the second leading cause of weather-related deaths in this country after floods. Even so, less than 100 deaths per year nationwide are attributed to lightning strikes. Florida leads the nation in lightning-caused deaths with about 10 a year—almost twice as many as any other state. Conversely, in the years 1959 to 1990 there were no lightning-caused deaths in Hawaii and less than one a year in California.[1] More than two-thirds of lightning-caused deaths occur in June, July, and August.[2]

Lightning threatens as a storm approaches. [Photographic Credit: Mike Hensler]

Overall, the thunderstorms that bring lightning are most prevalent in Southeastern, Midwestern, and Gulf Coast states. They occur much less frequently in New England, Hawaii, along the Pacific Coast, and along the Great Lakes. Most people struck by lightning are in open areas, such as beaches, or have taken shelter under a tree which is subsequently struck.

Cumulonimbus clouds, commonly known as thunderheads, are the tall and sometimes anvil shaped clouds that produce thunder and lightning. Their formation near the beach should be monitored closely. If lightning is observed, the proximity of lightning strikes can be roughly determined by timing the interval between a lightning flash and the subsequent arrival of thunder. Sound travels through the air at a rate of approximately one mile every five seconds, but light travels almost instantaneously. Therefore, a timed interval between observation of a lightning flash and the audible sound of thunder of twenty seconds, for example, would indi-cate a lightning strike at a distance of four miles.[3]

Lifeguards in areas heavily impacted by lightning strikes, particularly Florida lifeguards, should develop contingency plans for responding to lightning storms. Since lightning tends to strike the highest point in an open area, lifeguards should descend from towers or stands during these storms. Swimmers and beachgoers may be advised to leave the beach and seek shelter in automobiles or buildings. Static charge precedes a lightning strike, so lifeguards should be prepared to drop to the ground immediately if their hair suddenly stands on end.[4]

WATERSPOUTS

Waterspouts are tornadoes over water. They have an appearance of a narrow, vertical column touching the water. These formations can be deadly, and lifeguards should report any sightings immediately to the local bureau of the National Weather Service so that appropriate advisories can be issued. The tornadoes that form waterspouts pose a direct threat to both boats and aircraft. In addition, they may come ashore and threaten beach users. The primary danger from tornadoes is flying debris, so shelter and protection should be sought if it appears that a waterspout may come ashore.[5]

FOG

Fog is a cloud that forms near the earth's surface. Fog can result from several conditions that cause air to cool to its dew point. For example, when relatively cool air blows over warmer water, evaporation can occur, cooling the air and causing it to condense into tiny droplets. In fog, the most basic tool of the lifeguard for identifying persons in distress—observation—is negated. Swimmers and surfers may become disoriented and panic. Boaters may inadvertently run aground, threatening those aboard and any swimmers in the area.

Like some other weather conditions, fog may not be a major management problem simply because it will keep people away from the beach, but in some areas fog will not dissuade surfers and other beach enthusiasts from water recreation. It may arrive suddenly and unexpectedly, surprising those in the water.

When lifeguard observation skills from a fixed lifeguard tower become useless due to fog, many lifeguard agencies employ patrol procedures along the shoreline in vehicles or on foot, listening for distress cries. This is a particularly important procedure in areas with high boating traffic because serious boating accidents can occur in fog very close to lifeguard stations with lifeguard personnel left totally unaware of the situation.

WIND

Wind plays an important role in the generation of waves at all types of beaches, inland and coastal, but wind also affects beach operation in other ways. Strong winds may blow beach sand, causing discomfort and injuries to visitors. Wind can blow beach umbrellas over, which sometimes results in surprisingly serious injuries. Wind can blow balls and other floating objects away from swimmers, causing them to chase these objects into deeper water from which they are unable to return. Offshore winds can literally blow people on floatation devices away from the beach.

TEMPERATURE

Climate and weather affect air temperature at the beach and may put certain visitors at risk of a heat-related illness. This is particularly true at beaches where there is little shade. Although heat-related stress is often considered a problem of warm climate areas only, heat problems are also common at resort areas, where visitors are not properly acclimatized.

Heat is not the only concern. At many areas, climate, water depth, and primary currents can keep water very cold, with swimmers suffering from hypothermia. Although hypothermia is generally thought to be a problem only at beaches in the northern latitudes, water under 70 degrees Fahrenheit is considered by medical experts to be cold water. Many lakes, rivers, bays, and surf beaches in warmer climates have water temperatures below 70 degrees. Several factors will determine the extent of the effects of cold water on swimmers, including immersion time, relative air temperature, and wind.

SUN

Many people continue to practice sunbathing despite the fact that long term exposure to the sun causes accelerated aging of the skin and is believed to enhance the potential for contracting skin cancer. The most immediate danger from the sun comes from overexposure, which affects both beach visitors and lifeguards. Sunburns on the beach can range from minor redness of the skin to serious burns and "sun poisoning."

Problems with overexposure to the sun are not restricted to the more southern latitudes. Anywhere there is sun, there is the potential of injury from overexposure. Any significant exposure to the sun results in some degree of damage that is cumulative.

The problem of overexposure is compounded by the belief by some that a sunburn is a normal part of the beach recreation experience and that one or two episodes of overexposure each beach season will not be harmful. Indeed, some visitors accept and even look forward to a sunburn as tangible evidence that they enjoyed themselves at the beach. Lifeguards should monitor their beach crowd for persons who appear to be overexposed, paying particular attention to people with light skin, along with small children and babies who must rely on their parents to protect them. Dermatologists have found that sunburns, particularly when sustained by young children, can greatly increase the potential for contracting skin cancer later in life.

Lifeguards are particularly susceptible to sun-related injury. For a full discussion of this issue, refer to the chapter entitled *Lifeguard Health and Safety*.

FLOODS

Floods, particularly flash floods, are the greatest weather-related killers. Flood-related deaths outnumber all other weather-related deaths in the United States, with an average 110 deaths per year in the 1980s.[6] While flooding is not typically a threat to beach areas, lifeguards are often called upon to assist in flood rescues due to their aquatic skills and rescue equipment. Some lifeguard swiftwater rescue teams, such as the San Diego Lifeguard River Rescue Team, are essential components of local flood disaster response.

People are most often caught in floodwaters when they try to cross apparent low points in vehicles or on foot. They may become stranded or swept downstream. Floodwaters are extremely hazardous, perhaps even more so than heavy surf conditions, because floodwaters are relentless—there's no lull between sets of waves—and the water level may rise dramatically in a very short period of time.

Rescuers are seriously endangered by floodwaters also, and many rescuers have been killed in attempts to effect rescues in swiftwater flood conditions. Lifeguards who lack special training in swiftwater rescue should make every effort to avoid making a rescue that requires use of a boat or actual entry into the swiftwater environment. Instead, methods which allow rescuers to remain onshore should be preferred. For a further discussion of flood rescue considerations and basic techniques, refer to the chapter entitled *Special Rescues*.

OTHER HAZARDS

FLOTSAM

Flotsam is another environmental hazard at the beach. Flotsam is debris floating in the water. Such objects can be in the form of harmless seaweed or can be large, dangerous objects containing sharp edges or surfaces. Flotsam may take the form of hazardous materials or substances, which can cause a health threat to beach visitors. It is most evident after a storm or storm surf.

At surf areas, flotsam is particularly dangerous since it can be washed in at high velocity by surf action, injuring swimmers in its path. At both surf and flat water areas, flotsam that washes ashore without incident can continue to be dangerous, especially if it becomes buried and therefore hidden to beach visitors. Landed flotsam can then cut, stab, stub, and stick visitors walking along the beach.

Lifeguards should scan their water areas for flotsam and immediately investigate any unexpected floating objects. At surf beaches, it may be necessary to clear a water area until a large object floats in, so that it does not strike anyone. Regular patrols of beach areas by lifeguards are important to check for all hazards, including flotsam.

DRY LAND HAZARDS

The beach recreation zone does not stop at the water's edge. Environmental hazards also exist throughout the beach recreation area, including picnic grounds, adjacent cliffs, parking areas, along walks, and on trails. The beach itself can present hazards.

Sandy beaches are unique environments, seemingly perfect for recreation. Yet sand can be dangerous. Blowing sand, thrown sand, and uneven sand all can cause injuries. One of the most serious problems involving sand occurs when visitors attempt to dig a deep pit. When the pit reaches a point where the person in the pit is beyond waist deep, the person must bend down below the level of the pit to dig deeper. At this point, if the pit collapses on itself (and sand pits often do), the visitor may be completely buried and suffocate. Deaths have occurred this way on beaches around the world.

A related problem involves lifeguard emergency vehicles. Children often enjoy covering each other with sand up to their necks. Unfortunately, this can camouflage the covered child from a lifeguard driving an emergency vehicle. Caution is essential in all beach driving.

Sand beaches can also hide dangerous objects such as broken glass, nails, wood splinters, hypodermic needles, and countless other sharp or dangerous items. The problem is compounded when people actually use the sand to cover and dispose of litter such as glass containers, which may break and provide a hidden hazard to other visitors.

Improper disposal of hot charcoal or fire ashes poses a very serious hazard to beachgoers. Visitors may prepare picnics using small charcoal grills, disposing of the used but still hot coals in the sand and burying them. Unfortunately, buried coals can retain their heat for many hours, later causing second and third degree burns to the feet. This is a particular problem for infants who may wander away from their guardians and walk on discarded coals, but who may not understand how to get away from the burning sensation. Serious injuries causing lifelong deformity to children occur this way every year. A solution employed by some agencies is to maintain containers for disposing of hot coals.

Other dry land environmental hazards include rock outcroppings, cliff areas, and similar topographical features which provide beach visitors with opportunities to hurt themselves. Structures and improvements such as bathhouses, piers, floats and docks, parking lots, playgrounds, boardwalks, cycle paths, and so on can also inflict injury. Lifeguards should make it their business to be aware of all the potential hazards in areas under their responsibility, attempting to mitigate them as appropriate.

1   Williams, Jack, *The Weather Book,* Vintage Books, New York, N.Y.: 1992
2   Baker, Susan P., *The Injury Fact Book,* Oxford Unifersity Press, Second Edition, New York, N.Y.: 1992
3   *Lifeguard Training Manual,* Volusia County Beach Department
4   Ibid.
5   Ibid.
6   Williams, Jack, *The Weather Book,* Vintage Books, New York, N.Y.: 1992

CHAPTER NINE

DROWNING

CHAPTER HIGHLIGHTS

Statistical Indicators

Activities Associated with Drowning

Drowning Stages

Physiology of Drowning

IN THIS CHAPTER

Based on the experience of professional beach lifeguards, USLA believes there is a *two minute window* of enhanced opportunity for successful recovery and resuscitation of submerged victims. Thereafter, the chances of successful recovery decline very quickly.

Each year in the United States, thousands of people die or are seriously injured in aquatic accidents. Drowning is the third leading cause of accidental death in the United States and the second leading cause of accidental death for persons aged 5 to 44.[1] In some states, such as California, Florida, and Hawaii, drowning is the leading cause of injury death for persons under 15 years of age.[2] Moreover, death by drowning is only the tip of the iceberg for aquatic injury. For every child who dies by drowning, 14 are treated in emergency rooms and 3.6 are admitted for further treatment in hospitals.[3]

Prevention of drowning is a critical task for lifeguards, but timely effective medical aid after a near drowning incident is also essential. This is why lifeguards must be trained not only in rescue, but also in providing medical aid at a level adequate to provide life support for those injured in aquatic accidents.

Previous chapters of this text have described several environmental hazards that contribute to these tragic incidents, yet not all drownings can be attributed solely to environmental hazards. Human factors such as judgment, social pressures, inexperience, and intoxication are major contributors.

DROWNING ACCIDENTS

People of all races and ages, both male and female, are susceptible to drowning. No one is immune. There are, however, statistical data indicating that some age groups and populations are more prone to drowning accidents. In addition, certain activities have a high association with drowning.

STATISTICAL INDICATORS

National statistics have helped to identify the groups at highest risk of drowning. This is valuable information, but statistical data must be used carefully because statistics, by their nature, are indiscriminate. That is, they represent numerical averages which are not necessarily accurate in dealing with individuals. A member of a group which is statistically at high risk, for example, may actually be an excellent swimmer at little risk, just as a member of a low risk group may be a non-swimmer. Nonetheless, any clues which help lifeguards prevent drownings are valuable to all involved, as long as they are not misinterpreted or misapplied.

It would be completely inappropriate to prevent a member of a high-risk group from using a swimming area based purely on statistical data. On the other hand, it is most appropriate to pay particular attention to members of high risk groups who enter a swimming area, until their swimming ability can be evaluated through observation.

Gender

Males drown at a significantly higher rate than females. The ratio of male to female drownings is about 5 to 1. For boat related drownings, the ratio escalates to about 14 to 1.[4]

Young Males

Adolescent and young adult males are particularly susceptible to drowning. Those in the 17 to 20 year age range, for example, are about eight times as likely to drown as females of the same age. Males in these age groups are highly physically active and are known to be relatively frequent risk takers. It is often said that teenage males act as though they are immortal. They are the most likely people at a beach to recklessly dive from significant heights into unknown water or to enter obviously hazardous waters, for example.

Toddlers

Drowning is the leading cause of injury death for children in the one to two year age range. Unlike other age groups in which the frequency of drowning is slowly declining, it is actually increasing in children under one year of age and is remaining relatively static in those one to two years of age.[5] This is important information for beach lifeguards, and children of this age should be very carefully monitored, but most of these drownings occur in backyard pools or bathtubs, not at beaches. They typically result from failure to adequately fence off pools, and particularly from inadequate supervision by adult guardians.

Race/Ethnicity

The Journal of the American Medical Association and other authoritative sources have identified significant differences in drowning rates among various racial and ethnic groups.[6 7 8] However, these statistical trends vary somewhat on a regional basis. They appear to be associated with socioeconomic factors which, for example, can adversely impact access to swimming instruction.[9] Due to regional variations, USLA recommends that lifeguard agencies evaluate their own rescue statistics to identify at-risk populations in their local area.

Epileptics

Epileptics are disproportionately likely to drown. Epileptic seizures normally leave victims without control over their motor functions—a deadly circumstance in the water. Epileptics should be cautioned to advise lifeguards before swimming and to *wear personal flotation devices* during any activities in or around the water.[10]

ACTIVITIES ASSOCIATED WITH DROWNING

Many activities can result in drowning. The following are the most common in the open water environment:

- *Swimming*—Non-environmental factors that contribute to swimming deaths include poor swimming ability, alcohol and drugs, peer pressure (taking a dare, impressing friends), and carelessness or lack of good judgment. Acts of attempted rescue are another significant factors where would-be rescuers, reacting to the imminent death of others, drown in the attempt. Some studies suggest that 2% to 3% of drownings occur during rescue attempts.
- *Boating*—Each year in American waters, thousands of boating accidents occur, hundreds of which involve fatalities. Approximately 75% of recreational boating deaths result from drowning.[11] Alcohol use is believed to be a contributing factor in 50% to 90% of boating accidents.[12,13] The typical boat operator involved in a boating accident has little experience and no formal instruction whatsoever.[14] The vast majority of boats involved in fatal or injury accidents are motorboats less than 26 feet in length (including personal watercraft).[15]
- *Scuba Diving*—In recent years about 90 recreational scuba diving deaths per year have been reported to the Divers Alert Network or its predecessor.[16] Most of these occurred within the United States, but they include deaths of U.S. citizens traveling abroad. An additional 12 or so occupational diving deaths are reported each year. The annual incidence of reported recreational diving deaths is presently holding steady, although it has declined from the 1970s, when the annual average was about 35% higher.
  Most scuba fatalities result from drowning due to panic, entanglement, running out of air, or a heart attack. Most often, the diver runs out of air and is unable to surface in time. Florida and California have the highest diver populations and the highest numbers of associated deaths. Well over 900 cases of non-fatal decompression illness are sustained each year among U.S. scuba divers.[17]

- *Diving from Heights*—There are an estimated 900 spinal injuries sustained each year in the United States by people who dive from heights or even surface dive into shallow water, striking the bottom or a submerged object.[18] Over 80% of the victims are male, and the highest rate of injury occurs between the ages of 16 and 30.[19] Often, consumption of alcoholic beverages is involved as it inhibits natural fear. Death is sometimes the result. In other cases, permanent paralysis may be sustained. Body surfing injuries are similar to diving injuries when the body surfer surfs down the face of the wave and strikes the bottom. A major problem in diving injuries is that the victim may be quickly removed from the water by friends who are unaware of the spinal injury or who lack training in proper spinal injury management.
- *Alcohol consumption*: Alcohol use has been associated with as many as 50% or more of drownings.

DROWNING STAGES

The word *drowning* can be used to refer to a past event (e.g., "He died by drowning.") or an action in progress (e.g., "He's drowning."). The drowning process involves three distinct stages which can be interrupted through timely intervention:

1) *Distress*
2) *Panic*
3) *Submersion*

This process is usually progressive, but not always. Either of the two initial stages may be skipped completely, depending upon a variety of factors.

DISTRESS

There is sometimes a long period of increasing distress prior to the actual onset of a swimming emergency. These situations can involve poor or tired swimmers in water deeper than standing depth, swimmers caught in a current, or swimmers who experience cramps or trauma. During a distress presentation, swimmers are able to support themselves in the water with swimming skills or a floatation device, but have difficulty reaching safety. They may be able to call, wave for help, or move toward the support of others.

Some distressed swimmers do not even know they are in trouble and may swim against a current without at first realizing they are making no progress. A distress presentation may take a few seconds or can go on for minutes or even hours. As the strength of the swimmer ebbs, the distress presentation will progress to panic if the victim is not rescued or cannot make it to safety. Alert lifeguards on a properly staffed beach are usually able to intervene during the distress phase of the drowning process. In fact, it is not unusual for some victims to protest that they need no assistance because they have yet to feel distressed, though it may be clear to the lifeguard that they are in obvious jeopardy.

In-water distress is serious, but this phase of the drowning process does not always occur. If it does, rapid intervention at this stage can ensure that the victim suffers no ill effects and goes on to enjoy the rest of the day. USLA estimates that at least 80% of rescues at surf beaches are due to rip currents. In such cases, an initial distress phase is typical.

PANIC

The panic stage of the drowning process may develop from the distress stage, as the victim loses strength, or may begin immediately upon the victim's immersion in water. In the panic stage, the victim is unable to adequately maintain buoyancy due

Rescue from a rip current.

to fatigue, complete lack of swimming skills, or some physical problem. For example, a poor swimmer who falls off a floatation device in deep water may immediately enter the panic stage. There is little evidence of any effective supporting kick. The head and face are low in the water, with the chin usually extended. The victim focuses all energy on grabbing breaths of air, so there is usually no call for help. Panic has erupted.

The panicked victim may use an ineffective stroke similar to a dog paddle. Lifeguards refer to the appearance of victims in this stage as *climbing out of the hole* or *climbing the ladder*. The panic stage rarely lasts long because the victim's actions are largely ineffective. Some studies have suggested that it typically lasts between 10 and 60 seconds, but this stage can progress almost immediately to submersion unless a rescue is performed. Therefore, the lifeguard must react very quickly.

SUBMERSION

Contrary to common belief, most drowning incidents do not result in a person floating face-down in the water. Even in the enhanced buoyancy provided by salt water, persons without a floatation device who lose their ability to maintain buoyancy, rapidly submerge and sink to the bottom. In fresh water, which provides much less buoyancy than salt water, submersion can occur extremely rapidly. Submersion in and of itself is not fatal if the victim is recovered in time, but this can be a tremendously difficult task. Unlike the crystal clear water of the pool environment, open water is often murky and water visibility may be as low as zero. Currents and surf action can move the body a significant distance from the point of initial submersion. Once submersion occurs, the chance of a successful rescue declines dramatically. This makes intervention at the distress or panic phase crucial.

Based on the experience of professional beach lifeguards, USLA believes there is a *two minute window* of enhanced opportunity for successful recovery and resuscitation of submerged victims. Thereafter, the chances of successful recovery decline very quickly. In colder waters, successful recoveries have been documented after up to an hour or more of submersion, but these are extremely rare cases.

PHYSIOLOGY OF DROWNING

In a classic drowning presentation, breathing occurs in fitful gasps when possible and there may be coughing and sputtering as water is inadvertently drawn in with a breath. The inhalation of water into the lungs is known as water *aspiration,* while the swallowing of water into the stomach is water *ingestion.* Both of these usually occur. Victims may attempt to hold their breath to avoid aspirating water. If water gets into their mouth, which is usually unavoidable, they swallow it. A significant quantity of water is often ingested.

Drowning victims will start to lose consciousness and, at some point, will usually try to breathe underwater. The larynx, sensing an intrusion of water, closes in an uncontrollable muscular contraction known as a *laryngeal spasm.* While some water may be aspirated into the lungs initially, the laryngeal spasm usually closes off the airway to prevent further aspiration of water. As the victim loses consciousness, the laryngeal spasm eventually relaxes in most cases, allowing water to enter the lungs. This is not always the case, however, and some victims recovered from extended submersion are found to have very little water in their lungs. In addition to asphyxiation due to laryngeal spasm in the submerged victim, vomiting may also occur. In any case, brain death due to lack of oxygen normally begins soon after breathing stops.

Drowning or near drowning is not a simple case of suffocation underwater. In most cases the lungs are traumatized by aspiration of water. Even if the victim is rescued and revived, this traumatization will make it difficult for the lungs to transfer oxygen to the bloodstream and tissues.

TYPES OF DROWNING

Physiologically, drownings can be classified into four types, according to the mechanism of injury or death.

Wet Drowning

Wet drownings make up about 80% or more of all drownings.[20] In a wet drowning, water enters the victim's lungs upon relaxation of the initial laryngeal spasm. When this occurs in the salt water environment, the presence of even small amounts of aspirated salt water immediately begins to draw bodily fluids into the lungs through a process called osmosis. If the victim aspirates fresh water, the effect is different. Fresh water enters the bloodstream through the lungs, diluting electrolytes and causing a chemical imbalance called acidosis. Spasms occur in the bronchi, and the tiny sacs known as alveoli, which form the direct link for oxygen exchange between the lungs and the bloodstream, collapse. In either case, the results will be lethal unless the victim is quickly recovered and appropriate resuscitative efforts are initiated.

Dry Drowning

Dry drownings make up 10% or more of drowning cases.[21] These occur when the laryngeal spasm fails to relax and only a very small amount of water invades the lungs. The cause of death is simple asphyxia. Although dry drownings are unusual, some studies suggest that up to 90% of all successful resuscitations are from dry drownings, probably because the lungs remain better able to permit oxygen exchange during the resuscitation effort. A complication of resuscitation can be the larynx itself, which may continue to spasm, frustrating rescue breathing efforts.

Secondary Drowning

Secondary drowning is also known as near-drowning with delayed complications, or *parking lot drowning.* In this type of drowning, the victim reaches safety or is rescued after aspirating water. Although the immediate life-threatening situation has been resolved, delayed physiological complications occur. As has been described in the section on Wet Drowning, the physiological complications are different in salt and fresh water, but in either case, the victim can die as a result of the delayed effects of water aspiration. This can take place up to 96 hours after the event. It has been estimated that of all patients in near-drowning incidents, 5% will develop complications due to water aspiration and 25% of those will result in death.

Persons who have been rescued from near drowning are often in a stage of denial or embarrassed and simply want to walk away. It is very important that those who appear to have aspirated water be evaluated for signs indicating this and be advised about the potential for secondary drowning complications. Persons who have suffered a near drowning episode should be taken to the hospital or, at a minimum, carefully monitored by others for any signs of complications. This is particularly important for children whose drowsiness may appear normal, but may actually signal physiological complications.

Sudden Drowning Syndrome

Sudden drowning syndrome refers to sudden death caused by illness, physical conditions, or injuries that take place in the water but may not be related to classic drowning situations. For example, the shock to a victim who accidentally falls into cold water may trigger a cardiac arrest. Sudden drowning syndrome may take place when a person in the water is rendered unconscious, disabled, or dead due to situations that may include heart attacks, cardio-vascular accidents (strokes), epileptic seizure, head or neck injury, severe trauma, alcohol or drug overdose, and other conditions.

Sudden drowning syndrome is particularly difficult to prevent because it may occur with no sign of struggle whatsoever. The victim may have shown no prior indication of problems and be in a water area with no obvious hazards. It can be extremely difficult for a lifeguard with a large beach crowd under observation to spot a victim of sudden drowning syndrome who, for example, suffers an epileptic seizure and immediately sinks below the surface of the water with no apparent struggle.

1   Baker, Susan P. et al., *The Injury Fact Book,* Oxford University Press, 1992

2   Waller, A.E. et al., Childhood Injury Deaths: National Analysis and Geographic Variations, *American Journal of Public Health,* 1989; 79; 310–315

3   Wintemute, G.J. et al., The Epidemiology of Drowning in Adulthood: Implications for Prevention; *American Journal of Preventive Medicine,* 1988; 4:343–348

4   Baker, Susan P. et al., *The Injury Fact Book,* Oxford University Press, 1992

5   Brenner, Ruth A. et al., Divergent Trends in Childhood Drowning Rates, 1971–1988, *Journal of the American Medical Association,* 1994, 271–20, 1606–1608

6   Differences in Death Rates due to Injury Among Blacks and Whites, 1984; *Journal of the American Medical Association,* 1989, 261–2, 214–216

7   Brenner, Ruth A. et al., Divergent Trends in Childhood Drowning Rates, 1971–1988; *Journal of the American Medical Association,* 1994, 271–20, 1606–1608

8   Baker, Susan P. et al., *The Injury Fact Book,* Oxford University Press, 1992

9   Waller, A.E. et al., Childhood Injury Deaths: National Analysis and Geographic Variations; *American Journal of Public Health,* 1989, 79, 310–315

10 Ryan, C. Anthony, Drowning Deaths in People with Epilepsy, *Canadian Medical Association Journal,* 1993, 148(5), 781–784

11 National Transportation Safety Board, *Recreational Boating Safety Study,* 1993, national Transportation Safety Board, Washington

12 Ibid.

13 *Small Craft Advisory,* National Association of Boating Law Administrators, 1993, 9, 1, 8

14 National Transportation Safety Board, *Recreational Boating Safety Study,* 1993, National Transportation Safety Board, Washington

15 Ibid.

16 Dovenbarger, J.A., Ed., *1992 Report on Diving Accidents and Fatalities,* Divers Alert Network

17 Ibid.

18 Raymond, Chris Anne, Summer's Drought Reinforces Diving's Dangers, *Journal of the American Medical Association,* 1988, 260, 9, 1100

19 Kelly, Anne, Spinal Cord Injury, *Independent Living,* Feb-March 1991, 6, 1, 47

20 Kringsholm, B. et al., Autopsied Cases of Drowning in Denmark 1987–1988, *Forensic Science International,* 1991, 52, 85–92

21 Ibid.

CHAPTER TEN

PREVENTIVE LIFEGUARDING

Chapter Highlights

Preventive Actions

Special Operation Modes

Rules and Regulations

Public Education

Maintenance

Facility Design

In This Chapter

Lifeguards, more than any other providers of public safety, have an ongoing responsibility for accident *prevention*.

[Photographic Credit: Mike Hensler]

The primary role of many providers of public safety is one of responding to emergencies after they have developed. The main role of firefighters, for example, is often defined as fire *suppression*. That is, the fire has already started and the firefighter responds to extinguish it. While beach lifeguards also have a major responsibility for responding to emergencies, a lifeguard's primary role is *prevention*. This is a critical role because the worst outcome of water emergencies is death by drowning, and the drowning process can proceed very quickly. There are also many other types of injuries which can occur at the beach. Lifeguards, more than any other providers of public safety, have an ongoing responsibility for accident prevention.

At most lifeguard agencies, preventive lifeguarding measures are practiced in six major areas:
- Preventive Actions
- Special Operation Modes
- Rules and Regulations
- Public Education
- Maintenance
- Facility Design

PREVENTIVE ACTIONS

For every rescue effected, most lifeguards log tens, if not hundreds of preventive actions. Not all accidents can be avoided by preventive actions, and repeated warnings can become tiresome to both lifeguards and beach patrons; but timely preventive actions can reduce the number of rescues and injuries at a beach to manageable levels. They can prevent death.

Preventive actions may include directing visitors away from a rip current area or counseling poor swimmers in deep water. Persons with floatation devices may be advised to stay in shallow water. All preventive actions should be noted in the lifeguard tower log since they are a critical, if often unnoticed, aspect of lifeguard duties.

People also bring recreational equipment with them. Boats and other water vehicles can pose a significant hazard when operated improperly. Some boaters operate too close to swimming crowds, while others are inadvertently caught by waves, endangering the boat's passengers and swimmers alike as the boat is carried toward shore. While surfboards may not appear as hazardous as powerboats, they are capable of inflicting serious injuries when striking the human body. Many other types of recreational equipment can also cause injury.

In most areas with high levels of water activity, incompatible water users are separated by use of flags, lines, buoys, or other measures. In some areas, surfers are separated from swimmers in different water areas. In others, surfing is prohibited at periods of high swimmer attendance. In most states and local areas, boats are required to maintain a safe distance from swimmers.

Some lifeguards are vested with a lawful authority to take preventive actions. Failure to comply with lifeguard directions may be, in itself, a violation. In other areas, preventive actions are simply advisory, with the person having the option of compliance or non-compliance.

Although preventive actions are important in averting possible accidents and injuries, lifeguards must use good judgment in deciding when an activity

A motorboat buzzes a swim area. [Photographic Credit: Mike Hensler]

becomes too dangerous to permit. It is sometimes difficult to determine what activities should be considered unusually dangerous because occasional injuries are an inherent part of physical recreation. For example, throwing a Frisbee® may be viewed as an innocent act of recreation or may be seen as a potentially danger-ous activity, which could lead to the injury of someone in the immediate vicinity. One good rule to follow is that whenever a recreational activity of one person sig-nificantly threatens the safety of another, it should be stopped or modified. A high speed boat in the vicinity of swimmers is an example of an unusually dangerous activity.

Lifeguards who overuse preventive actions can create problems for them-selves and their agencies. Constant warning and overly intensive supervision can lead to serious confrontations, repeated complaints, or active non-compliance with requests. For example, many agencies have rules forbidding organized play of sports such as football on the beach because a player may inadvertently crash into other beach users, causing injury. On the other hand, on an overcast day, with few people on the beach, lifeguards may elect to allow such activity because it presents little hazard. Reasonable interpretations and good judgment are the key. Each agency, according to its own philosophy of preventive lifeguarding, should estab-lish guidelines for the use of preventive actions by lifeguards.

SPECIAL OPERATION MODES

Natural hazards can be intensified during periods of high surf, wind, fog, and other weather conditions. Unusually high beach attendance can also make safety more difficult to maintain. During these periods, many agencies initiate special operation modes. These may involve modified operations, actual beach closings, or beach advisories.

A sign advises swimmers of possible water contamination.
[Photographic Credit: Rob McGowan]

MODIFIED OPERATIONS

Certain water, weather, or crowd conditions may lead lifeguard supervisors to modify operations. This may include suspension of certain activities. For example, extremely high surf may lead to suspension of surfing in an area to help prevent possible injuries. High offshore winds may lead to restrictions on the use of floatation devices to prevent users from being blown far from the beach. Beach activities that take up a large amount of space may be curtailed or restricted during periods of heavy beach population.

Modified operations may also take the form of special lifeguard procedures initiated by the area supervisor. Fog patrols are an example. When rescue volume increases dramatically or weather draws unusually high crowds, lifeguard management must be prepared with plans to handle increased beach activity or hazards. The staff for a slow weekday may be completely overwhelmed on a busy weekend, and safety will suffer. On very busy days, some beaches use helicopter borne lifeguards to patrol and respond to hot spots.

BEACH CLOSINGS

Some conditions necessitate closing a beach area to swimming and other water activities. An example is water contamination. Decisions to close beaches to swimming call for serious judgment, and are usually made by area supervisors following specific, predetermined criteria. Once these criteria have been met, patrol lifeguards are informed and warning signs or flags are erected to inform beach visitors. Public address system announcements may also be broadcast regularly during such periods. Lifeguards then continue operations, but approach any visitors observed entering the water to advise them of the beach closing. When conditions allow reopening of the beach, lifeguards are notified, warning signs and flags are removed, and operations return to normal.

ADVISORIES

Lifeguard agencies lacking the authority to close beaches may instead initiate special advisories. Advisories are also utilized by agencies with closure authority when it is believed that outright closure is unjustified, but strong caution should be urged. When criteria for advisories are met, lifeguards are notified and warning flags or notices are erected to inform and warn the public. Regular lifeguard operations continue, but lifeguards may be required to approach visitors entering the water to verbally warn them against participation in certain activities. When conditions stabilize, lifeguards are notified of the suspension of the advisory and signs and flags are removed.

RULES AND REGULATIONS

Most agencies establish beach rules and regulations to help prevent accidents and injuries, as well as to ensure that all beach visitors can enjoy the beach experience without being unduly bothered by others. Lifeguards are usually provided with some degree of authority to enforce these regulations. Without such authority, it can be very difficult to manage a beach area because recalcitrant violators will quickly learn that the warnings will not be enforced and ignore them.

Lifeguard enforcement authority may be limited to issuing warnings which, if disobeyed, will ultimately be enforced by police officers summoned to the scene. While this system can be effective if police are readily available, it can also become very time consuming. Police are sometimes reluctant to become involved in disputes over beach regulations they consider of minor importance. For this reason, in some areas lifeguards are appointed as peace officers or law enforcement officers and authorized to enforce local or regional laws to the point of citation or arrest.

It is important for lifeguards to become completely conversant with the regulations that pertain to the beach area under their supervision. Effective enforcement often involves discussions with people who want a full explanation of the rules.

Enforcement of beach regulations requires tact and patience. Persons coming to the beach are in a recreational mode. Often they have driven long distances and had a difficult time finding parking. Perhaps they have had a very stressful work week. People coming to the beach want to play. Therefore, they may be be understandably unhappy if told that the form of recreation they want to practice must be modified or terminated.

In enforcement of minor beach regulations, lifeguards should normally approach in a friendly manner, perhaps first making conversation over unrelated issues. A negative reaction is less likely if the subject first sees the lifeguard as a nice person. The lifeguard should then explain the regulation and the basic reason for it. It is important that the person understand why the lifeguard is taking the time to enforce the regulation.

As an example, many beach areas prohibit glass containers because of the possibility of breakage and resultant injury to barefoot beachgoers. Unfortunately, beachgoers sometimes arrive unknowingly with all of their drinks in bottles. If the lifeguard approaches and simply states that bottles are not permitted, the beach patron may immediately consider the regulation capricious and react negatively. On the other hand, if the lifeguard explains that the intent is to prevent injury, most people will respond in an understanding manner.

In any enforcement contact, it is important not only to explain the regulation, but also clearly explain the action the person must take to come into compliance. For example, in the case of the bottle, after explaining the regulation the lifeguard might direct the person to remove the bottle from the beach to a nearby car. The person now knows what the regulation is, the reason for it, and what must be done to resolve the problem.

Another excellent technique in enforcement of regulations is to *provide alternatives*. The beachgoer told that football is impermissible on the beach may be very distressed. Perhaps this was the primary reason to come to the beach. Is there a nearby park that this person could visit instead? Is there an unused portion of the beach where football could be tolerated? Providing options shows concern for the person's needs and a desire to help.

Lifeguards involved in enforcement contacts should take care to display an even temperament. It may be very frustrating to observe that a person is acting in a seemingly reckless manner which endangers others, for example, but a display of anger on the part of the lifeguard suggests personal involvement and this is unprofessional. A display of frustration on the part of the lifeguard can also escalate tempers, whereas a calm demeanor is likely to reduce tension.

Informational signs are very valuable in enforcement of regulations. Most people who know the regulations will follow them. By posting signs explaining the regulations at beach accesses, the number of enforcement contacts can be significantly reduced. Informational signs should include pictograms as well as language so that those who do not read English can understand the message. It is a good idea to attempt to phrase the information in a positive manner, as opposed to a purely negative one. While a sign banning glass containers at the beach could state "No Glass Containers," a more positive approach might be to word it, "For Your Protection, Glass Containers Prohibited."

In many areas, the establishment of rules and regulations also means the establishment of special areas for certain activities. For example, surfing may be restricted to a specified water area. Boats and boardsailors may be restricted from designated swimming areas on bays or lakes. Rules and regulations may also

Signs divide swimming and surfing areas.
[Photographic Credit: B. Chris Brewster]

establish special procedures for participating in particular water or beach activities. Permits may be necessary for surfing or scuba diving and those activities may be restricted to established time periods.

In addition to beach rules and local ordinances, many beach areas are protected by national, state, or regional laws which regulate boat or aircraft traffic, or which are intended to protect the environment. Lifeguards should be knowledgeable of those laws and report violations to appropriate agencies for enforcement action.

The enforcement of beach regulations can result in an escalating confrontation when there is a refusal to comply. The goal is to avoid such an outcome. When it cannot be avoided, lifeguards without law enforcement training or authority are well advised to swallow their pride, back down, and contact police. Few beach regulations are of such great import that they justify risking injury to enforce. For a discussion of how to handle serious crimes in the beach area and protocols for summoning police, refer to the chapter entitled *Emergency Planning and Management*.

PUBLIC EDUCATION

An important aspect of preventive lifeguarding is public education. It is impossible to educate every beach user about all existing hazards immediately upon their arrival at the beach. They may also arrive at a time that lifeguards are off-duty. Public education gets the word out in a much more efficient manner than one-on-one contact.

[Photographic Credit: Rick Gould]

Public education programs include activities and materials developed to teach people about the hazards that exist in the aquatic environment and how they may avoid or escape some of those hazards. Public education programs also promote better understanding of lifeguard services and procedures, along with support for and patronage of lifeguard protected areas. The United States Lifesaving Association produces many educational publications available through local chapters.

SIGNS

Along with posting rules and regulations, many lifeguard agencies post signs informing beach visitors of particular hazards which may exist. Signs posted at entrance points can be extremely valuable, particularly in warning about unusual hazards which would not be evident to the average person. Regardless of how effective a lifeguard agency may be in providing local public education about the beach, many beach visitors are tourists, some from areas of the country with no beach. Informational signs may be the only public education that will reach them.

EDUCATIONAL MATERIALS

Printed educational information includes posters, bumper stickers, handouts, brochures, coloring books, and other materials designed to convey a message of safety or environmental awareness to the public. Many agencies will post public education materials at beach bulletin boards or in window displays and will provide visitors with handout material on request. Some agencies develop special brochures on local beach facilities, along with explanations of warning signals and tips for safe swimming.

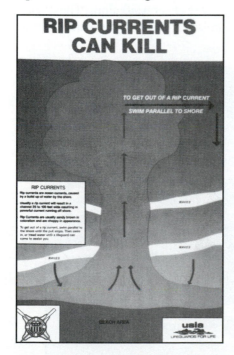

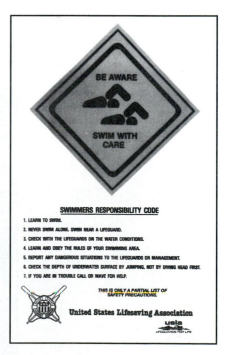

[Photographic Credit: Dave Foxwell]

Public education materials can also include films, tapes, and public service announcements distributed through the local media for inclusion in broadcasts and publications. Some agencies also send public information bulletins to the news media on a regular basis. This is known as a "news release." In some areas, special telephone lines are maintained with recorded information on local beach conditions and water safety information.

PUBLIC APPEARANCES

One of the most effective ways to provide public information is to have lifeguards attend special events, and deliver lectures to school or civic groups. In these cases, the investment of a few hours of time may provide concentrated delivery of the safety message to large numbers of people. These events also create "pass-along" information as the attendees tell friends and family about what they've learned.

It is a good practice to produce a slide show or video in preparation for such invitations. The next step is to contact school principals and the leaders of local civic organizations to offer services. In seasonal areas, it is best to attend schools just before summer recess when children are likely to visit the beach. Public appearances can continue through the beach season, either at the beach or in parks, campgrounds, or other recreation areas.

SPECIAL EVENTS

Lifeguard agencies sometimes work with local schools to sponsor poster contests, essay contests, and beach field trips relating to water safety. In some areas, lifeguard agencies tie in sponsorship of other special events, including concerts, fundraising events, and sporting events such as road races or triathalons. These special events include opportunities for spreading information on water safety or for generating support of lifeguard services.

Competitors line-up at the start line of a rescue board race.
[Photographic Credit: Chris Gierlich]

A major event at many beach agencies each year is National Beach Safety Week, sponsored by the United States Lifesaving Association. Beach Safety Week activities combine many public education programs with official proclamations and other public ceremonies. They can help draw media attention at a time when water safety education is very important to the beach-going public.

Lifeguard competitions also serve as public education events at many beaches throughout the United States. These events combine motivation for physical fitness and development of inter-agency relationships, with opportunities to show beach visitors and competition audiences the physical demands placed on open water lifeguards. USLA-sanctioned lifeguard competitions take place across the country, culminating each year at the USLA National Lifeguard Championships.

SPECIAL PROGRAMS

In addition to special events, many lifeguard agencies sponsor or assist ongoing programs to develop water skills and water safety awareness. Although beach lifeguards are not swimming instructors during work hours, many lifeguard agencies assist with Learn-to-Swim programs sponsored by local recreation departments. Other instruction programs sponsored or assisted by lifeguard agencies may include skin and scuba diving courses, surfing instruction, lifesaving training, and special "cross-instruction" courses offered to members of other local emergency services.

Some of the most successful programs offered by lifeguard agencies are junior lifeguard programs. The purpose of these programs is to provide youths with a sound aquatic background and acquaint them with the hazards of open water swimming, while exposing them to an environment that will teach them to act with courtesy, respect, and be good sports. Junior lifeguard programs often contain instruction in beach and water safety, lifesaving techniques and procedures, body surfing, bodyboarding and surfing techniques (in surf areas), development of swimming skills in all four basic strokes, competition opportunities with other junior lifeguard programs, volleyball and miscellaneous beach games and activities, field trips, and ecology. In many areas, junior lifeguard programs help agencies recruit and begin the training of future professional lifeguards.

Well run junior lifeguard programs are welcomed by local communities because they provide a positive youth program. They are generally supported by tuition fees. A good practice is to offset the cost of tuition with scholarships, based on financial need, thereby providing an opportunity for disadvantaged youths to participate.

MAINTENANCE

Beach maintenance is an aspect of preventive lifeguarding. With the exception of routine maintenance of lifeguard facilities and equipment, lifeguards should not be assigned to general maintenance duties, but every lifeguard has a responsibility for monitoring the beach and water for potential hazards. For example, large flotsam must either be removed by the lifeguard or reported immediately to beach maintenance crews for removal.

One purpose of routine beach patrols is to look for beach hazards, including broken glass, fire pits, and other sharp or hazardous materials. Lifeguard agencies must follow special procedures for protecting the public and themselves when any type of potentially hazardous material is found along a beach area, including potential medical wastes, and drums or containers that may contain toxic waste. In some areas, military explosives may float ashore from time to time. Usually, if explosives float, it is because they are intended to be used as markers in aquatic military exercises. Still, markers are meant to burn and some are highly explosive.

If hazards cannot be immediately removed from the beach area, lifeguards should keep people away from the area until the hazard can be removed. As a standard practice, beach patrons should be kept at least 100 feet back from any potentially explosive device, further if possible. The local bomb squad or fire department should be summoned for disposal.

FACILITY DESIGN

From conception to construction, all beach facilities should be designed carefully with public safety in mind. This is particularly true for any improvements such as roadways, parking areas, walkways, and beach houses. Facility designers and engineers will also look at ways to overcome natural hazards at the beach environment, which may include the installation of railings, the removal of water hazards, and even redevelopment of the sandy beach and swimming area.

While most lifeguard agencies are not directly involved in design of public improvements at the beach—except those which are directly related to lifeguard activities—many agencies are actively involved in designing safety into the beach environment. At many flat water beaches, swim lines are installed to mark the swimming area and provide emergency floatation support for people caught in deep water. To regulate boat traffic, special "No Boating" buoys may be placed at the perimeters of swim areas to warn boaters away from swimmers. Facility design may also include special safety considerations regarding docks, floats, and any play equipment installed on or near the water, including slides, diving boards or rope swings.

At surf areas, it is more difficult to install safety equipment in the water due to the dynamic conditions of tides and surf. Still, some beaches install swim lines or buoy markers to mark swim areas or protected zones.

For a discussion of lifeguard towers and other facilities, refer to the chapter entitled *Lifeguard Facilities*.

CHAPTER ELEVEN

WATER SURVEILLANCE

CHAPTER HIGHLIGHTS

Recognition and Assessment

Effective Water Observation

Coverage Systems

IN THIS CHAPTER

In emergency medicine there is often reference to a golden hour—the period of time after a traumatic injury during which effective medical intervention is essential to the saving of life. In open water lifesaving, such a time frame is an unheard of luxury. Lifeguards measure the opportunity for successful intervention not in minutes, but in moments.

[Photographic Credit: Mike Hensler]

To prevent injuries, or successfully intervene before a drowning occurs, the primary skill a lifeguard must employ is effective observation. Effective observation is not simply a question of vigilance. Accurate assessment and recognition of drowning victims is a skill which requires training, experience, extensive concentration, and good judgment. Experienced lifeguards can sometimes actually predict which persons at their beach will need assistance long before an emergency arises. They do so by using visual clues, many of which will be discussed in this chapter.

Surprisingly, it is not always obvious when a person is in distress in the water. Certainly many people in trouble become terrified and may yell for assistance, but often sounds from sources such as surf or other people playing will obscure any cry of distress. While some victims will wave for help in a classic manner, most are too busy trying to stay afloat to take the time to signal for assistance. Some victims simply submerge with no prior sign of a struggle whatsoever. Therefore, lifeguards must be adept at anticipating problems, recognizing when a person is in distress without hearing a yell for help, and understanding the subtle ways that persons in distress may telegraph their panic.

In emergency medicine there is often reference to a golden hour — the period of time after a traumatic injury during which effective medical intervention is essential to the saving of life. In open water lifesaving, such a time frame is an unheard of luxury. Lifeguards measure the opportunity for successful intervention not in minutes, but in moments.

RECOGNITION AND ASSESSMENT

In order to ensure successful rescue of people caught in the drowning process, it is important to be able to identify signs that can help indicate various drowning presentations. Once these signs have been recognized, the situation can be assessed and the lifeguard can respond appropriately.

DRY LAND OBSERVATION

If possible, observation of beach visitors should begin before water entry. There are a number of clues and statistical facts lifeguards can use to key in on persons in their area most likely to experience problems. Several indicators have already been covered in Chapter 9, particularly in the Statistical Indicators section. The following are some additional considerations. While these clues can suggest persons who merit particular attention, lifeguards should not exclude any water user from their surveillance.

- *Age*—Very old or very young people should be watched carefully. The second leading cause of accidental death among people aged 5 to 44 is drowning. It is the leading cause of accidental death for toddlers. Infants and toddlers can drown in water no deeper than their arm length due to their inability to easily get to their feet after falling over. Older children may lack the judgment or willingness to recognize their own limitations. Older adults may lack the physical strength necessary to fight an unexpected current, or quickly move away from a breaking wave.

- *Body Weight*—Persons who are overweight may become easily exhausted and are likely to be less able to move quickly to avoid a hazardous condition.
- *Pale or Extremely White Complexion*—If a light skinned person arrives at a sunny beach with no tan whatsoever, it is a reasonable presumption that the person is not a regular beachgoer and, therefore, may be inexperienced or unfamiliar with the open water environment. This is a particularly useful clue in an area frequented by tourists, since they may have a total lack of familiarity with local water conditions.
- *Intoxication*—Those who display a behavior pattern which suggests a probable impairment of normal physical coordination due to alcohol or drugs should be eyed as potential rescue candidates, particularly considering the high degree of drownings which involve alcohol. Slurred speech, an unstable gait, or erratic behavior are some examples of tell-tale signs.
- *Floatation Devices*—The only truly safe floatation devices are U.S. Coast Guard approved lifejackets which fit the wearer and which are properly worn. With that exception, floatation devices such as inflatable rafts, balls, and life rings can be *killers*. While floatation devices are sometimes used by accomplished swimmers, they are also used by weak and non-swimmers. Often non-swimmers use floatation devices to access deep water so that they can stay with friends who can swim, but if the non-swimming user of a floatation device becomes separated from the floatation device, submersion and death can occur very rapidly, with little or no observable struggle. One of the most chilling sights to a lifeguard is a floatation device offshore with no one around it.

  Parents of small children often give them floatation devices, believing they can pay less attention to their children as a result. It is not unusual to see very small children with inflated rings around their upper arms to assist in swimming, but if such devices deflate unexpectedly or fall off, death by drowning may be the result. No child or adult should use a floatation device without immediate supervision unless the person has the skill to easily swim to shore from the area where the device is being used.

  Some swimming areas actually ban use of floatation devices due to the danger they present. Since floatation devices can completely prevent a lifeguard from determining whether a person can swim at all, it should be assumed that a person using a floatation device is a non-swimmer, until the lifeguard is certain that the person is competent without the device.
- *Improper Equipment or Attire*—In most climates, under normal summer-like conditions, a swimmer is adequately equipped with only a swimsuit. Body surfers will usually don swim fins. In cold water, an experienced swimmer could be expected to wear a wetsuit to prevent loss of body heat and exhaustion. Depending on the conditions, absence of such equipment may be a clue to inexperience.

  Any person who enters the water wearing clothes, other than those designed for swimming, should be watched carefully. Clothes offer a negative buoyancy factor and restrict swimming ability. While some people with strong swimming skills may simply lack the funds to purchase swimsuits, the wearing of street clothes while swimming is a likely sign of a lack of water knowledge.

On the other hand, it is easy to dismiss from consideration a person who arrives at the beach with an impressive array of equipment under the assumption that the person must have extensive water skills. There is no guarantee, however. Particular attention should be paid to persons who have unusual difficulty donning the equipment or whose equipment fits poorly. The poorly fitting wetsuit, for example, may be borrowed by a non-swimmer from a friend who is a swimmer.

- *Disability*—Persons with physical disabilities are increasingly using open water areas for recreation. Some open water beach areas furnish ramps for wheelchairs to help wheelchair bound persons move across the beach. Other areas furnish wheelchairs specifically designed to move through the sand. Persons missing an arm or leg or with less obvious disabilities also swim.

  Physically challenged people usually know their limitations and make prudent decisions, just like other beachgoers, but just like other beachgoers, people with disabilities may overestimate their abilities. Given the same hazard (e.g., a rip current) and all other things being equal, a disabled person is likely to have more difficulty than a fully able-bodied person. It is important, however, not to presume that a disabled person is an incompetent swimmer. Lifeguards will find that just like able bodied swimmers, there are disabled swimmers who are very strong and some who are very weak. Lifeguards should make their evaluations on a case-by-case basis.

SWIMMER OBSERVATION

Once beach visitors are in the water, a number of signs can signal problems. The following are several of these signs:

- *Facing Shore*—The first indication of trouble from persons beginning to feel anxiety or experiencing distress is that they normally face shore or continually glance in that direction. This is a very important clue for a lifeguard, particularly at a surf beach where most swimmers will be facing away from shore, watching the waves. Even at a non-surf beach, groups of swimmers may be playing and facing each other, but one may be anxiously looking toward shore. In some cases an offshore platform may substitute for the safety of shore, and the swimmer may instead look toward this platform.
- *Low Head*—Competent swimmers remaining in a stationary location hold their heads high. They tread water, breaststroke, or float on their backs. The chin is usually clearly above the water level. Swimmers whose heads hang low in the water demand a focus of attention to determine competency.
- *Low Stroke*—This normally accompanies a low head and can be visualized as a stroke that is very low to the water with the elbows dragging.
- *Lack of Kick*—Under normal circumstances, the weak swimmer displays little or no kick. The lack of a break in the surface of the water should cue the lifeguard to a possible problem. In these cases, the body plane changes to a more upright position and little forward progress is made.
- *Waves Breaking Over the Head*—Most people who are competent at swimming in the surf dive under waves. When waves wash over a swimmer's head, with no apparent attempt to duck under them, it is a strong indicator that this is a rescue candidate.

- *Catching Large Waves Without Body Surfing*—The primary goal of a swimmer in distress is to make it to shore. These persons may be willing to pay the price of going over the falls of a large wave to accomplish this goal. Persons who allow themselves to be carried by a breaking wave, without making some attempt to body surf or duck under the wave, should be eyed very carefully. Often, weak swimmers who go over the falls on a breaking wave will find themselves disoriented and in worse shape than before.
- *Hair in the Eyes*—The natural instinct of people in control of themselves in the water is to brush the hair out of their eyes. People who make no attempt to do so are usually under stress and concerned about other things—like keeping their heads above water.
- *Glassy, Empty or Anxious Eyes*—Eyes can be a window to emotion. Experienced lifeguards can read the fatigue and fear in the eyes of a distressed person. Depending on distance, this may only be detectable with binoculars or not detectable at all.
- *Heads Together*—When other swimmers suddenly converge on a particular swimmer or simply cluster together, it may be an indication that one or more needs assistance. Often persons in distress are unable to signal to a lifeguard or don't think to do so. Instead, they call to the persons nearest to them for buoyancy or moral support. This request for aid may not be perceptible to the lifeguard, but the actions of other swimmers can suggest that a rescue is needed. When swimmers congregate for any significant length of time, the situation should be investigated with binoculars or in person.
- *Hand Waving*—Waving an arm, particularly in the water, is a natural sign of distress, perhaps because in water it is the only way to attract attention other than by yelling. This distress signal is constantly abused by persons waving to friends ashore or nearby in the water. Any person facing shore and waving should be assumed to be in distress until it can be ascertained that the person is all right. Waving by distressed swimmers is a relatively uncommon occurrence because they are usually more focused on using their arms to keep themselves afloat.

    The wave is a particularly important signal in the case of scuba divers who are generally taught in training that they should never wave unless they are in distress. Therefore, a wave from a scuba diver should result in a presumption that the diver is in distress and a scuba diver who waves when there is no distress should be counseled about the error.
- *Fighting or Being Swept Along by a Current*—Currents are a major source of distress. Lifeguards should know the locations and characteristics of currents that regularly present themselves in the same area. In addition, lifeguards at beaches susceptible to unexpected currents should be constantly on the alert for the appearance of currents and watch current areas with particular scrutiny. The first sign of potential distress in a current is the simple fact that a swimmer is moved laterally or offshore by the current. However, it is impossible to know whether the swimmer will be able to resolve the problem until the swimmer comes to recognize the pull of the current and tries to get out of it.

    Even waterwise swimmers may initially attempt to fight the current and strong swimmers may succeed in doing so, but once a swimmer begins to fight a current stronger than the swimmer's skills, the drowning process has begun and will only be resolved in one of three ways:

— the current relaxes
— the swimmer swims sideways to the pull of the current and gets out of it
— the person is rescued

When the swimmer concludes that fighting the current will be futile, and if the swimmer does not know enough to swim sideways to the pull of the current, panic will quickly set in. Therefore, as soon as a swimmer nears a dangerous current or becomes caught in it, experienced lifeguards begin preparing for a water rescue.

- *Erratic activity*—Any activity out of the ordinary should always be given close scrutiny. It may be someone who is showing off, horsing around, or perhaps disoriented and out of touch with the reality of the environment. Showoffs intentionally take risks to attract attention and often find themselves in over their heads.
- *Clinging to Fixed Objects*—Swimmers who are fearful or in distress sometimes try to cling to piers, rocks, pilings, buoys, or other apparent objects of security. This is often a good sign that the person is either too frightened or too exhausted to continue swimming, and it demands close scrutiny. In addition, aquatic life such as barnacles and mussels attached to these objects can cause significant injuries.

DROWNING PRESENTATIONS

There are two particularly obvious signs that a person has gone beyond initial distress and is in imminent danger of drowning, thus needing the most expeditious assistance possible. These are most typically displayed by persons with little or no swimming skills. Neither action provides any forward mobility.

- *Double Arm Grasping*—Usually the head is back, with the chin up, and both hands and arms are slapping at the water simultaneously and rapidly in an ineffective butterfly-type stroke.
- *Climbing the Ladder*—As the term implies, this action resembles the climbing of an imaginary ladder, an upward crawling motion.

EFFECTIVE WATER OBSERVATION

Firefighters, police, and lifeguards are all expected to respond quickly and efficiently once an emergency arises. Firefighters and police most often respond to emergencies based on reports from others who have observed the problem. While lifeguards also respond to such reports, a basic responsibility of lifeguards is to watch over water areas in order to locate persons in distress. In this sense, lifeguards report the emergencies *and* respond to them. In fact, the vast majority of lifeguard emergency responses are self-initiated and, therefore, effective water observation is a critical skill for lifeguards. They must be able to observe, evaluate, and respond to emergency situations efficiently and effectively.

OBSERVATION TECHNIQUES

Good observation techniques include the following basic points:
- *Visual Scanning*—Observation of a swimming area is accomplished through

visual scanning. The lifeguard sweeps the area from side to side with the eyes, checking quickly on each swimmer or group of swimmers. If a sign of distress is noted, further assessment of the person in apparent distress should take place. When a distress clue that is less than conclusive is noted, the lifeguard should occasionally scan the rest of the area quickly and return to evaluate the signs of distress further. *It is important that the lifeguard not forget to keep watching the remainder of the swimming crowd while making this evaluation.* If two or more lifeguards are working together at a station, one lifeguard may alert another guard to a distress sign and study that person or group while the other guard continues scanning. Scanning of the water should continue at all times that a lifeguard is on duty. Even when a lifeguard is talking to other lifeguards or a member of the public, scanning should continue. Professional beach lifeguards take great pains to avoid ever turning their back to the water, even when they are not specifically assigned to water observation. This is a matter of professional ethics. In some areas it is mandated by agency protocol.

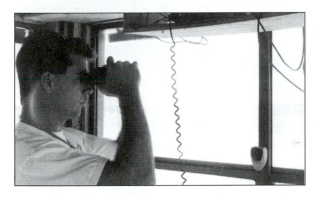

[Photographic Credit: William McNeely, Jr.]

- *Use of Observational Tools*—Binoculars are valuable tools for assessing possible distress signs over distance and should be available to all lifeguards assigned to water observation. When a potential problem is observed through visual scanning, lifeguards are encouraged to use binoculars to study the situation more closely. The use of binoculars can also let other lifeguards know that a lifeguard has noticed something and has ceased scanning to focus on a situation. However, since binoculars limit the field of vision in favor of focusing on a small area, they should not be used for continual scanning. Instead, lifeguards should scan with their eyes and use binoculars only when a distress clue warrants further investigation. Spotting scopes and high power binoculars mounted on tripods are used effectively by some agencies, particularly when large beach and water areas must be observed. These scopes sometimes have compass points on them so that coordinates for a boat in distress can be fixed.

  Sunglasses are also essential observation tools. Polarized sunglasses are highly recommended because they help eliminate glare, which can obscure large portions of swimming crowds. Sunglasses protect the eyes from blowing sand, wind, and fatigue. This is important to the health of lifeguards, but also to their level of vigilance.

- *Overlap*—Beaches with multiple lifeguard stations or locations generally divide the entire water area into sections or zones, but it is critical to provide for some type of overlap area between stations to avoid uncovered areas. A standard principle of overlap for a contiguous beach area with several towers is that each lifeguard is made responsible for the water area to the next staffed lifeguard station on either side. One important reason for this overlap is that it is very difficult to clearly define boundaries in the water.

Glare can be a serious problem. [Photographic Credit: Paul Drucker]

Lifeguards should never worry that they might be watching people in another lifeguard's assigned area or ignore distress signs there. Lifeguard administrators should take care to ensure that all lifeguards feel a sense of responsibility for the entire beach area so that egos do not result in a delayed response or lack of response due to fear of embarrassing a fellow lifeguard who may be missing a rescue. A strong sense of group responsibility is essential to effective beach lifeguarding.

- *Cross-Checking*—Glare caused by the sun can cause a serious problem, obscuring large swimming crowds, and essentially blinding lifeguards to a particular water area. Lifeguards must utilize a system of cross-checking to counteract this problem. Whenever a lifeguard assigned to water observation is unable to see a water area for any reason, lifeguards in adjacent locations, if any, should be advised to cross-check. On a beach with several staffed lifeguard towers, this is easily accomplished. In other cases, an alternative method is to post a lifeguard in a vehicle or on foot to cross-check areas with serious glare.

AREA OF RESPONSIBILITY

All lifeguard services should define an *area of responsibility* as clearly as possible. The area of responsibility is defined as that area of the water, beach, and related facilities wherein lifeguards are expected to be primary responders. The defined area of responsibility generally includes:

- *Water Areas*—Lifeguards are typically expected to be responsible for all water areas offshore of defined protected beaches, including those above and below the water surface.
- *Offshore Limit*—Some agencies define an offshore limit for lifeguard services, particularly for situations that may involve boating accidents some distance from shore. If such a limit is defined, lifeguards should be instructed on what other agency or agencies can be summoned if an emergency beyond the offshore limit is observed.
- *Beach Area*—Most lifeguard agencies are also responsible for observing beach areas and responding to emergency situations there.
- *Adjacent Facilities*—Many lifeguard agencies, while not actually responsible for observing activities in adjacent facilities such as parking areas and bathhouses, are subject to calls to emergencies that may occur in those areas.
- *Off-site Areas*—Off-site areas may include facilities, roadways, business districts, hotels, and residences that are not actually connected to the defined beach facility or park. Some lifeguard agencies are primary responders to emergencies in these areas due to their relative proximity.

    Regardless of the defined area of responsibility, lifeguards must avoid tunnel vision. While lifeguards should concentrate on the assigned area of responsibility, they are often the only organizational representatives at a beach available to quickly report problems that develop in adjacent areas.

PRIORITY ZONES

Once the overall area of responsibility has been defined, priority zones should also be defined. This provides lifeguards with a sense of the most important areas to concentrate on. The three major priority zones, in order of importance, are usually as follows:

- *Primary Zone*—The water is a lifeguard's top priority. The primary zone for each lifeguard station is the water area for which the lifeguard is personally responsible. On beaches with several towers, the primary water zone generally extends to the next staffed lifeguard station on either side. This zone automatically extends when lifeguards in adjacent stations are on a response or the adjacent station is closed.
- *Secondary Zone*—This usually includes adjacent water areas (including primary zones of other lifeguards), the beach, immediately adjacent park areas, the sky, and the water to the horizon. Less frequent scanning of this zone is required, but the lifeguard checks this zone regularly.
- *Tertiary Zone*—Generally, the tertiary zone includes all other areas within sight of the lifeguard. It could include adjacent streets and parking lots, for example.

COVERAGE SYSTEMS

Coverage systems are plans for providing protection to an area of responsibility. The development of a coverage system is a complex task for any emergency service. A fire chief, for example, must consider the size of the community served, the types of fires expected, the size and configuration of buildings and structures that must be protected, concentrations of commercial and residential areas, and other related factors. With that information, fire department managers can determine the staffing level and deployment needed to provide an adequate level of preparedness and response. This is a coverage system.

Like other emergency services, lifeguard agencies must develop coverage systems. Considerations in this process include the beach and water attendance, the size of the facility, the area of responsibility, the beach season, the water and marine life hazards, the scope of the service, and the past rescue experience. These factors help determine the number of lifeguards, their deployment, and daily scheduling.

BASIC COVERAGE PRINCIPLES

Basic coverage principles include the following:

- *Area of responsibility defined*—The first step to creating a coverage system is a clear understanding of the area of responsibility.
- *Operation period defined*—This includes the days of the year lifeguards will be on duty and the times of day coverage will be provided.
- *Protection provided with no break in service*—As with other emergency services, once lifeguard protection begins using established hours, protection must continue uninterrupted. While some lifeguard services may reduce coverage due to lower than expected crowd conditions, coverage should not be completely eliminated for routine breaks or meal periods. Instead, backup coverage should be provided for this purpose. It is an unacceptable practice for all lifeguards on duty at a beach to leave the beach unprotected for a lunch break. If supervisory personnel determine that coverage should be terminated early due to weather conditions or extraordinarily low attendance, beach patrons should be notified.
- Working conditions are reasonable and clearly understood: In many areas, working conditions are established through adherence to labor laws and employee contracts. Nonetheless, the paramount concern is that an atmosphere is maintained that ensures safety for both the employee and those being protected.

EXAMPLE COVERAGE SYSTEMS

As examples of how basic coverage principles are followed, the following are four different lifeguard operations.

1) Single Site Operation

Whispering Willows State Park is a small day area located on a pond. The area is open from 9 am to 8 pm daily, and gates control access to the 60-car parking lot. The beach is approximately 100 yards long and is protected from two lifeguard stands.

Three lifeguards are assigned to work at Whispering Willows, each working a 40-hour week during the summer season, composed of five eight hour days. One lifeguard has Monday and Tuesday off, the second has Wednesday and Thursday off, and the third has Friday and Saturday off. With this schedule, there are two lifeguards working each day except Sunday, the busiest day, on which there are three lifeguards.

The lifeguards cover the beach from 9 am to 8 pm on a rotating schedule. Each day, one lifeguard reports to work at 9 am and works to 5 pm. The second lifeguard working each day reports at noon and works to 8 pm. On Sunday, the third lifeguard working arrives at 10 am and works to 6 pm. Coverage is thereby maintained from 9 am to 8 pm, seven days each week, without a break in service. Lifeguards can take breaks during the double coverage period between noon and 5 pm daily. The lowest level of coverage exists during the early morning and late evening hours when attendance is lowest. The greatest coverage is provided midday, when attendance is highest.

[Photographic Credit:
Lucy Woolshlager]

2) Multi-Tower, Independent Operation

Lengthy Beach is a moderate-sized coastal town with a one-mile protected beach. The Lengthy Beach Patrol has established five lifeguard towers along the beach, providing continuous coverage over the one mile beach for the summer season. Fifteen beach lifeguards work 40-hour weeks in addition to supervisory staff, with three lifeguards assigned to each tower on a schedule very similar to that of Whispering Willows. On any given day, two lifeguards will work each tower and provide breaks for each other during the course of the operation day.

3) Multi-Tower Operation with Backup

Wide Island County provides lifeguard services from 12 towers during the summer over three miles of sandy beach. Twenty-one seasonal lifeguards are hired for forty hours each week, covering the beach from 9 am to 6 pm. Each tower operates with a single lifeguard. Two lifeguard supervisors work from vehicles to provide backup coverage during breaks and when a lifeguard leaves the tower on a rescue. Additional backup coverage is provided by other supervisory staff.

[Photographic Credit: Paul Drucker]

The Tower Zero system requires a main station with a commanding view.
[Photographic Credit: Rob McGowan]

4) Tower Zero Operation

Surf City, a major population area in a warm climate, operates a lifeguard service year round covering ten miles of beaches. There are several large, fixed observation towers with a wide area of view and numerous smaller, numbered towers spread along the beaches. During the busier season, the operation at Surf City is very similar to Wide Island County. The smaller towers are staffed by seasonally employed lifeguard personnel. The main observation towers are not numbered (hence the reference to "Tower Zero"). They are used primarily for overall observation and supervision of the area and are staffed by more senior personnel who coordinate responses and backup. The seasonal lifeguard personnel are relieved and backed up by mobile lifeguard units dispatched by lifeguards at the main tower.

In high season, lifeguards are on duty from dawn to dusk on staggered schedules. The first lifeguards on duty staff only the main observation tower. Those not assigned to water observation prepare equipment and patrol the beach. As mid-day approaches and more lifeguards arrive for their shifts, the smaller, numbered towers are opened, with preference given to those known to have high rescue activity and those furthest from the main tower. During the mid-day period all towers are staffed. As evening approaches, the smaller towers are closed one by one until all are closed. A lifeguard remains on duty in Tower Zero until the end of scheduled lifeguard protection.

During months of lower attendance, the small towers are not staffed and all observation is provided from the larger, fixed towers. From these towers, a smaller staff of lifeguards can observe the entire beach area using powerful binoculars and communicate with beach visitors over a public address system. They patrol the beach regularly in mobile lifeguard units and when trouble is noticed, mobile lifeguard units are dispatched to the scene.

CHAPTER TWELVE

COMPONENTS OF A RESCUE

CHAPTER HIGHLIGHTS

Recognize & Respond

Contact & Control

Signal & Save

IN THIS CHAPTER

While many rescues may seem quite simple, they actually represent a carefully planned response to a specific set of circumstances. The United States Lifesaving Association recognizes three basic components of every rescue.

To the beach visitor, rescues performed by lifeguards may seem dramatic, spontaneous events. Suddenly, a lifeguard springs from the station, runs to the water's edge and plunges in. The lifeguard quickly swims out to a person in distress (a victim) and contact is made. Returning to the beach, the lifeguard assists the swimmer to dry land and returns to the station, prepared for the next rescue to develop. Those who had riveted their attention on the sudden action, now go back to their recreational activities. It is all over, for now.

To the experienced lifeguard, most rescues are routine; but while many rescues may seem quite simple, they actually represent a carefully planned response to a specific set of circumstances. The lifeguard first recognizes distress or drowning signs, which are carefully and quickly assessed. The decision to respond is made. An entire backup network is alerted. Rescue equipment is selected based on the requirements of the rescue. The lifeguard plans an approach to the victim and carries it out. Throughout the approach, the lifeguard maintains constant visual contact with the victim. Upon arrival, the lifeguard calms the victim, signals to shore, and completes the save by bringing the victim to shore. Following these events, the lifeguard evaluates the victim for any complications, completes reports necessary to document the event, and prepares for another response.

The United States Lifesaving Association recognizes three basic components of every open water rescue. Each component includes specific steps. The three components of every rescue are as follows:

1) Recognize and Respond
2) Contact and Control
3) Signal and Save

Specific rescue procedures may differ somewhat from agency to agency, but these three rescue components are valid for all rescue situations, from wading assists to rescues with multiple victims. Each rescue includes all three components. What follows is a detailed description of each component and the subordinate steps involved.

A lifeguard with a victim in a rip current signals for assistance.
[Photographic Credit: William McNeely, Jr.]

RECOGNIZE & RESPOND

The first component of a rescue — *recognize and respond* — includes four steps:

1) Recognition
2) Alert
3) Equipment Selection
4) Entry

RECOGNITION

Before a rescue can take place, there must be *recognition* of distress. Typically a lifeguard determines through observation that a person needs assistance in the water. Perhaps a swimmer has fallen off a floating support in deep water or is being swept into deep water by a current. In some cases, lifeguards may be summoned to respond by beach visitors who have noticed something wrong in the water. Although it is unusual, the lifeguard may actually hear cries for help from the victim.

The 9-1-1 telephone system and the marine radio system are also sources of reports of emergencies, particularly for areas outside the direct observation of lifeguards. Occasionally employees of other public safety agencies observe and report the need for a lifeguard response. Regardless of the source of information, the process begins when a lifeguard recognizes the need for a rescue.

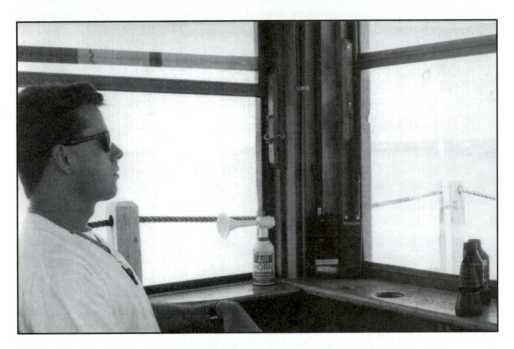

[Photographic Credit: William McNeely, Jr.]

ALERT

Before any lifeguard enters the water on a rescue, it is important that someone, somewhere knows that a rescue is being performed because the lifeguard will be exposed to a potentially dangerous situation and further assistance may be needed for the rescue. An *alert* to others triggers procedures that will provide backup assistance for the lifeguard. It will also ensure that other lifeguards begin to cover the water area of the lifeguard leaving on the rescue.

Each agency has its own alert procedures based on staffing levels and available communication equipment. A lifeguard may simply alert a station partner before responding to a rescue. At stations where lifeguards work alone, they may use a two-way radio to announce rescues or may trigger an alarm. Some stations are equipped with special telephone systems, allowing lifeguards to simply take a telephone off the hook. The off-hook telephone rings into a central switchboard, identifying the station involved. Other alert procedures may include air horns, whistle signals, and similar audible devices. Some agencies use flag systems, but this alert method is least certain in that it relies on other lifeguards who may or may not observe the signal.

The best alert systems allow for two-way communication, which enables the responding lifeguard to firmly establish that the alert has been received, to briefly detail circumstances of the response, and to request any special assistance which may appear necessary. The alert for a routine rescue may be very brief, such as, "Tower #1 in on one." The lifeguard in Tower #1 states that a rescue of one person is being initiated. Lack of additional information implies that it is routine. For further information on lifeguard communication, refer to the chapter entitled *Communication Methods*.

The importance of the alert cannot be over-emphasized. Alerts are standard practice in all emergency services, including fire departments, police agencies, and emergency medical services. Without an alert, lifeguards expose themselves to possible life-threatening situations without anyone else becoming aware. A significant component of drowning statistics is contributed by untrained people who drown while trying to assist other drowning people. Although lifeguard training significantly reduces this potential, lifeguards are at risk on every rescue.

EQUIPMENT SELECTION

Once the alert is made, or simultaneous to this notification, the responding lifeguard must make an *equipment selection*. Proper equipment selection requires a thorough familiarity with all rescue equipment maintained by the agency, a proper evaluation of the incident, and the foresight to consider ways that apparent circumstances of the incident may change during the response.

Sometimes the lifeguard who has observed distress develop may actually determine that other personnel should respond based on the availability of special rescue equipment. For example, a rescue boat may be very near the victim and signaled to effect the rescue. Equipment selection for more advanced equipment is covered later in this text. In our hypothetical rescue, the lifeguard selects a rescue buoy.

ENTRY

Once proper rescue equipment has been selected, the lifeguard determines the most efficient path to the victim and effects a water *entry*. It is very important to attempt to maintain visual contact with the victim throughout the rescue. Victims may move with a current or submerge prior to the lifeguard's arrival. In the latter case, lifeguards must be able to fix a last seen point.

The water can be very deceiving since there are usually no stationary objects. Lifeguards must find a way to get their bearings. Buildings, trees, and other stationary objects ashore can be used effectively. One of the best methods is to line up two stationary objects ashore that are one in front of the other. As long as these objects maintain the same position relative to each other, the lifeguard is staying on a consistent line.

The drowning process can progress rapidly through the distress and panic stages to submersion, so speed is important. To increase the speed and efficiency of entries, several points should be considered for swimming rescues:

- *Get there safely*—As important as speed may be in a water rescue, if the lifeguard is injured enroute to the victim, the victim may not survive. Speed is important, but lifeguards must protect themselves at all times.

A lifeguard enters the water to rescue a victim. Note the victim's head in the rip current. **[Photographic Credit: William McNeely, Jr.]**

- *Running on the beach is faster than swimming*—Running normally requires much less energy than swimming. In planning the entry, lifeguards should usually run down the beach to the point closest to the victim before entering the water.
- *Use the current if current is present*—If the victim is caught in a current, the best point for water entry will vary. For example, if the victim is caught on the edge of strong, out-flowing current from a tidal bay, the lifeguard could run to a point adjacent to the victim, jump into the center of the current and be swept past the victim. In this case, as in a river, the lifeguard may need to intentionally enter upstream and swim diagonally toward the victim.

    At a surf beach, if a victim is caught in a rip current moving perpendicular to the beach, the best entry point will usually be at the rip current feeder. The current then helps carry the lifeguard to the victim. At lower tides, rip current channels are sometimes bordered by sand bars that are waist deep or even shallower. The lifeguard may be able to run out on the sand bar to a point very near the victim before jumping into the rip current channel and swimming to the victim.

- *Run into the water as far as possible before beginning to swim*—Running in shallow water is faster than swimming. Upon entering the water, the best technique is to kick high out of the water while running to minimize the resistance of the water. This is called high stepping. At the same time, lifeguards should always be conscious of the potential for uneven bottom conditions that can inflict serious leg injuries.
- *Use surface dives to get to swimming depth*—On a gradually sloping beach, upon reaching deeper water the lifeguard will be unable to continue the running entry.

At this point, however, swimming may not yet be the fastest method of moving forward. Wading to swimming depth is a possibility, but it takes considerable energy and may be quite slow. At surf beaches, incoming waves will further impede forward progress. The lifeguard's goal is to present as little of the body as possible to the oncoming wave.

In such cases, when running is no longer effective, but swimming is not yet the fastest method of forward propulsion, a surface dive or surface dives should be used. At a surf beach, the lifeguard dives under incoming waves that are too large to jump over or through. As the lifeguard dives forward, the head and neck must be protected. This can be accomplished by fully extending the hands and arms forward as the dive is initiated.

A more advanced technique involves *porpoising* through shallow water to swimming depth. Porpoising is accomplished by springing forward into a shallow dive with the arms fully extended. If swim fins are used, they are held in each hand. As the forward glide slows, the lifeguard grabs the sand and pulls the feet under the body in a crouching position, then springs forward using the legs in another forward dive. This arcing dive-glide-recover pattern is repeated until swimming depth is reached. Porpoising can be used in both surf and flat water but is particularly effective in surf.

At beaches with a steep slope, the period spent running or porpoising through the water will be very brief. On the other hand, beaches with long, gradual slopes necessitate extensive running and porpoising through the water. Under either circumstance, the lifeguard begins swimming when the running or porpoising action is no longer faster than swimming.

CONTACT AND CONTROL

The second component of a water rescue—*contact and control*—includes the following three steps:
1) Approach
2) Contact
3) Stabilize

APPROACH

Once swimming depth is reached, the lifeguard approaches the victim as quickly as possible, using swimming strokes that will allow frequent checking on the position of the victim. The crawl stroke is best because it is fastest. Using the heads-up form of water polo players, the approaching lifeguard can usually maintain visual contact with the victim. In some situations, the lifeguard will be unable to see the victim no matter what stroke is used. This may occur when water conditions are rough or when a drowning presentation has progressed to a submersion. In these cases, the bearings that were taken on water entry become critical for fixing the last seen point of the victim.

To further assist, lifeguards ashore must be prepared to provide easily understandable signals to the lifeguard in the water. Upon losing sight of the victim, the responding lifeguard can turn to shore for this assistance. Audible devices, such as public address systems and whistle systems may be useful, but should not be

A lifeguard approaches a victim in a rip current. Note that the surf is not breaking in the rip current channel. [Photographic Credit: William McNeely, Jr.]

solely relied upon because the lifeguard in the water may not be able to hear them. Simple shore-based arm signals are as follows:

- *Move to right or left*—An RFD is extended to the right or left at the end of a fully extended arm by the lifeguard ashore.
- *Go further out*—An RFD is held vertically between two upraised arms.
- *Stay there*—Arms are extended horizontally to the sides without holding a rescue buoy.
- *Go outside the surf and wait*—An RFD is held horizontally in both hands over the head. This is generally used when a boat or helicopter is being sent to retrieve the lifeguard and victim.

In addition to these shore-based signals, other arm signals intended primarily for use by a lifeguard in the water can also be used by lifeguards ashore. These are covered later in the *Signal and Save* section of this chapter and in Appendix A.

Upon nearing the victim, the lifeguard should begin talking to the victim to provide reassurance and instructions. The lifeguard can watch the victim's eyes for signs of fright or panic. It is well worth taking the time needed to calm the victim because a panicked victim can be very dangerous. During the final stages of approach, the lifeguard should keep away from a position where the victim can grab the lifeguard.

Usually, the mere presence of another person in the water who seems calm and knowledgeable will have a significantly positive effect. The presence of the RFD also gives the victim immediate hope. The final few feet of the approach are covered with the rescue buoy extended, and the lifeguard using swimming kicks for thrust. The lifeguard assumes a defensive position by holding the rescue buoy and extending it toward the victim.

CONTACT

Contact with the victim begins when the victim grabs the rescue buoy or is otherwise connected to it. *Lifeguards should always avoid direct contact with victims in the water because they can panic, grab the lifeguard, and jeopardize the safety of both.* For purposes of this description, we will assume a standard rescue scenario in which the victim grabs an extended rescue buoy. The chapter entitled *Standard Rescue Equipment* provides information on more complicated rescues and proper use of a rescue tube.

If the victim grabs the lifeguard in panic, the lifeguard should immediately stop swimming and submerge. Victims almost always let go when this maneuver is used. If necessary, the lifeguard can push off from the victim using the feet, then swim away underwater and surface seven to ten feet away from the victim before extending the buoy again.

STABILIZE

Once control has been gained in a rescue, the lifeguard can begin to *stabilize* the victim. Informal studies of drowning situations have concluded that in most situations, once support in the form of a rescue floatation device has been provided, the panic experienced by the victim will quickly subside. The victim can regain normal breathing, wipe away hair and water from the face, and communicate with the lifeguard. Rationality returns, leaving the victim able to understand what is happening and what must be done.

In most rescue situations, lifeguards should take advantage of this reduction of panic before proceeding with the rescue. It is an excellent opportunity to explain to the victim what has happened, to assure the victim that the situation is now under control, and to rest before proceeding. Since the immediate crisis has been contained, there is usually no immediate need to proceed with retrieval to shore until extrication is planned and explained to the victim.

SIGNAL & SAVE

The third and final component of a rescue—*signal and save*—includes four steps:
1) Signal
2) Retrieve
3) Assess
4) Report

SIGNAL

The alert initiated by the responding lifeguard begins a backup procedure that directs the attention of shore-based lifeguards to the rescue and may bring other lifeguards or staff to the beach near the rescue scene. Once control has been gained and the victim has been stabilized, it is important to communicate with other responding staff. A *signal* should be made to other lifeguards.

Although each lifeguard agency may develop its own system of rescue status signals, the USLA has adopted four basic signals which all lifeguard agencies should utilize. These simple signals allow for national consistency and effective communication among lifeguards working for different agencies. Each signal, when given by a lifeguard in the water, should be repeated by lifeguards on shore. This lets the lifeguard in the water know that the signal was seen and understood. These signals can also be used by lifeguards ashore to communicate with lifeguards in the water.

USLA Approved Arm Signals

- *Under Control*—Also referred to as "no further assistance needed." The lifeguard touches the fingers together over the head, forming a large circle with the arms. An alternative is to touch the middle of the head with the fingertips of one hand, but this signal is not as visible. Either of these signals simulate the commonly used "OK" hand signal made by creating a circle with the thumb and forefinger. They are used primarily when the lifeguard has determined that the rescue can be accomplished without the help of others and the victim is stable. It is important to note that this does not mean lifeguards ashore can ignore the rescue in progress. The situation can deteriorate, and the lifeguard in the water will need to be able to signal the change to someone watching from shore.

 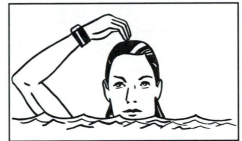

Under Control

- *Assistance Needed*—The lifeguard raises *but does not wave* one arm. The lifeguard in the water needs further assistance. This could be due to a badly panicked victim, multiple victims, an injury the lifeguard sustained in the response, etc. Backup should be sent immediately.

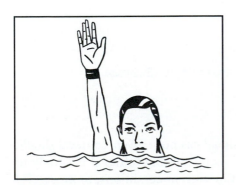

Assistance Needed

• *Resuscitation Case*—The lifeguard raises *and waves* one arm. In situations involving non-breathing victims, or those with seriously lowered respirations, backup staff must be advised that ventilatory support will be required once the victim is brought back to the beach. This allows backup staff to prepare resuscitation equipment for use once the victim has been retrieved. It also signals the need for in-water assistance. A single lifeguard in the water is rarely able to effectively manage a non-breathing victim alone.

Resuscitation Case

• *Code X*—The lifeguard raises both arms and forms an X overhead. This is the most serious signal of all. The lifeguard could not reach the victim in time. A swimmer is missing and presumed submerged. The lifeguard in the water believes that search and recovery procedures need to be initiated. This signal, developed and successfully tested in San Diego, allows a lifeguard in the water to advise lifeguards ashore of the need for immediate backup, without interrupting an initial search for the submerged victim by having to swim to shore. Lifeguards on shore receiving this signal should immediately take bearings to fix the point of the lifeguard, as well as prepare an appropriate response.

Code X (Missing Swimmer)

RETRIEVE

Once the victim has been stabilized and the signal has been given, retrieval should be planned. In calm water conditions, the objective during retrieval is simply to reach water of standing depth. In heavy surf or current conditions, more careful route selection is needed.

If the victim is in a rip current, the lifeguard usually needs to first swim laterally out of the current before swimming ashore. Rescues off rocky shores or near piers and other obstructions may also require lateral swimming before a turn is made toward the beach. Lifeguards should make every attempt to avoid swimming a victim to the beach through sets of very large surf. Lifeguards can either wait for a lull between sets of waves or swim the victim to deeper water for pickup by a lifeguard vessel or rescue helicopter, if available. Another alternative is to swim the victim to an adjacent beach area with less adverse surf conditions. While this will take time and energy, it may also be the safest method.

Once the route is planned, the victim should be instructed. In most cases, the victim will be able to assist by holding firmly onto the rescue floatation device and employing a flutter kick or frog kick. By using a backstroke, the lifeguard can maintain constant visual contact with the victim. If a crawl or breaststroke is used, the lifeguard should look back regularly to check on the victim.

Victims should be instructed to continue grasping the RFD until told that they can release it. Upon approaching shore, victims often become more confident or simply embarrassed and let go of the rescue buoy. In rip current rescues and in surf, a victim who releases the RFD prematurely can easily be recirculated back into the rip current.

While swimming to shore at a surf beach, lifeguards must remember to watch for incoming waves. If the victim will be taken in through large breaking waves, the victim should be advised of this and told how to prepare. The lifeguard gets behind the victim and hugs tightly under the armpits with the rescue buoy against the victim's chest. Just before the wave hits, the lifeguard can pinch the victim's nose with the thumb and forefinger and keep the rest of the hand over the victim's mouth to reduce the chances of water being swallowed or aspirated.

In situations where the victim is extremely weak or unconscious, the lifeguard will have to adapt the rescue buoy to provide support for the victim before beginning retrieval. Techniques for proper use of rescue buoys in these cases are detailed in the chapter entitled *Standard Rescue Equipment*.

REMOVE

Once shallow water is reached, it may be a simple procedure to remove the victim to shore. In most rescues, the victim needs little or no further assistance. Some agencies have established policies that require lifeguards to escort all victims completely out of the water to dry sand, even if the victim appears to need little or no assistance.

In some situations, victims will need assistance in leaving the water. Perhaps a weak or tired swimmer is having trouble maintaining balance or wading ashore. Other victims may be unconscious or barely lucid. In these situations, lifeguards will have to carry or assist the victims.

Lifeguards should consider several important points when removing victims from the water. First, lifeguards must have the strength and ability to extricate a victim without assistance. Although there are often other lifeguards, staff, or visitors present to assist with extrication, there may be times when a lifeguard will have to accomplish removal alone. Second, lifeguards should use extrication techniques that minimize the possibility of personal injury. Victims may be large, overweight, or of no assistance to the lifeguard. Finally, lifeguards should use techniques that protect the victim from injury during extrication, both from the terrain that must be covered and from the removal technique itself. Two simple removal techniques are offered in this chapter that consider these points.

When victims are able to assist to some degree during the removal process, a *shallow water assist* is recommended. To execute this technique, the lifeguard simply drapes one of the victim's arms around the back of the lifeguard's neck, supporting the victim's waist with the other arm. Then the victim is gently directed out of the water to dry sand and assisted in sitting or lying down on the beach.

When the victim cannot assist in the removal process, a *longitudinal drag* is recommended. Place the hands under the victim's armpits and attempt to support the head with the forearms. Then drag the victim up the beach.

Lifeguards remove a rescued victim from the water.
[Photographic Credit: William McNeely, Jr.]

If there are two lifeguards available and if any spinal injury is suspected, use the *underarm spinal stabilization method*. This method is described in the chapter entitled *Medical Care in the Aquatic Environment*.

ASSESS

Assess all victims for possible complications after the rescue. This can be done rather informally in routine cases. Does the person have a steady or unsteady gait? Are the eyes clear? Does the person appear alert? Does the person seem fully oriented? In most cases, this will be adequate.

It is a good practice to ask all victims if they are all right upon reaching shore. Can they take a deep breath without pain? Do they think they swallowed or inhaled water? In most cases, it will be obvious if a person is feeling poorly, but lifeguards must remember the tendency of victims to deny problems. Often upon the completion of a rescue everyone on the beach is watching. The victim feels very embarrassed and just wants to get away. The lifeguard should never release victims until reasonably certain they are fine.

REPORT

The rescue *report* is critical to all lifeguard provider agencies. Rescue reports, including name and address of the victim, should be completed for every rescue performed by lifeguards. The reporting form should include information such as the name of the lifeguard, the time of day, and the date. A basic *Incident Report*, suitable for recording rescues, minor medical aids, and similar lifeguard actions can be found in Appendix B.

USLA defines a water rescue of a swimmer as any case in which a lifeguard physically assists a victim in extrication from the water when the victim lacked the apparent ability to do so alone. Providing verbal commands or advice to swimmers in the water is considered to be an aspect of preventive lifeguarding but not a rescue.

Statistics generated through the filing of rescue reports often provide the single most important information in determining needed levels of lifeguard staffing. While stories about rescues are sometimes fascinating, agency administrators need hard facts about the volume of rescue activity when budget-based decisions need to be made. This makes the accurate reporting of rescues critical to lifeguards concerned about ensuring that staffing levels meet the need. Some lifeguard supervisors tell their personnel that, "If you don't record it, it didn't happen." While in truth the rescue may have taken place, statistically it did not happen if a rescue report wasn't filed.

USLA compiles annual statistics on the number of rescues performed at beaches throughout the United States. Each open water lifeguard agency should report the rescues they perform annually, using the USLA national lifesaving statistics form found in Appendix B. Reports should be submitted within a month of the end of each calendar year. Seasonal agencies should report at the close of the season.

CHAPTER THIRTEEN

STANDARD RESCUE EQUIPMENT

CHAPTER HIGHLIGHTS

Rescue Floatation Device

Swim Fins

Rescue Board

Spinal Stabilization Device

Boat Tow

IN THIS CHAPTER

The rescue floatation device (RFD) has become the principal piece of rescue equipment used by professional lifeguards in the United States. The use of swim fins is indicated in rescue situations involving longer approach swims and deep water rescues involving currents. The rescue board is like no other piece of equipment and lifeguards must practice rescue board skills often to develop and maintain proficiency.

Special training and the use of rescue equipment are essential to professional lifeguard operations. These are primary factors separating professional lifeguards from amateur lifesavers. The rescue equipment described here is the mainstay of professional beach lifeguard agencies—the core equipment which should be available to all beach lifeguards.

Lifeguard agencies provide rescue equipment for several reasons:

- *Lifeguard Safety*—Drowning victims are desperate for buoyant support. A panicked victim is therefore a very real threat to an approaching lifeguard. The victim may attempt to grab the lifeguard, forcing both underwater and into a mutually life-threatening situation. Buoyant rescue devices provided to victims usually have an immediate calming effect as the primary source of fear (submersion) is eliminated. This allows the lifeguard to safely complete the rescue.

- *Speed*—Because the success of some rescues will depend greatly on how fast a lifeguard can reach a victim, equipment has been adapted or developed to decrease lifeguard response time.
- *Support of the Victim*—To reverse the drowning process, buoyant support must be provided for the victim. This support must be sufficient to maintain the victim's breathing passages above the water surface.
- *Increased Efficiency*—Many rescue devices provide increased efficiency for the lifeguard by augmenting the lifeguard's swimming skills or by providing support for the victim so that the lifeguard can devote more energy to swimming. For example, rescue floatation devices (RFDs) increase the speed with which victims can be removed from the water and allow the rescue of multiple victims by a single lifeguard.

In the open water beach setting, most lifeguard rescue equipment consists of devices used during in-water rescues, rather than extension devices such as reaching poles or throwing devices (ring buoys, etc.), which are more typically found in the pool environment. This is not to suggest that these types of equipment are useless. Open water recreation areas with floats, docks, or piers may provide lifeguards with extension or throwing devices since drowning presentations may occur at those facilities within easy reaching or throwing distance. Open water lifeguards assigned to flood rescues in swiftwater also use throwbags and similar devices very effectively.

At open water beaches, however, it is a very rare situation that allows for an effective throwing rescue and this text will not cover such rescues in detail. Suffice it to say that if a victim can be easily and reliably rescued by throwing a line or extending a pole, this method should be given due consideration. At the same time, lifeguards must always be prepared to enter the water when such methods are ineffective.

RESCUE FLOATATION DEVICE

The rescue floatation device (RFD) has become the principal piece of rescue equipment used by professional lifeguards in the United States. The three major components of an RFD are:
- A floatation device
- A lanyard
- A harness

RFDs should always be available in an adequate number to allow all lifeguards at a beach to use one if a major rescue develops. In many areas, RFDs are assigned to lifeguards as pieces of personal equipment, for which they are responsible during all duty hours. At other agencies, RFDs are assigned to locations rather than lifeguards. When lifeguards leave these locations, they are always expected to take an RFD along. Some agencies require the use of an RFD on all rescues in addition to other equipment that may be selected.

There are good reasons for such policies:

- *Constant Readiness*—If a lifeguard is away from the station for some reason, a fundamental piece of rescue equipment will always be at hand for a sudden response. Some agencies forbid the storage of RFDs at the station, preferring that lifeguards carry the RFD to and from the station each day in anticipation of an early or late rescue.

- *Identification to the Public*—RFDs are very distinctive and recognizable, even more so than uniforms. When help is needed, people will quickly see and identify the person carrying an RFD as a lifeguard. The RFD also helps to symbolize the authority of the lifeguard when approaching a beach patron. In a rescue situation, the RFD helps identify a lifeguard during water entry, which may help to clear the way on a crowded beach or avoid confrontations. When a lifeguard responds to a rescue with an RFD (even a shallow water assist), people will often focus their attention to the water area, which can be helpful in bringing family members to the scene to help with information or ensure better future supervision. In the water, a victim seeing a swimmer approach would have no way of knowing this person is a lifeguard without the presence of the RFD.

- *Identification to Fellow Lifeguards*—Like other people at the beach, life-guards are easily lost in the crowd, but the characteristic shape and color of the RFD can identify a patrolling lifeguard easily on a crowded beach. In the water, the RFD clearly identifies the lifeguard on a rescue. As a signaling device, the RFD helps lifeguards in the water identify lifeguards on the beach and the instructions they are giving. At some larger agencies, RFDs of differ-ent color can identify special lifeguards or lifeguard supervisors.

- *Multiple Uses*—RFDs can be used in conjunction with other equipment and taken along without interfering with other devices. RFDs can be adapted to almost any rescue situation. With a boat tow (described later in this chapter) attached to the rear of the buoy, an RFD can be used to swim a boat away from the surf. They can be modified to carry and store special rescue equip-ment, such as one-way breathing masks. They can be used for a wide variety of signals on the beach and in the water and rescue buoys are even useful as self-defense tools in particularly dangerous public confrontations.

In general, commercially manufactured RFDs are preferable to custom-made devices because of their proven design and durability. The different types of RFDs each have distinctive characteristics, and many lifeguard agencies prefer one type over another for various reasons. For example, agencies that often encounter multi-ple rescue situations may prefer a large size rescue buoy because of the extra buoy-ancy it provides. Other agencies may supply lifeguards with various types of RFDs with instructions to use certain types in particular situations.

TYPES OF RESCUE FLOATATION DEVICES

Rescue Buoy

Rescue buoys are also known as rescue cans, torpedo buoys (torps), diamond buoys, and Burnside buoys. The latter name stems from one of the lifeguards involved in their modern development. Since the first rescue buoy was developed in 1897 by Captain Harry Sheffield for a South African lifesaving club, the design has evolved significantly but the general shape and manner of use remain.

The first rescue buoys were made of sheet metal, then copper, then aluminum. These metal versions had an elongated elliptical shape, rounded in the middle with pointed ends. Line was run from end to end down both sides of the buoy, secured through eyes at the points. The victim would hold on to the line while being pulled ashore. These historical pieces of lifesaving equipment were of great value in their time but are no longer considered appropriate for use in lifesaving.

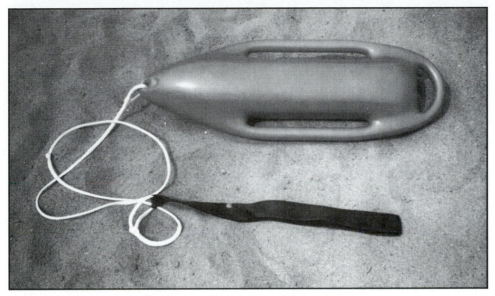

Rescue Buoy [Photographic Credit: Dan McCormick]

The most widely employed design of rescue buoy in current use is molded from lightweight, hard plastic. This air-filled (but not inflated) buoy has handles molded into the sides and rear of the buoy, which allow the victim to maintain a firmer, more comfortable grip during rescue than is possible with rope. Rescue buoys are available in different sizes for different conditions. They are very durable and highly visible.

Advantages of the Rescue Buoy:
- Multiple Victims—Rescue buoys have high buoyancy, allowing the simultaneous support and rescue of several victims.
- Victim Avoidance—A rescue buoy can be pushed to a victim from several feet away, allowing the lifeguard to avoid being grabbed by a panicked victim.
- Durability—Rescue buoys are generally very durable.

Limitations of the Rescue Buoy:
- *Lack of Victim Security*—Victims can't be attached to a rescue buoy as they can to a rescue tube.
- *Hard Exterior*—Although softer than the original metal design, modern rescue buoys are still hard plastic and can cause injuries.

Rescue Tube

The rescue tube, also known as the Peterson tube after the lifeguard who designed it, is a flexible foam buoy with an embedded strap and a vinyl skin. The embedded strap is connected to the lanyard leading to the lifeguard. Attached to one end of the strap is one or more rings. On the other end of the strap, a snap hook is attached.

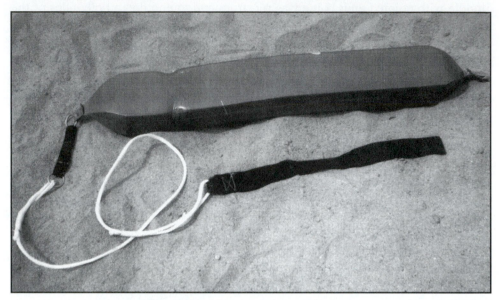

Rescue Tube [**Photographic Credit: Dan McCormick**]

When the tube is bent, the hook can be snapped to the ring, creating a closed loop. In a rescue situation, the tube can be wrapped around the victim and secured. This is particularly useful when taking a victim through breaking surf, wherein the rescuer and victim might otherwise be separated. Rescue tubes are available in several sizes. Overall, the rescue tube is not as widely used as the rescue buoy.

Advantages of the Rescue Tube:
- *Hydrodynamic*—The rescue tube creates very little drag against the lifeguard towing it.
- *Secures the Victim*—The victim is actually wrapped in the buoy.
- *Rescue Boat Use*—The soft design keeps rescue tubes from bouncing around in a rescue boat.

Limitations of the Rescue Tube:
- *Single Victim Use*—The rescue tube can be used for more than one victim, but is designed for a single victim.
- *Low Buoyancy*—Rescue tubes have a relatively low buoyancy compared to rescue buoys.
- *Requires Physical Contact with Victim*—Snapping a rescue tube around the victim requires physical contact with a possibly panicked victim.
- *Requires Extra Maneuver*—Unlike the rescue buoy which is simply pushed to the victim, the rescue tube requires that the lifeguard take an extra step of wrapping and snapping.

- *Fending Off*—Rescue tubes cannot be effectively used to fend off a panicked victim.

The snap of a rescue tube can cause lacerations or other injury. This is very unusual, but it is best to secure the tube around the victim to avoid this problem. In regard to maintenance, rescue tubes are particularly susceptible to environmental degradation. They should be stored in an elongated position out of the sun.

RESCUES WITH RESCUE FLOATATION DEVICES

The basic use of an RFD is described in the chapter entitled, *Components of a Rescue*. The following additional factors must be considered:

- *Water Entry*—In addition to the floatation device, RFDs are equipped with a lanyard and a harness, which is attached to the lifeguard. The lanyard and harness can trip the lifeguard during the entry run. Care should be taken to unwrap the RFD and don the harness without letting the line become a hazard. RFDs should be carried into the water until the lifeguard needs to begin porpoising or swimming, since a dragging RFD is dead weight and may collide with beach visitors. At surf areas, lifeguards should expect to feel extra drag after waves pass by, which is caused by the force of the wave against the RFD.
- *Removal from Water*—In many situations, lifeguards can simply drop RFDs as they move to assist or carry victims from the water. In some surf conditions, however, an unsecured RFD could be washed with force against the lifeguard or victim, potentially causing injury. If heavy surf conditions are present, lifeguards may want to carry the RFD completely out of the water or have the victim do so.
- *Fouling*—If the lanyard becomes wrapped around an object, the lifeguard can be placed in serious jeopardy. For example, the lanyard could become wrapped in the propeller of a rescue vessel. For this reason, it is essential that the attachment between the lifeguard and lanyard allow for quick release.
- *Lanyard Length*—The length of the lanyard often reflects the personal preference of each lifeguard. In general, however, the lanyard must be long enough at least to allow the buoy to clear the kicking feet of the lifeguard while swimming, plus a foot or two. If buoys are shared at an agency, this measurement should take into account the lifeguard with the longest legs. At the same time, a long lanyard is more likely to become fouled and to trip the running lifeguard.

Rescue Buoy

Contact & Control: In most presentations, victims will quickly grab and hold tightly to the rescue buoy handles or ropes for support and subsequent retrieval. In some cases, a victim may be so unresponsive that lifeguard assistance is needed. In these situations, the lifeguard should move to the rear of the victim facing the victim's back while keeping the rescue buoy in front of the victim. Then the lifeguard reaches under the victim's arms to grasp a side handle of the rescue buoy. The rescue buoy is pulled close to sandwich the victim between the rescue buoy and the lifeguard. The rescue can now proceed, with retrieval being made through kicking the feet. It can be difficult to bring a victim ashore in this manner for obvious reasons. Therefore, additional lifeguard assistance should be considered.

A lifeguard makes contact with a victim. [Photographic Credit: Annette Kennedy]

Retrieval: If a victim must be moved through a heavy surfline where there is still deep water, the lifeguard should move behind the victim and sandwich the victim between the lifeguard's body and the rescue buoy in the position just described for unresponsive victims. Then the lifeguard moves through the surfline carefully by kicking the feet, checking behind frequently, and informing the victim when to expect the force of a wave.

A lifeguard prepares to bring a victim through the surfline using a rescue buoy. [Photographic Credit: Annette Kennedy]

Rescue Tube

Contact and Control: Perhaps the most valuable feature of the rescue tube is that it can be securely be wrapped around the victim. It should always be used in this way, not as a device to be held by the victim. In most presentations, the lifeguard should first be concerned with establishing control by providing the support of the tube to the victim and letting the victim stabilize. Then, if possible, the lifeguard can direct the victim to move on the tube to a position where the victim is facing the tube with both arms over it and the tube is nestled under the armpits. The lifeguard can then move to the rear of the victim and bring the ends of the tube together for connection. Note that this requires the lifeguard to come into direct contact with the victim, which should not be done until the lifeguard is certain that the victim will not panic and grab the lifeguard.

If the victim is unconscious or unresponsive, the process of securing the victim in the tube is more difficult, since the tube is often much more buoyant than the victim. When facing the victim, the lifeguard can pull one arm over the extended tube to armpit level, then carefully work the other arm over the tube to the same position and connect the tube from the rear of the victim. Another technique is to swim to the rear of the victim and provide support with one hand under an armpit while placing the tube in front of the victim's face. From that point, the lifeguard can lift one, then the other arm of the victim over the tube to the armpit level and finally connect the tube at the victim's back.

Retrieval: If a victim must be moved through a heavy surfline, the lifeguard moves to the rear of the victim and holds on to the tube and victim with the lifeguard's face to the victim's back. The lifeguard should check behind frequently while kicking toward shore and advise the victim when to expect the force of a wave.

SWIM FINS

At many lifeguard agencies, swim fins are issued as part of the lifeguard's basic rescue equipment. The obvious advantage to use of swim fins is the added speed and power that they give to the responding lifeguard. In rocky areas, swim fins provide protection for the feet. They can also be useful during search and recovery procedures requiring diving.

USE AND SELECTION OF SWIM FINS

The use of swim fins is indicated in rescue situations involving longer approach swims and deep water rescues involving currents. They are also useful when lifeguards need to provide additional support to victims in deep water, such as situations involving resuscitation. Deep water rescues under heavy surf conditions may indicate the use of swim fins, as may multiple or mass rescues. Swim fins are not, however, indicated in shallow water rescues or in rescue situations a short distance from shallow water. In these situations, the time necessary to don swim fins can delay response.

The most common design of lifeguard swim fins.
[Photographic Credit: Dan McCormick]

Lifeguard agencies are usually very particular in selecting or approving swim fins for lifeguard use. Swim fins must fit the lifeguard precisely, so fins are usually selected and assigned to individual lifeguards. The type and style of swim fins are also important. Shoe-type fins are usually unacceptable because they frequently fall off. Adjustable heel-strap styles are generally less dependable than solid heel-strap styles. Swim fins which float or have neutral buoyancy are very useful because a lifeguard can remove them, if necessary, without fear of loss.

RESCUES WITH SWIM FINS

Entry: When swim fins are used on rescues, the lifeguard dons the RFD harness, then grabs the RFD and lanyard in one hand and both fins in the other, running with them into the water. On a sand beach entry, it is preferable to run or porpoise until forward progress would be expedited by swimming. Upon entering the water with swim fins, the lifeguard drops the RFD and places one fin in each hand. At this point the fins can be used as paddles (one in each hand) until the lifeguard is in water approximately chest deep. The lifeguard can also porpoise, holding the heel strap of each fin in each hand. Once swimming becomes the most expeditious manner of making forward progress, the lifeguard stops and dons the fins. Rarely can this be done with the head above water and, therefore, lifeguards who use fins must be adept at donning them blind. When the fins have been donned, the lifeguard can turn and swim to the victim. Swim fins should not be worn while running on the beach or in shallow water.

An exception to this guideline is a water entry in a rocky area. Swim fins can be put on immediately in this situation, as they provide protection for the feet. High strides will cut down the resistance caused by the swim fins.

Retrieval: Once the lifeguard can stand, most lifeguards begin by walking backward, as this can be done effectively without removing the fins. Once shallow water is gained, the lifeguard removes the fins and carries them for the remainder of the rescue. In rare instances, the lifeguard may need to discard the swim fins during this rescue component in order to better provide victim support. Fins that float are particularly useful in such situations as they can be more easily recovered.

Lifeguard Rescue Board
[Photographic Credit: Dave Foxwell]

RESCUE BOARD

Rescue boards (known also as paddleboards and rescue surfboards) are a valuable piece of rescue equipment that evolved from the surfboard. While surfboards and rescue boards have a common ancestor, today's lifeguard rescue boards should not be confused with surfboards. Although these devices may have a similar appearance, rescue boards are designed primarily for rescue, not surfing.

A rescue board is a buoyant, lightweight craft approximately 10 feet to 12 feet long and shaped to move quickly through the water. Most commercially produced rescue boards are manufactured from a shaped, reinforced core of polyurethane foam, which is then covered with a skin of fiberglass, epoxy, or other compounds. To increase stability, a skeg (fin) is attached to the bottom of the board at the rear, acting somewhat like the keel of a ship.

Rescue boards may be equipped with rope or inlaid handles for use by lifeguards and victims, and with eyelets to allow for towing. Most lifeguard agencies prefer commercially manufactured rescue boards to custom-made devices, although some larger agencies are producing high-quality rescue boards to their own specifications. The primary use of a rescue board is water rescue of swimmers. They can also be used in boat rescue and, if necessary, as a backboard to remove an injured victim from the water, although the latter use should only be as a last resort.

Advantages of the Rescue Board:
- *Speed*—When used properly under the right conditions, rescue boards can allow lifeguards to cover considerable distances much faster than swimming with fins, making them useful in rescues involving long approaches.
- *Buoyancy*—Rescue boards are very buoyant and can support numerous victims. Increased buoyancy can also be useful during situations where resuscitation must be provided in deep water. In calm water, rescue boards can even be used to administer rescue breathing. When rescuing a single victim, the victim is almost completely removed from the water, significantly increasing the sense of security.
- *Lightweight*—Unlike a boat, the low weight of the rescue board allows it to be carried, launched, and operated by one lifeguard and easily transported atop a lifeguard vehicle. On the other hand, a rescue board is heavy and unwieldy compared to a rescue buoy and cannot be easily transported by a lifeguard on foot over a long distance.
- *Platform*—The deck of the rescue board provides an excellent platform from which the lifeguard can observe the swim area. This makes the rescue board a rudimentary patrol device and a useful tool in surface searches of swim areas.
- *Usefulness in Flat Water*—Rescue boards, while based on the design of surfboards, are ideal for the flat water environment. In flat water, rescue boards are almost always the fastest method of accessing victims other than power boats.

Limitations of the Rescue Board:
- *Surf Conflicts*—A rescue board is difficult, if not impossible, to move through heavy surf. A swimming lifeguard can more easily penetrate heavy surf than a lifeguard on a rescue board. Trying to return to shore with an incapacitated victim is very difficult in sizable surf. Loss of the rescue board in the surf is a considerable risk. If the board is lost, the lifeguard may be left without equipment and lose contact with the victim, not to mention the possible hazard for other swimmers presented by an uncontrolled rescue board. For these reasons, it is advisable to carefully consider use of a rescue board in large, breaking surf, and it is suggested that lifeguards doing so always wear swim fins and take an RFD. This way, if the rescue board is lost, the lifeguard will retain the ability to effectively complete the rescue.
- *Lack of Maneuverability*—Rescue boards operate best when paddled in a straight line with occasional small corrections made in direction. A congested swimming area may present the lifeguard with too many obstacles to move around enroute to the victim. Similarly, congested swimming areas may provide the lifeguard with difficult obstacles during retrieval.
- *Design and Maintenance Problems*—Rescue boards are expensive to purchase and maintain. Because they are built for speed and lightweight, rescue

boards can be damaged (dinged) easily, which could contribute to periods when the equipment is unusable because of maintenance requirements. Unrepaired boards can cause injury to both lifeguards and victims.

- *Skill Requirements*—The rescue board is like no other piece of equipment, and lifeguards must practice rescue board skills often to develop and maintain proficiency. Without proper skills and practice, the rescue board can be an awkward piece of equipment that can be dangerous to beach visitors.

Rescues With Rescue Boards

Entry

When a rescue board is used, direct launching into the water may be preferred to moving down the beach with a cumbersome board to the point nearest the victim. Often, the speed of the board will offset the longer paddling distance.

On most days, a lifeguard can move a rescue board to the water by lifting the board up at the middle and carrying it pointing ahead toward the water at the lifeguard's side. Some boards are equipped with handles or carrying slots to facilitate this. On windy days, the wind may cause the board to sail during this carry and the board may become very difficult to manage. Should this situation present itself, the nose (front) of the board can be lifted and the tail (rear) of the board allowed to drag on the sand. Dragging the board is considered very bad form under normal conditions, since the practice will eventually wear away the board's protective covering. During the launching process, an RFD can be dragged behind the lifeguard or carried with the board.

In flat water, boards should be launched and mounted at about knee depth. This is important, since attempts to launch a board in shallower water may result in the skeg catching on the bottom, which will stop the board and throw the lifeguard off. As the lifeguard approaches the water, the rescue board is held with one hand on each rail (side) and the top side of the board facing upward. The board is held to the side of the lifeguard on a flat plane with the nose facing toward the open water. When the appropriate depth is reached, the lifeguard throws the board forward, without letting go, and the lifeguard's body then follows the direction of the board. In a continuous, fluid motion, the lifeguard mounts the board in either a prone or kneeling position. This technique requires considerable practice to master.

Effective use of the rescue board requires a considerable amount of balance and awareness of the orientation of the board. If the lifeguard lies too far forward, the nose dives beneath the surface of the water, slowing or stopping it abruptly. If the lifeguard's center of gravity is too far toward the tail, the board will become unstable. The ideal position leaves the board flat on the surface of the water with the nose out.

In surf conditions, one objective of launching a rescue board is to carry the board past as many incoming waves as possible. Once the water becomes approximately waist deep, the board can be placed on the water and sledded along the water's surface at the side of the lifeguard. When waves threaten to lift the board above or out of the lifeguard's reach, the lifeguard can swing up onto the deck of the board with the upper body, letting the wave lift both the lifeguard and the board temporarily off the bottom while the lifeguard's legs trail beside the board. When the wave passes, the lifeguard can regain footing and proceed.

Once deep water is reached, the lifeguard must commit to paddling. The board is mounted, and a paddling position is assumed. The rescue board must be kept headed directly toward any incoming waves to keep them from throwing the board off to either side. Like surface diving through waves, the aim with a rescue board is to present the smallest possible forward surface to the incoming wave.

The initial goal of using a rescue board in the surf is to get out beyond the breakers. A lifeguard who is swimming can easily duck under breaking waves, but when breaking waves land on a lifeguard on a rescue board, the lifeguard is exposed to the full force of the wave. In this case, the lifeguard may lose the board or may be thrust into the board by the incoming wave, causing injury. The lifeguard may also be pushed a significant distance shoreward.

When approaching the incoming foam line of a wave that has already broken, the lifeguard should adjust body weight somewhat toward the tail so that the nose rides up over the foam line. When a wave approaches that will break on the lifeguard, the lifeguard should try to force the nose of the board down by leaning forward in a push-up position. This helps keep the board from being lifted and carried shoreward by the breaking wave.

Heavy surf conditions may call for an action of rolling the rescue board through the waves (turtling). To employ this maneuver, the lifeguard inhales deeply just before the impact of the oncoming wave and rolls the board over so that the bottom of the board faces toward the sky and the lifeguard hangs underneath. Once the wave has passed, the lifeguard turns the board over and continues paddling.

Approach

There are two basic positions for paddling a rescue board: the prone position and the kneeling position. In both positions, it is important to maintain a good trim —a position where the board remains flat on the water. In practicing paddling, each lifeguard will find a position on the board that results in the board staying in trim.

The prone position (lying face down on the board) is the easiest to master, since a low center of gravity is maintained for a very stable ride. Arms are used in a butterfly stroke motion or a crawl stroke, with the hands and arms dug into the water deeply for efficient movement. The prone position, however, uses muscles that are not commonly exercised, resulting in a tired lifeguard over a relatively short distance. For distance paddling, many lifeguards prefer the kneeling position.

[Photographic Credit: Mike Hensler]

Lifeguards in a competition demonstrate knee paddling. [Photographic Credit: Mike Hensler]

The kneeling position is usually assumed from the prone position. After a few strokes to develop momentum and stability, the lifeguard moves from the prone position to kneeling by holding onto the rails and pulling the knees up to the center of the board, spread somewhat to maintain stability and trim. The head is kept down to maintain a low center of gravity and the arms dig in deeply to grab water and pull it back. Arms are recovered with hands low and elbows high.

To make small changes in the direction of the board, several techniques can be used. These include dragging a foot, shifting weight, or reaching out and pulling water from the direction of the turn. If the lifeguard wants to turn the board completely around, the lifeguard stops the board by sitting on the deck with legs hung over both sides. The lifeguard then slides back on the board, which picks the nose up. Then, by using an eggbeater kick and/or by paddling with the hands, the board can be twirled to the desired direction.

Approaching a victim with a rescue board should be done in a manner that will place the nose of the board just slightly to one side of the victim. When the lifeguard has drawn nearly beside the victim, the lifeguard slips off the far side of the board, placing the board between the lifeguard and the victim. Then, if necessary, the lifeguard moves the board to the victim using a swimming kick and reaches over the board to pull the victim to the support offered by the board.

Retrieval
Once the victim has been stabilized and the signal has been made, the retrieval process can begin. There is no requirement that victims be loaded onto rescue boards for retrieval. In many situations, lifeguards can simply begin swimming kicks that will move the board and the victim toward shallow water while holding the victim's arms on the board. In other situations, victims may stay in the water and hold onto rescue board handles or the trailing RFD while the lifeguard mounts the board and paddles in.

More skilled lifeguards may choose to bring a strong, conscious victim aboard. One way to do this is to begin by treading water at the nose of the board and stabilizing the board for the victim by holding both sides of the nose. The victim is then instructed to mount the board facing the nose. Once the head and shoulders are supported by the board, the lifeguard can assist by pulling the legs onto the deck, if necessary. The lifeguard can now push the board and its passenger to shore from the water or can carefully mount the board from the tail to assume a position over the victim's hind quarters with the victim's legs on either side. The lifeguard adjusts the board's trim and begins to paddle to shore.

If the victim is unconscious or unable to mount the board using the foregoing procedure, an alternative method of bringing the victim aboard the rescue board involves rolling the board. The lifeguard dismounts the rescue board and turns it over, bottom side up. The middle of the overturned board is positioned between the lifeguard and the victim. Both of the victim's hands are pulled across the board so that the victim's armpits are against the rail opposite the lifeguard. The rescue board is then turned back over, rolling it toward the lifeguard. The victim will now be lying across the rescue board, in a position perpendicular to its length. The final step is to move the victim's body carefully onto the board in a lengthwise position.

In flat water, bringing the victim to shore simply means moving the rescue board to shallow water. Surf conditions complicate retrievals of victims on rescue boards. At many agencies, lifeguards are instructed not to bring victims through breaking surf on rescue boards. Instead, victims are transferred to boats or life-guards with RFDs outside the surf zone for retrieval.

If a victim must be brought through breaking surf on a rescue board, no attempt should be made to catch or ride waves with victims aboard. Lifeguards should keep the board perpendicular to waves and shift weight heavily toward the tail of the rescue board when caught by a wave. This may include moving the victim to the rear of the board and sandwiching the victim between the board and life-guard while holding both rails.

Removal from the Water
In most situations, lifeguards must either tend to the removal of the rescue board or removal of the victim. Rescue boards should not be left unattended, especially in moving or turbulent water. In many cases, another lifeguard may help with removal of the rescue board while the responding lifeguard deals with the victim.

Maintenance

Care is a must for a rescue board. The board must be kept in a waxed or "non-skid" treated condition. It should be inspected daily and any holes or cracks repaired. Any opening in the skin of the board will allow water to seep in and ruin it. Rescue boards should never be leaned upright against other objects as the wind can sail them into people. They should be stored horizontally or fully secured if stored vertically.

SPINAL STABILIZATION DEVICE

Several sources of spinal injury are present at all open water beaches. These may include shallow water diving, body surfing, underwater objects, wave action, dry landfalls, and other activities. Therefore, every lifeguard agency should have spinal stabilization devices available for immediate use. All lifeguards should be fully trained in the necessary techniques. For a discussion of the recognition and treatment of spinal injuries in the aquatic environment, refer to the chapter entitled,

Medical Care in the Aquatic Environment.

SPINAL STABILAZATION DEVICE COMPONENTS

Spinal stabilization devices consist of three parts: spineboard, head and neck immobilization devices, and fastening devices to hold the person to the spineboard. Use of spinal stabilization devices may be regulated by local emergency medical service authorities and they should be used in a manner consistent with agency protocol and training.

Spineboard: The spineboard is also known as a backboard. A spineboard is a rigid flat surface to which the backside of a person, including head, trunk, legs, and feet can be attached. The most basic version of a spineboard is a flat, rectangular piece of wood of dimensions slightly greater than that of an average male lying supine. Better versions have handles in the sides to improve the grip of rescuers. The most advanced models for aquatic use are made of plastic and metal. These devices float and are slightly contoured. They have handles and specially designed areas for securing straps.

Head and Neck Immobilization Devices: Neck immobilization devices were initially known as cervical collars (C-collars). The original versions lacked reliable support for the neck. Modern versions are quite rigid and significantly reduce any neck movement. These may be known as hard collars, Philadelphia collars, or by actual brand name. Further stabilization to prevent head movement is provided by head immobilizers. These are placed on either side of the head as the body lies on a spineboard. They may be commercially manufactured or improvised objects and include sandbags, rolled towels, etc.

Fastening Devices: Fastening devices are used to secure the trunk, head, and legs to the spineboard. These may be pre-designed harnesses, heavy tape, or Velcro straps.

BOAT TOW

The boat tow is one of the simplest and least expensive pieces of rescue equipment a lifeguard will use. It can make the difference in successfully rescuing boats worth tens of thousands of dollars and the persons aboard. A boat tow is simply a length of line approximately six feet long, with a loop spliced in one end and a large snap hook on the other end. When a boat is observed to be in distress, perhaps disabled and drifting toward rocks or surf, the lifeguard runs the boat tow through the rear handle of a rescue buoy and pulls the snap end through the loop end of the line. The snap end of the line is then pulled tight.

There is now a six foot piece of line securely fastened to the rear handle of the rescue buoy, with a snap hook on the far end. The lifeguard swims to the boat, clips the hook into the bow eye of the boat, and then swims the boat away from danger.

This process is surprisingly effective for vessels up to 30' long and larger. There are several important considerations, however. Swim fins are highly desirable when using a boat tow as little progress will be made without them. The lifeguard must always be prepared to jettison the rescue buoy if the vessel is caught by surf while the tow is underway. Additionally, a position must be maintained so that the lifeguard is not caught between an incoming wave and the boat.

The goal in using a boat tow is to pull the vessel from immediate danger. Obviously, a swimming lifeguard cannot keep a boat away from danger indefinitely, but once the boat is away from immediate danger the skipper can be directed to deploy an anchor, if available. If a rescue boat is available, it is dispatched to take over the tow.

CHAPTER FOURTEEN

SPECIALIZED RESCUE EQUIPMENT

Chapter Highlights

Emergency Vehicles

Rescue Boats

Aircraft

> **In This Chapter**
>
> Most rescue boats can support the operator(s) and several victims completely out of water. Thus, rescue of a victim and removal from the water can take place almost immediately, effectively resolving the victim's distress while still offshore.

This chapter introduces some of the specialized rescue equipment employed by lifeguard agencies. It is intended to provide an overview of the capabilities and basic techniques for employing specialized rescue equipment. Extensive training and further information will be needed prior to actual use.

EMERGENCY VEHICLES

One of the most useful pieces of emergency equipment employed by lifeguards is the emergency vehicle. Emergency vehicles may be all terrain vehicles (ATVs), pick-ups, sport-utility vehicles, and the like. Emergency vehicles offer the advantage of increased speed, range, and payload as compared to a lifeguard on foot. Specifics vary from agency to agency, but in addition to rescue floatation devices (RFD), the typical emergency vehicle will carry such essential equipment as a two-way radio, public address system, extensive medical aid and trauma kits, resuscitator, flares, wetsuits, extra fins, and face plates, marker buoys for search and recovery, cliff rescue gear, a rescue board, spinal immobilization device, and a stretcher. At some lifeguard agencies, emergency vehicles are equipped with semi-automatic defibrillator units for use by suitably trained personnel.

Emergency vehicles are of use not only for responding to serious emergencies on the beach, but can also serve as mobile lifeguard stations. Their mobility allows a single lifeguard to cover a large area effectively. Although it depends on the area served, lifeguard emergency vehicles should be equipped with four wheel drive. Full size emergency vehicles should also be equipped with emergency lights and siren.

Of paramount concern in the operation of emergency vehicles is safety. As the size and speed of the rescue vehicle increases, so does the possibility of injury to lifeguards and beach patrons. Some basics of emergency driving are:

- Drive as safely as possible, as quickly as possible - if you don't get there, you're of no help
- If an injury is caused in the act of responding to an emergency, the purpose is defeated

Even routine driving of emergency vehicles on the beach can pose hazards. Lifeguards must always use extreme caution. Serious injuries have been sustained in instances where beach patrons, particularly small children, unexpectedly sat down in front of or behind a lifeguard vehicle while the vehicle was momentarily stopped. For this reason, before leaving from a parked position the driver should check behind, beneath, and in front of the vehicle. This inspection requires only a few seconds and it ensures a safe path.

The three most dangerous moves are backing up, right turns, and driving up over a berm. During these maneuvers the driver's visibility is obstructed. Berms should be ascended or descended at obtuse angles. Prior to ascending or descending the berm, the best visibility can be attained if the vehicle is positioned with the berm on the driver's side.

Lifeguard vehicles can carry extensive amount of rescue and medical aid equipment. [Photographic Credit: Mike Hensler]

[Photographic Credit: Rob McGowan]

People are not alert for vehicles on the beach. Lifeguards should not make the mistake of believing that because the vehicle is big and brightly colored, people will know it is there. Small children have a tendency to run in front of lifeguard vehicles toward their parents when a vehicle approaches. Parents will sometimes bolt in front of the vehicle to protect their children. Heightened caution is needed when traveling past pier pilings or other obstructions, such as large rocks, as people can suddenly appear from behind these sight obstructions.

If the vehicle is to be parked on the beach or in a public area, it is a good idea to delineate the vehicle's parking area by use of traffic cones or flags. The area should then be kept clear of people at all times.

RESCUE BOATS

Rescue boats were first used in this country by the original American life-savers in the 1800s. The variety and sophistication of lifeguard rescue boats have advanced a long way since then, although some agencies still employ variations of the traditional lifesaving craft. Larger, more advanced lifeguard agencies now utilize motorized vessels for their rescues.

Los Angeles County Baywatch [Photographic Credit: Conrad Liberty]

ADVANTAGES OF RESCUE BOATS

Size and Stability

Most rescue boats can support the operator(s) and several victims completely out of water. Thus, rescue of a victim and removal from the water can take place almost immediately, effectively resolving the victim's distress while still offshore. In a multiple victim rescue where several victims are swept out by a flash rip current, lifeguards in a boat at the head of the rip can quickly pluck numerous distressed swimmers from the water, returning them to shore at a later time. This can assist lifeguards effecting rescues with RFDs who, instead of taking their victims in through the surf, can simply swim victims to the waiting boat. For this reason, in large surf conditions a rescue boat on the outside of the breakers is invaluable.

Patrol and Observation

Rescue boats are very good tools for lifeguard patrols. Lifeguards can patrol from them for long periods without inordinate fatigue. Equipment, including communications equipment, can be carried and stowed in rescue boats, essentially making them mobile lifeguard stations. Rescue boats can also carry additional RFDs or personal floatation devices (PFDs) for use by lifeguards and persons in distress.

Rescue boats can provide a platform on the outer edge of the swimming area or within the area, allowing the lifeguard to be closer to potential victims. Although they should not be used to substitute for observation by a lifeguard on land, rescue boats elevate a lifeguard in the water, allowing better surveillance than a swimming lifeguard or one on a rescue board.

[Photographic Credit: Leon Skov]

Speed

Often motorized rescue boats can move to a rescue location more quickly than free-swimming lifeguards and can cover longer distances with minimal lifeguard fatigue. They are particularly valuable at facilitating a rapid response to remote beach areas or other vessels in distress. Some types of motorized vessels can move through large surf with ease and can be reliably operated inside breaking surf. For lifeguard agencies serving large geographic areas, motorized rescue boats can respond to emergencies many miles away faster than vehicles impeded by traffic problems ashore, and upon arrival, the vessel is already outside the surf, where the problem is likely to be. Manually powered vessels are slower in comparison and more apt to be deterred by surf conditions, but they may be faster than swimming lifeguards under some circumstances.

Versatility

Some agencies use boats to effectively mark the limits of the swim area and staff the boundary with lifeguard boat operators. Rescue boats can be used for general crowd control when water users need to be separated or swim area boundaries exist. During special events such as open water swimming competitions, lifeguards in rescue vessels can easily monitor the status of swimmers on the course.

Boat Rescue, Enforcement, and Firefighting

For some lifeguard agencies, a major responsibility of the rescue boat fleet is response and assistance to boaters in distress. Rescue boats can be equipped for marine firefighting and lifeguards from several American lifeguard agencies are primary responders to boat, marina, and pier fires. Rescue boats can also be very valuable in the enforcement of boating safety regulations. One of the most frustrating experiences for a lifeguard is watching an errant boater buzzing a swimming crowd. This is extremely hazardous, but the land based lifeguard can do little about it. A lifeguard in a rescue boat can quickly resolve such a problem. Moreover, lifeguards from some agencies use rescue boats for general law enforcement, including enforcement of boating safety and environmental regulations.

San Diego lifeguards battle a boat fire. Note that lifeguards are wearing full fire-fighting gear. **[Photographic Credit: San Diego Lifeguard Service]**

LIMITATIONS OF RESCUE BOATS

Size

Rescue boats can be large and heavy. Unless berthed at a dock or pier, launching a boat can be a strenuous process that may take more than one lifeguard. Because of their size and weight, boats can be dangerous in heavy surf and must be handled expertly in negotiating a surfline during a rescue. The boat can become a hazard to swimmers should it be overcome by surf.

Crowded Beaches

Large concentrations of water users can cause problems in effecting rescues from boats because of the size of the boat and the area necessary to maneuver. Crowds can also make launching and recovering a boat difficult and hazardous. Like motor vehicles on the beach, rescue boats must often be maneuvered very close to people and must be operated with tremendous caution.

Wind and Waves

Because of their high profile in the water, boats can be subjected to problems from wind and waves. Although these problems can be overcome with good operating skills, weather conditions can complicate a boat rescue to the point where some other rescue equipment may be better indicated.

Expense

Boats can be expensive to purchase and operate, depending on their size and equipment. Training requirements are proportional to the complexity of the vessel.

Personnel Requirements

Boats require operators. This may be obvious, but under most circumstances a rescue boat operator cannot leave the boat to effect a rescue. This is different from a lifeguard in a rescue vehicle, for example, who can park the vehicle and leave it to rescue a victim. On the other hand, in many cases the rescue boat can be brought directly alongside the struggling victim, unlike a vehicle. A properly equipped rescue vessel includes a throwable floatation device in case the victim cannot be immediately assisted.

TYPES OF RESCUE VESSELS

A wide variety of boats can be employed by lifeguards in carrying out their responsibilities. The following describes the types most commonly employed by lifeguards at American beaches. Some agencies have boats of several types, employing different boats for different purposes. Lifeguards from these agencies can select the best tool for the job, depending on the circumstances of the rescue. Other agencies focus on a single boat design for purposes of economy and to help reduce training time.

Inshore Rescue Boats (IRBs)

Inshore rescue boats (IRBs), also known as inflatable rescue boats, were first employed by the lifesavers of Australia and New Zealand. These boats are typically 12 feet to 14 feet in length and utilize a small outboard motor of 25 to 35 horsepower for propulsion. Most often they are staffed by an operator and a crewmember, who sit on the inflated gunwale while holding handles. The relatively low weight of these craft allows them to be moved and launched easily. To keep the vessels light, fuel cans are replaced with fuel bladders made of a synthetic material. Because they are operated in very close proximity to swimmers, a propeller guard is commonly attached to the outboard.

[Photographic Credit: B. Chris Brewster]

IRBs are perhaps the most versatile boats available to lifeguards. Used by trained operators, they can successfully handle very large surf conditions. IRBs can easily be operated in the surfline for extended periods of time. These boats are fast because they draw little water as they float across the surface. They can be launched from a beach or returned to the beach with relative ease. As a result, a nearby harbor is not needed and response is immediate.

When necessary, an IRB can hold two to three victims. In a mass rescue situation, the IRB can be used as a raft to which many victims can cling until brought to the beach by swimming lifeguards. IRBs can be successfully employed in very close proximity to large swimming crowds with limited danger presented.

IRBs have drawbacks. They are small open boats in which the operator and crew can be subjected to heavy bouncing over waves and wet conditions. A well trained operator can turn an IRB on a dime, but when used to tow other vessels, IRBs can be difficult to steer because of the lack of an effective keel. They require constant though inexpensive maintenance. When caught in the wrong orientation by a breaking wave, IRBs can be flipped. Even in this circumstance, however, they are generally less hazardous than other types of rescue boats because of their soft sides. Properly employed restart procedures can result in complete salvage of an outboard motor that has been fully doused.

Personal Watercraft

The invention of the Jet Ski® created a market of boaters that perhaps never existed before. Over the years, these jet powered craft have attracted competition from a variety of manufacturers. The original Jet Ski® requires the operator to stand while riding, but small jet powered craft that the operator sits astride have since become the most popular design.

These small boats are generally under 12 feet in length, and steered through use of a jet of water, the direction of which is usually controlled by handlebars. Collectively, these small jet powered craft have become known as personal watercraft (PWC), because they allow only one or two riders.

[Photographic Credit: Mike Hensler]

PWC can be effective rescue craft under certain circumstances and many American lifeguard agencies utilize them. Although generally heavier than the IRB, they too can be launched from the beach. Their extraordinary speed makes it essential that the operator take care not to become launched into the air over a wave.

The rescue capabilities of personal watercraft are limited. Since most hold only an operator and passenger, the rescue capacity of a standard sit down model is just one victim. Furthermore, it can be difficult to pull a victim aboard a personal watercraft because they ride so high in the water and can roll. Some agencies utilize floating sleds, which they tow behind the personal watercraft, with a lifeguard lying on it. The lifeguard can then pull a victim onto the sled and rapidly bring the victim to shore.

The greatest value of PWC is that they are relatively inexpensive motorized rescue boats with great speed. While their value in breaking surf is limited, they can be very valuable in open water swells or flat water conditions. Like the IRB, personal watercraft leave the operator exposed and often wet. They can be operated near large swimming crowds, but their hard hulls are unforgiving if a swimmer is struck.

Rigid Hull Vessels

Some lifeguard agencies operate large, motorized, rigid-hull vessels, equipped for full service response to swimming rescues, boat rescues (including fires and towing services), and other emergencies. These vessels can be equipped with a full complement of rescue and emergency gear such as two-way radios, firefighting equipment, positioning equipment, medical gear, scuba gear, depth finders, and public address equipment. In some agencies, these vessels combine traditional lifeguard duties with those of harbor patrol, general law enforcement, and special rescue missions.

[Photographic Credit: Conrad Liberty]

Some rigid hull rescue vessels are designed for work inside the surfline.
[Photographic Credit: Mike Hensler]

Rigid-hull vessels are particularly useful for offshore rescues or long distance responses to remote beach areas. They can carry numerous victims from the head of a rip current and can accommodate a victim on a stretcher or even allow full CPR. Some lifeguard agencies actually utilize rigid-hull rescue boats inside the surf in a manner similar to an IRB, but this is not common and requires unique skills. Large, rigid-hull rescue boats offer the greatest degree of protection for operator and crew.

Depending on their size, most larger rigid-hull vessels are either difficult or impossible to beach launch. A nearby harbor is usually needed, along with docks and storage facilities.

Rowed Boats

At most major beach areas in the United States where rescue boats are employed, manually powered (rowed) rescue boats have been replaced by motorized rescue boats, but in a few areas such as New Jersey and the Great Lakes, rowed rescue boats are still common. They are descendants of the first American beach rescue boats and are typically known as lifeboats, surfboats, dories, or rowboats. Usually, they are rowed by one or two lifeguards.

[Photographic Credit: Al Shorey]

Manually powered boats include hollow draft surf rescue dories. These are designed to cut through the surf while retaining adequate stability, and can be used as an effective observation platform. Rescue dories feature a square stern that facilitates foot placement for the rear crewmember who can propel the boat from a forward facing standing position. The square stern also allows boarding of the victim over the transom. On the surf beaches of the Great Lakes and at many other inland lakes, a wide variety of wood, fiberglass, and aluminum boats are employed.

[Photographic Credit: Paul Drucker]

Rowed vessels are dependable in that they do not rely on motors, which can fail. Compared to powered vessels, however, rowed vessels are very slow and easily delayed or even stopped by surf conditions. In most cases, a swimming lifeguard responding from the beach will reach a distressed victim far more quickly than a vessel which is launched and rowed to the victim. On the other hand, when deployed outside the swimming crowd, the lifeguard aboard a rowed rescue boat can quickly observe and rescue a distressed victim.

For a discussion of dory rowing techniques, see Appendix D.

Kayaks

The least expensive type of rescue boat is the kayak. Kayaks are also the least versatile type of rescue boat. Kayaks used in lifeguarding are plastic, highly maneuverable craft that can carry a personal floatation device (PFD) and limited medical gear. They are lightweight and easily carried to the water's edge by a single lifeguard.

Kayaks provide a relatively dry platform for patrol and observation. Lifeguards in kayaks can sit in an erect position, easily observed by swimmers. These craft can be useful for rapid approach, control, and stabilization of a victim. With minimal skills, lifeguards can propel kayaks quickly through light and moderate surf. Kayaks are particularly useful in choppy, light surf conditions that make the use of rescue boards or dories difficult.

USE OF RESCUE BOATS

The following is an overview of the techniques commonly used to operate lifeguard rescue boats. Actual operation, particularly of motorized rescue boats in the surf environment, requires extensive training under the supervision of a skilled and experienced operator.

Alert

The most common source of alert to the need for a rescue boat response is observation by a shore-based lifeguard. A rescue boat may be sent because the victim is a significant distance from shore, or there are multiple victims, or a patrolling rescue boat is close to the rescue. There are a variety of other reasons to utilize a rescue boat, but these are the most common.

Lifeguards patrolling in a rescue boat are usually not the first to observe victims in distress because they are at a low point, unable to make broad observations of a large swimming crowd. Despite this fact, lifeguards in a rescue boat can sometimes evaluate persons in apparent distress more directly than those ashore because of their relative proximity to the victims. The lifeguard on the beach must make an evaluation largely on the actions of the swimmer, deducing the skills and panic level from visual clues. The lifeguard in a rescue boat, however, may be able to simply ask the person if help is needed.

At some agencies, lifeguards in rescue boats are expected to patrol unguarded beaches that, due to remoteness and low attendance, lack on-site lifeguard supervision. In these cases, they may be the only source of supervision, albeit sporadic. Lifeguards in rescue boats may be alerted to vessels in distress by observation of a flare or by a marine radio broadcast.

When lifeguards ashore spot a problem that calls for a rescue boat response, they must have a method to immediately alert the rescue boat crew. Likewise, when lifeguards in a rescue vessel observe persons in distress requiring their assistance, they need a reliable method to advise lifeguards ashore of the incident so that proper backup can be sent. The most reliable method of ship to shore communication is the two-way radio and most modern lifeguard agencies equip their rescue boats with such equipment. This can be problematic for small rescue boats which lack a waterproof location for even a hand held radio, but there are several sources of waterproof bags that effectively resolve this problem.

When radio communications break down, or in cases where radio communications are not available, it is important to have some other method. These may include airhorns, flags, etc., but it must be emphasized that such methods are unreliable and very limited in that lifeguards ashore cannot provide details on the nature of the rescue, while lifeguards in the rescue vessel cannot provide information on victim status or other observations. Lack of two-way radio communications significantly limits the usefulness of rescue boats.

Entry

When a drowning presentation is detected on boat patrol, lifeguards can move directly from alert to contact and control of the victim. Beach-based boats, however, will have to go through an entry. At flat water beaches, boats can be positioned at the water's edge with the bow of the boat in the water, ready for response. At surf beaches, boats will usually be positioned on the beach close to the waterline. Some agencies utilize rollers placed under the bow of the boat to facilitate launching. If significant tidal changes are present, the boat will need to be moved regularly to keep it close to the water.

Boats should be prepared for instant use, with all equipment aboard and accessible. Proper preparation and maintenance is required to ensure that, when an emergency occurs, the boat is fully serviceable. A motorized rescue boat, for example, will be of little use and perhaps seriously impede an expeditious rescue response if the motor won't start. For this reason, lifeguards should never completely rely on a boat response to a rescue. A lifeguard ashore should always be prepared to effect the rescue if the boat response encounters problems. At some agencies it is a standard practice to send a lifeguard from shore in all cases, even when a boat is responding from nearby. The shore based lifeguard can always return to shore if the boat based lifeguards complete the rescue first.

Flat water entry is straightforward — lifeguards simply push off from shore and respond, but surf entry in a rescue boat can be very challenging, depending on the size of the surf. It is important to select an area with few or no swimmers around. There is always the possibility of losing control of the boat in the surf and having the boat pushed to shore by incoming waves, striking swimmers. It is also difficult to see over waves to determine whether a swimmer is ahead and, if the operator is focusing on getting through breaking waves, attention can be distracted.

The primary rule of operating a rescue vessel inside the surfline is that the boat should be kept perpendicular to incoming waves and foam lines of broken waves. This presents the least resistance to the power of the waves and allows the design of the vessel to efficiently deflect wave energy. Skilled operators of powered craft can learn to take broken waves at almost parallel angles while the vessel is moving forward at significant speed, but this requires advanced training.

When a manually powered rescue boat is employed by a single lifeguard in the surf environment, the lifeguard will push from the stern into the water with the bow perpendicular to incoming waves. The boat is pushed to a comfortable rowing depth, usually waist deep. The lifeguard then vaults over the stern, enters the vessel, and begins rowing. Likewise, a personal watercraft operated by a single operator is pushed to a depth needed to operate, started, and the operator jumps aboard.

Beach based vessels which utilize two lifeguards are IRBs and sometimes dories. Entry with an IRB or a dory with a crew of two persons is quite similar. At first, both lifeguards push the boat toward an adequate depth for rowing, or for the outboard to be dropped from the cocked position without striking bottom. Once this depth is reached, one lifeguard jumps into the vessel while the other keeps the bow perpendicular to oncoming waves. The goal is to prepare to exert forward momentum adequate to make way against the waves before the second lifeguard boards the vessel. The IRB operator starts the engine, while the first lifeguard in the dory simply assumes a rowing position. Once the lifeguard in either vessel determines that forward progress can be made which will allow the boat to make headway without further assistance from the lifeguard in the water, the latter is advised to jump into the vessel.

The position of the operator of an IRB is usually sitting on the port (left facing forward) pontoon near the stern. The crewmember sits on the opposite (starboard) pontoon toward the bow. These positions help keep the vessel balanced.

In a dory, the rowing position can be a standing one, facing forward (known as "boating") or a sitting one facing toward the stern. The latter position requires less skill and allows for more efficient rowing, but it is more difficult to maintain visual observation over the victim in this position. Directions from beach based lifeguards may be needed.

An essential role of the lifeguard in command of a rescue boat is to avoid taking a direct hit from a breaking wave. This can injure the crew or swamp an IRB, killing the engine. It can significantly impede the progress of a manually powered rescue boat or carry it all the way to shore in the foam line. In the case of a PWC, it can knock the operator completely off the craft. In any case, the rescue boat response is slowed or curtailed, and persons inshore of the boat can be threatened by the unpiloted incoming boat.

In larger surf, boat operators time their approach to breaking waves carefully, often hanging inshore of the breakers until the boat can be moved quickly forward between breaking waves. The inside of the surf break is a difficult area in which to maneuver because the water is moving shoreward so quickly and the water is heavily aerated, providing low buoyancy, but the break itself is most dangerous and should be avoided by proper timing of the boat operator. In large surf, operators of IRBs may move the craft back and forth inside the breakers, waiting for the right moment to make it through.

When a two person rescue boat is clearly about to be caught by a breaking wave which will break directly on top of it, the lifeguard in command of the vessel advises the crewperson. In an IRB, the crewperson braces by grabbing the bow line and lying face down between the bow pontoons, head first. This maneuver adds weight to the bow which reduces the chance of the boat riding up the wave and being flipped. On a PWC, the best action on the part of the operator is to flatten to the seat. In a motorized craft, the operator may decide to try to punch through the wave with a last minute burst of speed. This may allow the boat to avoid much of the power of the wave which would otherwise break directly on the vessel. In any case, a direct perpendicular orientation to the wave is critical or the boat will likely broach and be pushed ashore.

Great care must be taken if the rescue boat rides up the steep face of a wave about to break, and when the bow plunges downward on the other side. Powered vessels are very susceptible to being launched over an incoming wave and becoming airborne. Lifeguards can be seriously injured or even ejected from the boat. Personal watercraft are particularly prone to this problem due to their high power and speed, but any boat can become airborne given the right circumstances. The goal in all cases is to get to the other side of the wave without being caught in the break, and try to stay in contact with the water at all times. This is done by using no more forward power than is needed to get past the wave and by rapidly decelerating as soon as it is clear that the boat will reach the other side.

Contact and Control

Safely approaching a victim with a rescue boat, particularly in rough conditions, requires great skill and extensive practice. The obvious goal is to rescue the victim quickly without further injury. If an oar, propeller, or boat hull strikes the victim, injury is likely. In rescue boats with two persons aboard, if a safe approach will be difficult or the victim's condition is poor, one lifeguard can simply enter the water with an RFD to assist the victim, then swim the victim to the waiting rescue boat.

In flat water or gentle swells outside the surfline, a manually propelled rescue boat is rowed within ten to twenty feet of the victim, then a fast rowing pivot is performed to present the stern to the victim. Stern presentations are preferred for rowed rescue boats because the transom is the most stable area of the vessel. The lifeguard then backs toward the victim. If there is only one lifeguard aboard, the lifeguard ships the oars and moves to the stern to assist the victim aboard. If there are two, the sternmost lifeguard provides this assistance.

In these same conditions, an IRB is simply brought alongside the victim and the victim is brought in over a pontoon with the assistance of the crewmember (preferably over the mid to forward portion of the port pontoon). The transom is not used because of the hazard presented by the outboard. On a personal watercraft, the victim is helped aboard with a one arm assist from the operator who must take care not to allow too much weight to shift to one side. If a rescue sled is towed, the boat is positioned so that the victim can be grabbed by the lifeguard on the sled and held there in a prone position.

The most difficult area to effect a rescue is inside breaking surf. Generally, only the IRB and personal watercraft are suitable for rescues in this zone because they are best able to maintain position inside breaking surf without being overcome. In either case, the ideal is to bring the vessel alongside the victim, maintaining a constant bow out (toward the breaking surf) position. The victim is then brought aboard as previously noted. It is particularly important to effect this action very quickly when inside the surfline, for obvious reasons.

Highly skilled IRB operators utilize a maneuver in critical rescues between breaking waves which can rapidly extricate a victim. This involves approaching the victim at moderate speed and turning sharply around the victim in a counter-clockwise direction. This brings the port pontoon down to water level. The crewmember leans over from the starboard side and grabs the outstretched arms or armpits of the victim. The victim is then rolled into the boat. Due to the hazard involved, this technique is appropriate only for highly skilled operators in critical situations.

Larger rescue vessels generally approach the surfline from the outside and back down into the waves, keeping the bow out. A crewmember then jumps into the water and brings the victim out to the rescue boat. Great caution is needed in operating large rescue boats near the surf because of the danger involved in having a large, hard-hull vessel overcome and pushed into the beach toward swimmers.

Retrieval

Once the victim has been brought aboard the rescue vessel, expeditious retrieval to shore is not normally necessary. Exceptions include cases where the victim needs medical attention or where the rescue vessel is immediately needed for response to other emergencies. Under normal circumstances, however, lifeguards can take the time to carefully consider the return route to shore.

For flat water, the rescue boat is simply returned to shore. Manually powered boats are best beached stern toward the beach to allow the victim to exit over the transom. Powered vessels must usually be beached bow first.

Returning to shore in significant surf conditions requires careful planning and timing. The lifeguard in charge should first select the best area for this return. Considerations include avoiding areas where swimmers are present, selecting areas with less severe surf breaks (if available), and bringing the vessel to a safe shore area (devoid of rocks, debris, etc.).

Powered vessels that can be beached are usually able to outrun incoming surf. The operator waits to gauge the incoming sets of waves, then simply drives straight to shore between breaking waves. As an IRB approaches shallow water, the operator kills the engine and raises it to the cocked position. This is very important because striking even a sandy bottom can damage the engine and transom.

Rowed boats usually cannot outrun the surf. When returning to shore in surf conditions that threaten to overwhelm the boat, the stern lifeguard can ship oars and drop over the stern in order to stabilize the boat by holding onto the transom with the hands and extending the body to act as a sea anchor and rudder. Some agencies prefer that dories are pivoted so that the bow is toward the waves and the boat is rowed backwards toward shore for a more stable ride. This often depends on the design of the craft. Either of these maneuvers may be impractical depending on surf size. If there is a significant hazard in retrieval of the victim to the beach, an alternative is to simply swim the victim to shore with a crewmember from the rescue boat or a lifeguard from shore.

AIRCRAFT

Few lifeguard agencies have aircraft available for regular use. However, many agencies have rescue, medical, and law enforcement aircraft they can call upon when needed. Fixed wing aircraft can be useful for covering wide areas in the case of a search, but are of little value in transporting a lifeguard to a rescue or evacuating a victim. Of all the forms of transportation available to lifeguard services, the helicopter is the fastest and most versatile.

Lifeguards and a Coast Guard helicopter crew prepare to extricate a victim by hoisting the stretcher from a beach area bordered by high cliffs.

Helicopters can transport lifeguards over long distances expeditiously, then drop them to victims. Properly equipped helicopters can lift victims and lifeguards from the water and some can even land on the water. This is particularly valuable in very large surf conditions where the victim is taken outside the surfline or in rescues of persons aboard offshore boats.

Seal Beach, California lifeguard Steve Cushman jumps to the aid of two people whose boat had capsized in large surf. Both were successfully rescued.
[Photographic Credit: Los Angeles Times]

Helicopters are ideal in searches for persons lost at sea because of their high vantage point and mobility. When necessary, they can be used to transport medical supplies to offshore locations or drop pumps to sinking vessels. Helicopters can provide night lighting for water and cliff rescues and can be extremely valuable in flood rescues when victims are trapped by moving or rising water. Some lifeguard services develop a working agreement with a helicopter provider that results in having a helicopter on standby for problems which may arise from large surf conditions, heavy crowds, or inclement weather.

VICTIM EXTRICATION

There are two primary methods of extricating victims from the aquatic environment using helicopters — hoist and static line. The hoist is typically available on larger helicopters specially equipped for rescue, notably those of the U.S. Coast Guard. Using a powered reel, a cable is lowered to the victim from a hovering helicopter, the victim is secured and the helicopter continues to hover as the victim is reeled up. The victim is then swung inside to safety.

The static line method is used by smaller helicopters which lack powered hoists. This involves a line hung from the helicopter to which the victim is attached. The victim is lifted from danger as the helicopter gains altitude. This technique is somewhat more difficult because the victim must hang from the static line as the helicopter pilot flies the victim to safety, and the victim must then be gently set down.

The U.S. Coast Guard generally uses a yoke system to attach the rescue line to the victim. This is simply a circle of material similar to fire hose. The yoke (also known as a horse collar) is placed over the victim's head and under the armpits with the hoist line on the victim's front side. As the victim is hoisted, the circle closes and the victim holds the sides. This method is very rapid.

Static line rescue systems typically employ a pouch made of netting attached to the end of the line. The net is lowered into the water and the victim climbs inside. Once the victim is secured, the helicopter pilot lifts off. An injured victim in a stretcher can be evacuated using either the hoist or static system, as long as a proper harness is used that will keep the stretcher level and the victim is properly strapped inside.

A third extrication method, often used in flood rescue, is to have a helicopter actually touch down one skid or even land completely, allowing the victim to climb inside. The one skid method is extremely challenging for a helicopter pilot in that flight must be maintained simultaneous to touching a stationary object. The simple addition of weight to one side of a helicopter from a victim boarding can cause the aircraft to yaw, creating the potential for loss of airworthiness.

Helicopters build up static electricity which is discharged upon touching the ground. In order to create a partial discharge without hazard when a metal cable is lowered to the lifeguard or victim, it is best to allow the cable to first touch the ground or water. When aboard a boat, an insulated boat hook should be used or at least lifeguard personnel can slap at the stretcher or basket to provide a partial discharge before actually grabbing it and guiding it onto the boat. Once this contact is made, there is no further concern for this discharge as the winch cable will continually ground it to the boat and into the ocean water.

It is vital that a cable or line attached to a helicopter never be secured to a rescue vessel, unless it is a small rescue vessel being hoisted. Helicopters must have the freedom to move according to changing wind currents and cannot in any way be secured to substantial surface craft.

When removing a victim from a boat, helicopter pilots often prefer to head into the wind, maintaining minimum airspeed, for stability. This requires that the boat be headed in the same direction at the same speed.

LANDING ON A BEACH

If a helicopter has to be landed on a beach, lifeguards must create and maintain a secure landing zone (LZ) of adequate size. As a general rule, an LZ which is 100 feet in diameter should be considered a minimum. Helicopter pilots also appreciate the existence of a wind indicator in the immediate area, but outside the LZ. This can simply be a flag atop a lifeguard station, for example, or a smoke bomb. Another option is to draw a large arrow in the sand pointing toward the prevailing wind direction.

The rotor wash of a landing or departing helicopter creates a small windstorm which can carry sand for hundreds of feet. It can also blow beach items like umbrellas and tents which may then injure beachgoers. These should be moved back or collapsed before a helicopter is landed.

A helicopter landing on a beach always draws a crowd. Adequate crowd control measures should be implemented prior to landing. It is good practice to summon local police well in advance of landing a helicopter on a crowded beach so that they can assist in securing the LZ. Lifeguards should remember that they are not immune from the problems of rotor wash. Most experienced lifeguards take shelter behind emergency vehicles or other stationary objects to protect themselves during landing and take-off.

While helicopters are extremely valuable for lifeguard rescue, extensive training is needed before lifeguards can properly employ them. Lifeguards must be conversant with protocols needed in approaching a helicopter on the ground because the blades can be lethal. When working in close quarters with a helicopter, it is important to keep eye contact with the pilot if at all possible and be prepared to back off quickly, if necessary. Helicopters hovering over water can create a tremendous amount of water disturbance and noise which can be very disorienting and curtail verbal communication.

These concerns notwithstanding, with proper skill and training of the personnel involved, helicopters are an invaluable tool for lifeguards. It is strongly recommended that lifeguard agencies with the local availability of helicopters conduct training exercises and create contingency plans for their use.

LANDLINE

The landline appears to be a descendent of the breeches buoy apparatus which was used by the first American lifesavers to rescue persons aboard foundering ships. The typical landline device is a length of line (usually 200 yards or more), with a snap hook on the lead end and a spliced loop or snap hook on the trail end. It is kept coiled on a reel or laid in an easily transported, open container. Some agencies keep their landlines in inexpensive plastic laundry baskets.

Rescue buoy attached to a landline on a reel. [Photographic Credit: Dave Foxwell]

The landline provides an added level of security and safety for lifeguard and victim by establishing a link with assistance on shore. The lifeguard dons the harness of the landline or attaches the line to an RFD and responds to the victim. Once control and stabilization are attained, assistants on shore can retrieve both the lifeguard and victim or victims by pulling in the line. Therefore, while the lifeguard must swim the line to the victim, once the victim is reached no further swimming is necessary.

While use of the landline has declined over the years, it remains in wide use along the New Jersey shore and on some beaches in New York, New England, and around the Great Lakes. The agencies which presently use landlines indicate that they are most effectively employed in the following applications:

- Rescues from the neck of a rock beach rip current—the victim can be guided away from sharp rocks or reefs at the sides of the neck, or from other rocks and sea growths along the rescue route
- Intermittent, rapid moving rip and onshore current situations where strong surf prevents effective use of rescue boards, dories, or IRBs
- Lateral current situations, as in river rescues
- Rapid moving rip and onshore current situations that threaten to carry the victim onto adjacent groins or a rocky shore
- Landlines can be adapted to boat rescues, crowd control and many other situations where a length of line can be useful

Some drawbacks of landlines include:

- Landlines require more than one lifeguard to perform a rescue
- Landlines contribute to drag on the swimming lifeguard and can slow the approach to a victim
- Landline rescues are limited by the length of the line
- Problems can be encountered with crowds, piers, or other obstructions to the clean play of the line

LANDLINE RESCUE TECHNIQUES

Landline rescues are similar to RFD rescues with the exception of the retrieval phase. There are two primary landline procedures based on the number of lifeguards available.

Two Lifeguards

The first, or responding lifeguard, dons the RFD and attaches the landline to the RFD using the snap hook on the landline. The responding lifeguard then enters the water and approaches the victim as the line plays out. The second or assisting lifeguard monitors the line and tends to any tangles that may occur. The responding lifeguard controls and stabilizes the victim, secures the victim to the RFD, or sandwiches the victim as described earlier, then signals the assisting lifeguard who pulls the line in toward shore. When shallow water is gained, the responding lifeguard signals for cessation of the pull and removes the victim from the water.

Three or More Lifeguards

The initial responding lifeguard takes an RFD and proceeds with a free swimming entry, approaching, contacting, and stabilizing the victim. The first assisting lifeguard dons the harness of the landline, or attaches an RFD to the landline snap hook, and swims the landline out to the responding lifeguard and victim. The line is then fastened to the responding lifeguard's RFD. The second assisting lifeguard on shore monitors the landline, tends to any tangles that may occur, and pulls victim and responding lifeguard toward shore when signaled.

Additional responding lifeguards assist by keeping the line free of obstructions while it is being played out, in assisting in landline retrieval and controlling spectators who might interfere. They can expedite the playing out of the landline by

A second lifeguard helps play out the line as the rescuer swims to the victim. [Photographic Credit: William McNeely, Jr.]

Two lifeguards retrieve a rescuer and victim on the end of a landline. [Photographic Credit: William McNeely, Jr.]

holding it above their heads through the surf to minimize drag. If there is a possibility of the initial landline not being long enough to reach the victim, a second landline should be placed in preparation for use.

ADDITIONAL LANDLINE CONSIDERATIONS

- It is important to move the landline to the entry point before commencing the rescue. The entry point may be on the beach directly perpendicular to the victim or at a point along the beach to which onshore currents may carry the victim.
- An alternate way to select an entry point when a rip current has carried a victim at an angle to the shore is to place the landline on the shore perpendicular to the point where the responding lifeguard anticipates the victim will be when contact is made, then run to the base of the rip, enter the water, and use the speed and force of the rip to help overtake the victim. This technique is known as the pendulum.
- If use of the landline results in unmanageable tangles or exceeds the length of line available, the landline should be immediately discarded and a free swimming rescue performed.

- Landlines are pulled in while facing the victim, either hand-over-hand or by holding the landline and walking backwards away from the water.
- When retrieving the landline, assisting lifeguards must closely monitor the lifeguard and victim for signals to cease pulling, and for swells and waves overtaking the lifeguard and victim. Speed of retrieval is less important than steady pulling. An exception to the latter is when landline retrieval must be slowed or stopped while the swell or wave passes the lifeguard and victim, to prevent them from being temporarily submerged. No hand signals are involved. The technique and timing of this retrieval pause should be practiced in drills.
- After landline rescue, the equipment must be carefully recoiled and prepared for immediate use.
- If a second landline rescue is initiated for multiple victims, assisting lifeguards must be certain they know which lifeguard and victim are being supported to avoid confusion during retrieval.

CHAPTER FIFTEEN

SPECIAL RESCUES

CHAPTER HIGHLIGHTS

Rip Current Rescues

Multiple Victim Rescues

Surfer and Bodyboarder Rescues

Scuba and Skin Diving Rescues

Fugitive Retrieval

Suicide Attempts

Fog and Night Rescues

Rock and Jetty Rescues

Pier Rescues

Boat Rescues

Rescues Without Equipment

Defenses

Automobile Accidents in Water

Aircraft Accidents in Water

Cliff Rescues

Flood Rescues

IN THIS CHAPTER

Lifeguards must be constantly aware of the dangers presented by people experiencing panic in deep water. Distressed swimmers often move toward responding lifeguards and may, in desperation, grab the lifeguard for support. In unusual situations, some victims may even choose the support of the lifeguard over the support of an extended RFD and make a quick grab for the lifeguard during approach and control. Lifeguards must be prepared to counter these advances with appropriate defenses.

A lifeguard leaps to rescue a submerging swimmer beside a capsized boat.
[Photographic Credit: Leon Skov]

The majority of rescues are routine, requiring basic rescue skills covered earlier in this manual. Yet not all rescues are of a routine nature. This chapter will explore special rescue situations and offer techniques that can help lifeguards react to situations beyond the scope of a single victim in distress in deep water. Regardless of the complexity of a rescue, however, the three points of a rescue are always followed. These are:

1) Recognize and Respond
2) Contact and Control
3) Signal and Save

RIP CURRENT RESCUES

The United States Lifesaving Association estimates that rip currents are the primary source of distress in over 80% of swimmer rescues at surf beaches. Rip currents can pull people into deep water very quickly, creating an immediate hazard to those with moderate or poor swimming ability. Non-swimmers will rapidly submerge after being swept into deep water by a rip current. Even strong swimmers can tire and panic in a very short period of time as they swim against a rip current.

Regardless of the equipment used for rip current rescues, two basic techniques can be used to the lifeguard's advantage in these situations:

- Use the power of the rip current for victim approach—When a rip current pulls victims away from shore, most attempt to fight it by swimming against the current. A lifeguard who swims with the current toward the victim can use its power to rapidly approach the victim.
- Avoid the rip current when retrieving a victim—Once contact and control are accomplished, the lifeguard should normally plan a retrieval outside the rip current. This may not always be necessary, but there is little point in fighting a strong rip current when it can be easily avoided. To do so, the lifeguard swims parallel to the shore until well away from the current, then swims directly to shore. Another option is to swim diagonally toward shore. Since some rip currents pull diagonally away from shore, care must be taken to avoid swimming directly into the force of the current when taking a diagonal course toward the beach.

Rip currents usually dig a channel in a sandy bottom, leaving water deeper than that on either side. Therefore, simply moving to the side of the current channel will often help to quickly locate shallow water. This lessens the distance the lifeguard must swim with a victim. In strong and lengthy rip currents, swim fins and the skill required to don them quickly are essential.

In cases of multiple victims or rip currents pulling far offshore, it may be best to swim victims with the current to an offshore rescue boat. In such cases, the power of the rip current can be used to approach victims and to retrieve them to the offshore location.

MULTIPLE VICTIM RESCUES

It is not uncommon for a lifeguard to be faced with a rescue where two or more people are caught together in a distress or panic situation. These multiple victim rescues (also known as mass rescues) present unique challenges.
Multiple victim rescues commonly occur when:

- A panicked person grabs others for support, incapacitating them and causing a multiple victim situation.
- A current sweeps several people to deep water.
- A boat suddenly capsizes or sinks, forcing victims into the water.

The two keys to successful rescue of multiple victims are *floatation* and *back-up*. Adequate floatation is essential to allow lifeguards to gain control of a rescue. Panic is usually greatly diminished once victims have something to hold on to which keeps them above the water. This also lessens the need for immediate assistance. The victims may still be caught in the current, causing alarm, but the immediate fear of submersion is eased once they are provided with floatation.

If available, a lifeguard selecting equipment for what appears to be a mass rescue should take more than one RFD. At beaches where multiple victim rescues occur with regularity, larger rescue buoys should be standard equipment since they can provide floatation to more victims.

A rescue board can be extremely valuable for a mass rescue. Although it is difficult to retrieve victims to shore using a rescue board in a surf environment , the superior floatation of a rescue board can provide support to numerous victims while

A lifeguard using two rescue buoys pulls three victims to safety. [Photographic Credit: Mike Hensler]

awaiting other lifeguards to swim them to shore. The rescue board is particularly valuable at a calm water beach where the lifeguard can quickly access the victims, then move slowly toward shore with all of them holding on to it.

Backup is often critical on mass rescues. Information provided in the initial alert by the lifeguard who first spots the emergency unfolding is very important. If this lifeguard advises that backup is needed, it can be sent promptly, at the same time as the first lifeguard enters the water. If no backup is immediately available and the lifeguard is unable to control the situation adequately, other swimmers nearby with floatation devices can be solicited to help. For example, several victims can hold onto a surfboard until lifeguards arrive to bring them ashore.

A rescue boat is an excellent tool for a mass rescue. If it is large enough, the victims can be brought aboard. If not, the boat can simply be used as a raft for floatation until the victims can be ferried ashore by swimming lifeguards.

As a general rule, a lifeguard should not swim past one victim to reach another. If the lifeguard approaches a victim and sees another further out, the lifeguard may choose to tow the first victim to the second, or leave the RFD with the first victim and physically support the second until backup arrives. In cases where several victims are some distance apart, the lifeguard should try to select the person in the greatest distress, assisting that victim first, and then move to the next distressed person and so on. Swim fins are particularly valuable when a lifeguard must support a victim without an RFD. Rescues without equipment are discussed later in this chapter.

Rescue boards are sometimes useful in multiple victim rescues because they can provide floatation to several victims at once.

[Photographic Credit: B. Chris Brewster]

SURFER AND BODYBOARDER RESCUES

In general, surfers and bodyboarders have better than average water skills and have an excellent floatation device with them. In the surf environment, most use leashes so that they do not lose their board. It should not be assumed, however, that a surfer or bodyboarder will never need rescue just because they have floatation. Not all users of these devices are skilled. Leashes can break and injuries sometimes occur when a fiberglass surfboard or the skeg strikes a person.

Signs of surfer or bodyboarder distress include:

- *Bodyboarders who try to paddle the board*—Bodyboards are designed to be propelled by kicking and most users employ swim fins. The use of arm strokes by a bodyboarder indicates weak ability and possibly distress or panic.
- *Surfers who try to kick the board*—Surfboards are designed to be propelled by paddling, not kicking. A surfer who attempts to kick may be showing signs of distress or panic and this certainly demonstrates weak ability.
- *Surfers who attempt to propel the board sideways*—This is a sign of a novice surfer with extremely limited ability.
- *Weak paddling or kicking*—Surfers who make little progress while paddling, and bodyboarders with a weak kick.
- *Continually falling off the board*, or hopping off the board, and trying to swim.
- *Losing the board*

- *Caught by a rip current*—Experienced surfers and bodyboarders may use a rip current area to quickly make their way offshore, just as a lifeguard might, but most avoid these areas once they reach the surfline. Waves usually don't break well in a rip current due to the depth of the rip current channel and conflicting water movement. A surfer or bodyboarder who lingers in a rip current area is probably a novice and will tire quickly.

When surfers or bodyboarders need rescuing, the three components of a rescue are employed. In many cases, the board can be used to help stabilize and control the victim prior to retrieval. Caution should be used, however, in entering the surfline with a victim who has a surfboard as the board can cause serious injury or be lost to the waves, injuring swimmers toward shore. One alternative is to allow the board to be pushed ashore by the waves in an area where swimmers will not be endangered, then to swim the victim in with an RFD. Another is to use a rescue boat.

Occasionally surfers and bodyboarders become trapped outside the surfline at rocky beaches. This occurs because the victim is able to paddle out through the surf, but is fearful of being injured on the rocks upon return to shore. The responding lifeguard may also conclude that a safe retrieval is unlikely, particularly in large surf. In these cases, it is usually best to summon a rescue boat or helicopter for assistance outside the surfline.

In all rescues of wave riders, spinal injury should be considered a possibility. Sometimes the victim will go over the falls — that is, be caught by the breaking wave and dumped in its force. If the victim strikes bottom or is torqued in heavy surf, spinal injury can result.

SCUBA AND SKIN DIVING RESCUES

In many beach areas, people skin dive (diving with mask, fins, and snorkel) and scuba dive (using compressed air tanks). Lifeguards are encouraged to become certified scuba divers. This training provides extensive insights into the sport and helps in understanding scuba rescue techniques, as well as the physiology of diving injuries. For a full discussion of diving injuries, refer to the chapter entitled *Scuba Related Illness and Treatment*.

Skin diver rescues are no different than those of swimmers, with the exception that a typical source of panic is having the mask fill with water. Often simply removing the mask resolves the problem. Since skin divers do not breathe compressed air, they are not susceptible to related problems.

Scuba[1] diving rescues are more involved. Prior to diving on their own, all scuba divers should be fully trained by an instructor who is certified by a nationally recognized scuba training organization. Reputable dive shops will not provide compressed air refills to persons without a certification card.

In addition to a mask, snorkel, swim fins, and often a wetsuit, divers use a tank of compressed air (not pure oxygen) and a regulator. The regulator reduces the pressure of air coming from the tank to a lesser pressure which can be breathed without damaging the lungs.

Divers also use weight belts and buoyancy compensators. Weight belts are used to counteract the natural surface buoyancy of a fully equipped diver so that the diver can submerge more easily. Once submerged, however, divers become progressively less buoyant as they descend. The buoyancy compensator (BC), which is most often an inflatable vest, is then gradually inflated by the diver using compressed air from the tank. Divers attempt to maintain neutral buoyancy or to be slightly positively or negatively buoyant, to aid in ascending or descending. This may require frequent adjustment to the amount of air in the buoyancy compensator when moving from one depth to another.

The recognized depth limit for recreational diving is 130 feet. Recreational divers should not descend below this depth.

Divers can experience distress for all of the reasons that swimmers experience distress, but the vast majority of deaths are directly attributable to diver error. Equipment failure is rare. The most prevalent factors contributing to diver deaths are insufficient air, entrapment, and rapid ascent. Insufficient air and rapid ascent are closely related, as running low or out of air causes the diver to ascend rapidly. Other contributing causes include panic and alcohol or drug use. The degree of physical conditioning is a significant factor in diver deaths while cardiovascular disease is a particular contributing factor.[2]

Running out of air is demonstrative of very poor judgment and is a factor completely under the control of the diver (except in the rare case of equipment malfunction). Divers are strongly encouraged to use the buddy system, diving in pairs, so that if one diver has trouble the other can assist. About 50% of diving fatalities are sustained by solo divers and divers who have become separated from their buddy. For this reason, a lone diver may be viewed as a high risk-taker. When two divers embark from shore and one surfaces alone, lifeguards should be very concerned. This means the buddy is now diving alone and may be in distress.

Divers may be entrapped due to entanglement in weeds (particularly kelp) or fishing line or inside a confined space, such as a submerged wreck or cave. Divers are encouraged to carry knives to cut themselves free of entanglement.

Divers over 40 years old and those who are obese should maintain strong physical conditioning for scuba diving. Diving gear is heavy on the surface and its use can strain the cardiovascular system. An obese diver should be viewed as a high risk candidate for rescue.

Lifeguards with experience in diver rescue know that preventive lifeguarding involves sizing up divers before they enter the water. Lifeguards can ask divers if they are certified and their level of experience. They can be sure the weight belts are fastened with quick release buckles and note the location of the buckle. They can look for ill-fitting equipment, which may indicate that it is borrowed and the diver is a novice. If divers are drinking alcohol before a dive, they should be counselled not to dive. Good judgment is critical while diving and alcohol impairs judgment. It is good practice to warn divers of any unusually rough or hazardous conditions. Responsible divers will simply avoid diving on a day when conditions are poor.

Divers use hand and arm signals to indicate when things are going well. The most commonly used is the OK hand signal, made by forming a circle with the thumb and forefinger. Another is the overhead OK signal, which is similar to the USLA approved arm signal for lifeguards. The diver touches one hand to the top of the head, forming a circle with the arm. Divers also use hand and arm signals to indicate distress. A wave is a sign of diver distress, but it is not the only evidence that a diver is in trouble.

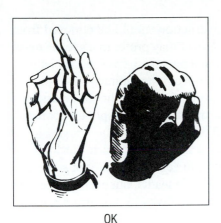
OK

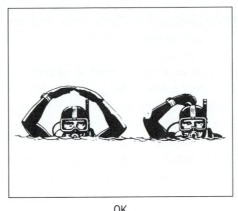
OK

Assistance Needed

Signs that a diver is in distress may include:
- Sounding a whistle or waving toward shore
- Surfacing alone with no sign of the buddy
- Surfacing and remaining motionless
- Breaking the surface very suddenly or even explosively
- Removing the mask or other equipment in a hurried manner
- Swimming toward shore, but making no progress

Diver rescues follow the three components of all rescues: recognize and respond; contact and control; signal and save. The initial alert to other rescuers prior to entering the water is particularly important in the case of scuba divers. In these rescues there is a heightened potential for physiological complications contributing to the distress, and diver rescues are generally more difficult than those of free swimming persons.

Caution should be used in the approach. Divers often have spears or spearguns with them, which can be lethal. They should be handled very carefully and always kept pointed away from other swimmers.

When approaching a diver in apparent distress, the lifeguard should ask about the nature of the problem, if it is not obvious. Divers have their own source of buoyancy, though they may become panicked and unable to use it. Other sources of distress are a physiological problem related to diving, a current, or separation from the diver's buddy. The presence of a lifeguard usually reduces fear significantly.

If the diver is having a buoyancy problem, there are two immediate options. The simplest is to pull the quick release buckle on the weight belt, jettisoning it. This, of course, results in loss of equipment and should be avoided unless clearly necessary for rescue. The other option is to inflate the buoyancy compensator (BC). The RFD may provide sufficient buoyancy, but if a diver is negatively weighted, inflating the BC or releasing the weight belt is sometimes necessary and can increase comfort of the diver significantly.

The buoyancy compensator is usually inflated via breathing into a mouthpiece or by triggering a valve attached to the scuba tank. Some BCs also have a CO_2 cartridge which can be triggered to immediately and fully inflate the BC. These techniques should be practiced by lifeguards working in areas frequented by divers.

Once buoyancy has been stabilized, any obstruction should be removed from the diver's face and an airway ensured. A relaxed diver may prefer to leave the mask on and even continue breathing from the tank. For a panicked diver, it may be necessary to remove the mask and snorkel or regulator from the mouth.

If a diver advises that a dive buddy is missing, the diver should be asked if this is normal, or if the diver is concerned. Some divers routinely split up upon diving and separation in and of itself is not unusual for them.

A swimming lifeguard with buoy and fins is ill-equipped to perform an underwater search for a missing diver who may be in very deep water or some distance away. Usually, such searches require trained dive teams, but even so, the first responding lifeguard can make a few quick surface dives to perform a cursory search and look for bubbles on the surface.

If a diver is observed beneath the surface entangled in something, a surface dive should be performed in an attempt to assist. A knife in the possession of either diver can be very helpful in such cases. If a diver is observed beneath the surface who appears lifeless, the lifeguard should dive down, release the victim's weight belt, and swim to the surface with the victim. The BC should not be inflated unless this is necessary to bring the diver to the surface — rapid inflation of the BC of a submerged diver can cause the diver to rocket to the surface. Upon reaching the surface, the lifeguard should signal for assistance and begin rescue breathing.

Retrieval of a conscious, distressed diver is essentially the same as for any victim, but it is complicated by the heavy equipment and relative lack of mobility of the diver. The RFD is provided and the lifeguard swims the victim to shore. Surf rescues of divers can be hazardous because the tank and regulator can strike the lifeguard, which can cause serious injury and loss of consciousness. Appropriate caution should be utilized and, if necessary, the equipment can be removed.

Rescued divers should be evaluated carefully for physiological complications related to breathing compressed air. Sometimes these problems are instantaneous while at other times they become evident after the dive. Such complications can be life-threatening and should be taken very seriously. Often lifeguards learn of such problems when an afflicted diver walks up to the lifeguard for medical advice. For information on recognition and treatment of diving illness, see the chapter entitled, *Scuba Related Illness and Treatment*.

Lifeguards in rescue boats should be made aware of divers submerged in the patrol area so that they can be avoided. Divers sometimes use a floatation device to mark their location and to warn boaters. The most common is an inner tube with a diver flag. The flag is either red with a diagonal white stripe or the alpha flag, which is a white and blue flag with blue dovetails.

FUGITIVE RETRIEVAL

Lifeguards at some agencies have police powers; at others they do not. Regardless, occasionally suspects of crimes attempt to elude arrest by escaping into the water, and lifeguards are called upon to retrieve them. Often suspects in such cases are actually very poor swimmers and simply desperate to get away. In these cases, superior water skills place lifeguards at a tremendous advantage. There are several important considerations in these cases:

- *Consider the possibility of a weapon involved*—Lifeguards should determine if a weapon is involved before any approach. A handgun may be usable even after being submerged, and a knife is an obvious hazard.
- *There is no rush*—While police officers often become very concerned in these cases and desirous of immediate action, rapid intervention is not called for unless the suspect is in imminent danger of drowning. Many times, it is best to simply watch the suspect and wait. In fact, the more time passes, the more fatigued the suspect becomes, reducing the likelihood of effective resistance.
- *Wait for police backup*—If qualified law enforcement personnel are not at the scene, summon them and wait for their arrival. The situation is better controlled by leaving the suspect in the water than by bringing the suspect to shore, creating potential problems on land.
- *Maintain personal safety*—The primary concern of the lifeguard in these cases should be personal safety. Avoid any confrontation likely to result in injury.

If it is decided to approach the fugitive, it is highly recommended that two lifeguards be involved, allowing one to approach from the rear. Upon approach, lifeguards should first try to talk the fugitive into surrender. A reminder to the fugitive that there is no escape may be successful. Often, the simple fact that persons are approaching in the water causes the suspect to realize the hopelessness of the situation and give up.

If this is unsuccessful, the lifeguards should place themselves in a position that requires the fugitive to turn away from one lifeguard. The lifeguard who is able to get behind the fugitive immediately throws an arm over the shoulder and across the chest. The wrist of that arm is grabbed by the other hand for additional control.

If the fugitive is a poor swimmer, the control of the lifeguard may cause a cessation of resistance. If not, the lifeguard should try to kick in toward shore while maintaining a grasp of the fugitive. If control is lost, kick away. As in the case of a panicked victim, the best escape if the fugitive grabs the lifeguard is to submerge and wait until the fugitive lets go to surface for air.

SUICIDE ATTEMPTS

It is not uncommon for people to try to take their own lives in or near the water. People may jump from piers, cliffs, or bridges. They may swim directly out into large water bodies. They may even attach themselves to weights. While many of these suicide attempts will occur at more remote areas or at times when lifeguards are not present, lifeguards may be called upon to respond.

The most difficult aspect of a suicide presentation is that those attempting suicide typically do not want to be rescued. They may swim away from approaching lifeguards and not hold on to extended RFDs. In these situations, it may be necessary to take physical control using techniques described for fugitive retrieval. Another option is to stay nearby, but wait for the person to tire. This will ultimately help to reduce resistance. The lifeguard must stay near enough, however, so that if the person intentionally submerges, immediate retrieval from below the surface is possible.

It is recommended that two or more lifeguards participate in approaching a person attempting suicide, as those responding can expect resistance during initial contact and rescue and perhaps beyond removal from the water. Response to a suspected suicide attempt should automatically trigger a call for police assistance, since a weapon may be involved and police will eventually be needed to transport the person to a treatment facility.

Responses to suicide attempts involving jumpers attached to weights can be particularly difficult for lifeguards, as these presentations are often sudden and involve immediate submersion presentations. Search procedures should be initiated upon arrival at the scene and may require tools necessary to free victims from attached weights.

A consideration in suicide attempts is that they may occur in response to having contracted a life-threatening communicable disease that appears incurable. Lifeguards should always employ appropriate universal precaution. For more information on universal precaution, see the chapter entitled *Lifeguard Health and Safety.*

FOG AND NIGHT RESCUES

Fog and darkness have a similar effect in drastically reducing visibility. Both tend to significantly reduce beach activities and, therefore, the volume of rescues is also diminished. However, lifeguards must be prepared for rescues in these conditions.

Fog can appear unexpectedly and may be associated with the hot weather that attracts large crowds to the beach. Also, fog may not be present inland from the beach and clear weather there can encourage people to plan a beach visit only to arrive at a fogged-in facility. This can place lifeguard services in a position where protection of swimmers must continue when the primary means of victim recognition—visual scanning—is lessened or eliminated.

Some lifeguard agencies simply elect to close the beach to swimming as a safety precaution in fog conditions or at night. In other areas, foggy conditions will activate special fog patrol procedures. When approaching fog is noticed, warnings should be issued to beach visitors. Public address systems can be used to make these warnings and announcements, or other audible signals can be made at regular intervals once fog shrouds the beach.

Since visual observation is no longer effective, fog patrols should be commenced to place lifeguards closer to the water's edge in vehicles or on foot. While on patrol, lifeguards should be constantly alert for cries of help or the sound of boat engines from boats mistakenly operated close to shore.

Fog patrols are best made in teams of two lifeguards. If a rescue is indicated, one lifeguard can enter the water as the other lifeguard remains on shore to call for backup assistance and to sound an audible device (such as a vehicle horn or siren) at regular intervals. This device serves to help the responding lifeguard determine the direction of shore and helps backup find the location of the response. In surf conditions, shore direction can be determined generally by swell direction and the sound of crashing waves, but lateral position along the beach may be uncertain.

Lifeguards who become lost in the water in foggy conditions or in the dark should stop and listen for waves, voices, lifeguard fog alarms, vehicle traffic, or other noises that may indicate the direction of shore. In most coastal areas, when wind is present during fog, it is likely to be blowing toward land. Calling for help can also be effective. The lifeguard who starts swimming toward shore should stop frequently to re-check current position using the clues previously mentioned. Some lifeguard agencies provide special RFDs for night and fog responses which are equipped with underwater flashlights or waterproof strobes for better identification in the water.

Fog can be particularly dangerous for boats suddenly caught in a fog bank without electronic positioning equipment. Lifeguards should be prepared for this possibility and continue regular patrols in an effort to locate wrecked vessels.

ROCK AND JETTY RESCUES

When compared to smooth, sandy beaches, rescues from rocky shores can be quite difficult and dangerous for lifeguards, especially in surf conditions where incoming waves can throw a lifeguard into the rocks. Usually, rocks have shellfish such as barnacles and mussels attached to them. These can cause serious lacerations. Urchins may be present in tide pool areas. Rocks can be very slippery, particularly when seaweed is attached, and it is easy to fall during response and retrieval.

While rescue procedures at rocky areas involve the three basic components of all rescues (recognize and respond, contact and control, signal and save), special considerations are in order. The following is a partial list:

- Water entry over rocky areas sometimes can be made easier by donning swim fins for foot protection prior to entering the water. Another option is amphibious footwear. The benefits of foot protection should be weighed carefully against maneuverability.

A lifeguard on a personal watercraft attempts to pull a hapless boater out of pier pilings. [Photographic Credit: Mike Hensler]

- Use of a wetsuit can greatly diminish the potential for injury from striking or being abraded along rocks.
- Shallow diving entries can be made from ledges, docks, and outcroppings, but should be made with great care to avoid a head injury. Keep hands extended above the head and plan the shallowest dive possible. In surf conditions, dives can be planned for entry into the high point of a wave rather than the trough between waves. Wait for the upsurge of the arriving wave and jump into it.
- Begin swimming as soon as possible upon entry into the water, even in knee to waist-deep water. Continue to keep the hands in front to feel for and fend off rocks.
- Avoid ducking under incoming waves unless water depth is known.
- Once the victim has been approached and controlled, retrieval should be made away from rocky shores if at all possible, especially in surf conditions. This is an excellent indication for a boat pick-up. Another option is a long retrieval swim to the relative safety of a neighboring sandy beach.
- If it is absolutely necessary to make a retrieval to a rocky shore in surf conditions, stay close to the victim during retrieval through rocky areas rather than towing the victim behind on the RFD. Reach through under the arms of the victim (from the victim's back) to grasp the RFD and use the RFD to fend off rocks during retrieval.
- A primary rule for lifeguards involved in rescues near rocks is to protect themselves first. The lifeguard will be of no assistance if injured, and a serious injury to the lifeguard will greatly delay assistance to the victim.
- The greatest aid to lifeguard response at rocky areas is experience and knowledge of the area. Those who work at a beach with rock areas should get to know those areas well by studying them regularly in all weather and tide conditions. Underwater rock formations should be of particular interest.

PIER RESCUES

At many surf beaches across the United States, piers have been constructed extending out past the surfline, supported by pilings. Unlike piers at flat water beaches, surf piers are usually constructed at a considerable height over the water to protect the pier deck and any buildings or improvements installed on the pier from high surf. Among other uses, piers provide fishing opportunities, scenic promenades, and special activity or amusement areas for beach visitors.

While surf piers can be renowned local attractions for beach visitors, they can pose challenges for lifeguards. Pier pilings can create or magnify rip currents. They are unyielding to those pushed into them. People sometimes fall or jump from piers. Piers can become attractive if not dangerous challenges for imprudent surfers, power skiers, boardsailors, and boaters who may try to operate around the pilings.

To save time on a rescue response near a pier, some lifeguard agencies will train lifeguards to respond by jumping from the pier rather than approaching from the water. Special training and regular practice is required for this entry method.

To safely accomplish entry from a pier, the lifeguard must know the water depths at every point around the pier. These water depths can be affected by tides or other vertical movement of water. The water will be deeper if the lifeguard times the jump to enter the water on an incoming swell.

Entries from piers should be made feet first. The proper entry method is to hold the RFD in one hand and swim fins in the other. Jump well clear of the pier, preferably on the side that is away from incoming surf. The RFD is raised over the head vertically with one hand and the swim fins with the other. The legs are crossed to protect the groin. Eyes are focused on the horizon to avoid eye injury upon water contact. As the feet hit the water, the lifeguard should let go of the rescue buoy. This helps to avoid shoulder injury as the buoyancy of the RFD might otherwise pull on the arm during submersion.

A problem with piers is that victims are frequently drawn toward the pilings for support. The sharp-edged mussels and barnacles that grow there can cause painful wounds, as can water movement, which grates the victim's skin against the rough surface of the piling. Still, lifeguards can have difficulty in convincing victims to release the piling in favor of the support of the RFD. In some situations, it will be necessary to forcibly remove the victim from the piling. Once this has been accomplished, the lifeguard can retrieve the victim away from the pier and to shore. Careful maneuvering may be necessary around other pilings, with the RFD placed in a position to be used as a fender.

BOAT RESCUES

Distressed boats can present lifeguards with several rescue situations, ranging from stalled craft needing assistance to serious boat collisions. Sailcraft, including boardsailors, can also get into serious trouble, often due to inexperienced operators. How a lifeguard agency responds to boat rescues often depends on the equipment available to lifeguard staff.

A lifeguard pulls a swamped vessel out of the surfline as his crewmember, who swam the tow line in, sits beside the owner in the bow of the swamped vessel. [Photographic Credit: Annette Kennedy]

In larger agencies, lifeguard rescue vessels can be called on for a wide range of boat rescues, including towing and firefighting. At smaller agencies, lifeguards may have to respond to serious boat accidents as first responders, relying on other agencies or individuals to provide the equipment necessary for the safe recovery of boats and their passengers. Whatever the response policies of a lifeguard agency, there are several points for lifeguards to consider when making boat rescues:

- *Distress Recognition*—Recognition clues for potential boat rescues can be very obvious or very subtle. A collision, capsizing, fire, or explosion indicates a clear need for immediate assistance. Yet, other presentations can be deceiving to the lifeguard. Boardsailors who appear to be in control of a craft may actually be trapped offshore, unable to return against the wind. Small capsized sailcraft may indicate problems or they could be engaged in training exercises. While experience often helps the lifeguard to recognize potential boat rescue presentations, the following signs may indicate the need for assistance:
  - Crews working on a boat engine
  - People on board waving anxiously toward shore
  - A boat positioned broadside to the wind or waves
  - Boats with no one on board or on deck
  - Boats continually circling
  - Sailcraft continually "in irons" or with the sail ruffling but catching no wind
  - Repeated falling by a boardsailor, especially when no progress is made toward shore
  - Any boat approaching a surfline or swim area with obvious lack of control
- *Alert*—In determining if a response is necessary, lifeguards should remember the established area of responsibility. Boat problems outside of it should be reported immediately to the proper agencies for their response. If a lifeguard response is appropriate, the alert should contain enough information to inform backup staff of the situation and the required equipment.
- *Equipment Selection*—Rescue boats, rescue buoys, and swim fins are good equipment choices for response to boat rescues. If a swimming approach is to be used, a boat tow should be fastened to the rescue buoy. If there is any indication of spilled fuel in the water, face masks should be taken for eye protection.
- *Approach*—Great care should be taken in approaching any craft still under power. Advise the skipper to turn the engine off and keep it off while lifeguards are in the water around the boat. Also, carefully evaluate the potential for fire, such as a spilled fuel slick. During approach, identify people in the water who are most in need of assistance and approach them first. If appropriate, encourage people to stay with the boat for support and direct them to don PFDs while awaiting backup assistance. When there are people in the water, it is important to determine, as soon as possible, that all passengers are accounted for. In general, it is important to gain permission to provide assistance from the boat captain or owner of any upright, floating vessel before aid is rendered. When approaching a boat drifting toward a surfline, it is important to avoid approaching shoreward of the vessel. A disabled vessel may overturn at any moment, pushed by the wind and waves. Instead, approach from the seaward side.

- *Signal*—Once initial control has been gained and the situation is assessed, signal ashore to indicate if backup response is necessary. In serious boat accidents, lifeguards should continue to stabilize victims while awaiting backup assistance. If passengers are able to assist, engines should be stopped and sails should be dropped. In flat water conditions or well outside breaking surf, anchors may be dropped. When backup assistance arrives, injured passengers can be immobilized if necessary and extricated to stable vessels for retrieval.
- *Retrieval (flat water)*—In minor presentations involving disabled boats or inexperienced operators, the lifeguard can offer to retrieve the boat and passengers. Small, capsized sailboats can often be righted. Swamped or capsized small craft can usually be towed ashore with passengers aboard or holding on. Boardsailors can drop their sail across the board and be towed ashore while riding the board. To assist by towing, uncoil the boat tow and have the boat operators attach it to the bow of the craft to be towed. The lifeguard can then swim, paddle, or row while towing the rescued vessel and passengers.
- *Retrieval (surf)*—Disabled vessels approaching a surfline present a very dangerous situation for passengers, lifeguards, and beach visitors. Should the vessel enter the surfline and be catapulted through it, serious injury and damage could occur. To prevent this, often lifeguards will have to assist by keeping the craft out of the surfline while awaiting backup assistance in the form of a rescue vessel.

Depending on surf conditions, towing a vessel up to about thirty feet in length usually can be accomplished by a single lifeguard equipped with a boat tow and swim fins. Upon approaching a boat (from the seaward side), the lifeguard should gain permission to give assistance and request that all lifesaving equipment be donned by the passengers or at least placed on deck. Request that running engines (if providing no propulsion) be stopped and that sails be dropped. If anchors are being used but are not effective in stopping progress toward the surfline, they should be pulled up. Uncoil the boat tow and toss the free end to an occupant with instructions to secure it to the bow. The lifeguard can now swim the boat away from the surfline to calmer water to await rescue vessel assistance.

If towing cannot prevent a disabled boat from entering the surfline or if the boat swamps, passengers should be directed to jump off to the seaward side. The lifeguard must be prepared to jettison the RFD, which, if attached to the tow line, may pull the lifeguard with the boat through the surfline. Rescue efforts in the water are now focused on people who have abandoned the craft, while efforts on shore focus on clearing the water and minimizing damage to the boat.

RESCUES WITHOUT EQUIPMENT

Lifeguards should avoid attempting a rescue without proper equipment. Lifeguard equipment increases the efficiency of rescue while providing additional safety for the lifeguard. All on-duty lifeguards should be provided with the necessary equipment to effect rescues.

Still, lifeguards must be prepared to effect rescues without equipment if it is unavailable. For professional lifeguards, rescue presentations when equipment is not available will most often occur during off-duty hours. In a typical scenario, the off-duty lifeguard may be at an unguarded beach on a day off. Suddenly, a drowning presentation is recognized. The off-duty lifeguard feels a moral obligation to assist, even though rescue equipment and backup assistance may be unavailable. Another possibility is in a multiple victim rescue where the lifeguard provides a buoy to one victim and must swim to another some distance away.

Considerations for rescues without equipment:

- *Alert*—It is critical to ensure that someone, somewhere knows that a rescuer is in the water on a rescue. Call for help. Draw someone's attention. Direct bystanders to go to the nearest phone and call 9-1-1.
- *Equipment Selection*—Look around. Can something nearby be adapted to use as rescue equipment? Are there ring buoys mounted nearby? Does anything float that can be pushed out to the victim? Can some object be extended to the panicked victim to avoid direct contact? A shirt? Rope? Many items may be used to improvise rescue equipment.
- *Approach and Contact*—A rescuer without equipment should approach a victim from the rear. This can be difficult or impossible because the victim's tendency is to turn to watch the rescuer. Swim wide and circle around the victim or surface dive in front of the victim and swim under and past the victim to surface behind. Sometimes victims are merely panicked, but can swim in with encouragement. If so, avoid contact and try to talk the victim to shore. If this is not the best option, approach the victim from behind and move swiftly to control the situation. If the victim is clothed, try grabbing their collar and tow using a side-stroke. If this is not feasible, one of the following three tows may be effective:
    - Cross-Chest—Throw one arm over the victim's shoulder and across the chest to the opposite waist. Immediately secure the victim between the arm and hip. The victim's shoulder should be secured in the rescuer's armpit. Concentrate on keeping the victim's face out of water. Informal studies of drowning victims show that while this control method supports the victim and maintains an airway, it may not place the victim in a position that produces a feeling of security, with the face and head out of the water. Expect struggling to continue as the victim attempts to lean forward out of the water.
    - Modified Cross-Chest—Quickly place an arm under the victim's arms and across the chest/abdomen of the victim to secure the victim between the arm and hip. The victim's buttocks should be supported on the rescuer's hip. This position usually provides the support that allows the victim to sit forward and remove the head from the water. Panic usually subsides more quickly. However, this position may result in the lifeguard remaining nearly or fully submerged, due to the added weight being supported out of the water. This position should be used when there is a short retrieval distance to standing depth.
    - Armpit Tow—The rescuer takes a position on the back facing the victim's back. The hands grasp the victim under the armpits with the arms slightly bent at the elbow. The rescuer kicks in, using a frog kick. The major advantage of this retrieval method is that the victim is kept high in the water. The major disadvantage is very limited control. It is not appropriate for a surf retrieval.
- *Stabilize*—Attempt to reduce the victim's panic while providing support by using a breaststroke or sidestroke kick. Additional support and momentum

can be gained by sculling or pulling the water with the free arm. If difficulty is encountered in controlling the victim, the free arm can be moved to lock onto the supporting arm, pulling the victim more tightly to the supporting hip. If this is unsuccessful, move the free arm to the victim's back and quickly push the victim away. Swim away, reconsider the approach, and try again to gain control.

- *Retrieve*—Once control is gained, turn and make progress toward shore using breaststroke kicks, scissor kicks (regular or inverted), and shallow arm pulls (strokes used by the leading arm during sidestroke).
- *Assess*—Treat or resuscitate the victim if necessary. Monitor breathing for signs of complications and be prepared to assist responding personnel in completing the necessary reports.

DEFENSES

A lifeguard responds to a rescue presentation where several people have been swept suddenly into deep water by a current. The lifeguard enters the water and approaches the group, studying people to determine those most in need of assistance. Pulling the RFD in to approach a victim, the lifeguard feels a hand on the back, quickly followed by a vise-like grip around the head, applied by a panicking swimmer who could not wait for assistance. For the moment, the rescuer has become a victim.

Lifeguards must be constantly aware of the dangers presented by people experiencing panic in deep water. Distressed swimmers often move toward responding lifeguards and, in desperation, may grab the lifeguard for support. In unusual situations, some victims may even choose the support of the lifeguard over the support of an extended RFD, and make a quick grab for the lifeguard during approach and control.

Lifeguards should avoid situations that include:
- presenting their backs to unsupported or unstabilized victims
- moving through or among a close group of unsupported or unstabilized victims
- placing themselves in a position where a panicking person can jump from a support onto them

Victim behavior in these situations is quite uniform. The victim will grab at any exposed part of the lifeguard and quickly pull that person into a hugging position at the highest point of support, usually the head. The victim sees that the lifeguard is buoyant and tries to climb to safety.

The lifeguard is pushed downward as the victim puts weight on the lifeguard for support. The victim is now supported with the head out of water and the lifeguard is submerged or strangled, making breathing difficult or impossible. People experiencing the panic of a drowning presentation can demonstrate extraordinary strength. Children can incapacitate adults.

The best defense is to simply go limp and submerge. Since the victim grabs the lifeguard in an attempt to climb up for air, if the lifeguard no longer provides buoyancy, the victim will almost always immediately let go.

In unusual cases, when submerging is ineffective, defenses against these advances follow the same principles of self defense taught in many martial arts courses. Anticipation of the victim's movements and quick, decisive actions by the lifeguard can often prevent the establishment of a firm head hold.

Defense techniques include:

- *Turn toward the attack*—At the first sign of unknown contact or movement, quickly turn to face the source. Bring the lead arm up in a sweeping, blocking movement.
- *Assume a tuck position*—Drop the head lower to the shoulders, draw the knee or knees up and present feet and arms toward the attack. Present as small a target as possible toward the victim. Lean back away from the attack.
- *Block and push*—If the victim is close enough, the lifeguard should not hesitate to block an attack by placing a foot on the victim's chest, pushing away, and swimming in the other direction. The lifeguard should continue to face the attack while swimming to safety.
- *Be prepared to ditch the RFD*—In some situations, panicking swimmers may use the boat tow attached to the RFD to pull themselves toward the lifeguard instead of toward the floating buoy.

Defenses from head holds include:

- *Turn and submerge*—The chin should be brought close to the body and to the side to keep it from catching. Reach up and push the victim's arms away over the head.
- *Execute the escape*—Move quickly and decisively. Use leverage over sheer strength.

In a front head hold, the victim is facing the lifeguard with arms around the lifeguard's head or neck. If submersion does not result in release of the hold, place the hands on the hips of the victim and push away while tucking in the chin. Once the release is effected, swim back and away from the victim.

In a rear head hold, the victim is behind the lifeguard with arms around the lifeguard's head or neck. The lifeguard should grab a breath of air and submerge, turn the head and tuck the chin to one side. When ready, the lifeguard drops the shoulder to the side where the head is turned and quickly turns to face the victim. Leverage can then be applied to the hips, as described earlier, to break the hold and escape from the victim.

AUTOMOBILE ACCIDENTS IN WATER

In many localities, beaches are directly adjacent to highways and other roads. In these areas, vehicular accidents can occur which result in a submerged vehicle. These presentations can be complicated by victim entrapment and possible injuries associated with the vehicle accident. Lifeguard response to vehicle submersion accidents often involves a coordinated effort with local police and rescue agencies.

The objectives of automobile rescue are to:

- Determine the exact location of the submerged vehicle
- Determine the number and location of vehicle occupants
- Respond necessary equipment and personnel to the scene
- Plan and execute measures to extricate accident victims for resuscitation and treatment

These types of accidents are relatively rare, so lifeguards are typically seen as the experts who are expected to handle the situation. Lifeguard agencies with

experience in vehicle submersion accidents have established special emergency plans for dealing with these incidents to ensure rapid and professional response.

Once a submerged vehicle accident has occurred, emergency plans are activated and all responding agencies are notified. These agencies may include police, fire and rescue agencies, and special responders such as wreckers (removal of victims may require extrication of the vehicle first). If the lifeguard agency is first on the scene, free-diving lifeguards usually try to determine the location of the vehicle and make initial attempts at locating and extricating victims. The ideal tool for such quick dives is the bail-out bottle, a small scuba tank that can be strapped on the waist. Used by lifeguards certified in scuba, along with a mask and swim fins, immediate underwater search can be initiated. The alternative is free diving by lifeguards. One clue to finding a submerged vehicle is rising bubbles.

When a fully submerged vehicle is located, a marker buoy should be fastened to it. An RFD is an excellent alternative if the lanyard is long enough. While initial dives take place, specially trained lifeguard dive teams should respond and prepare to enter the water. Other responding lifeguards or personnel should inspect the scene for victims who may have escaped the vehicle prior to immersion, or interview witnesses in an attempt to determine how many people were in the vehicle.

In-water lifeguards must quickly determine the location of the submerged vehicle and determine if extrication of trapped victims is possible. Lifeguards cannot assume that all victims will be in the vehicle. Checks of the surrounding water, especially pilings or other structures close to the accident scene are important, particularly at night. Lifeguards should also assess prevalent currents to devise a search pattern.

The greatest hazard in rescues of persons trapped in submerged vehicles is laceration from exposed metal and jagged glass. There is also potential for entrapment, so lifeguards should use great caution in entering a submerged vehicle and be prepared to release the RFD harness, if necessary. Petroleum products are often present in the water. These can be toxic, particularly to the eyes. A mask should be used and care taken not to swallow the water. Approach should be from up-current, if there is one.

The value of pre-planning such responses stems from their unusual nature and the extreme emergency presented. The possibility of a person trapped and in imminent danger of death always creates a very high degree of concern on the part of lifeguards and bystanders. It is important to stay calm and to operate as quickly and safely as possible.

AIRCRAFT ACCIDENTS IN WATER

The attraction that water and the beach has for people can also draw aircraft. In many areas, it is not uncommon for air traffic to be heavy along beaches, especially helicopters and small, prop-driven airplanes. Near-shore crashes happen occasionally.

Lifeguard response to aircraft accidents should be handled in a manner essentially similar to that of automobile accidents in the water. The aluminum used in aircraft is likely to leave jagged edges following a crash, and aircraft fuel is very toxic, so great caution and proper protective gear are appropriate.

One important consideration for lifeguard agencies near airports is the possibility of a major airliner crash. Many airliner crashes with multiple casualties have occurred in the water. These cases are especially challenging due to the number of victims involved. Rescue boats are extremely valuable. Lifeguard agencies near major airports should have contingency plans worked out with airport authorities and local safety responders.

CLIFF RESCUES

Some lifeguard agencies have jurisdiction over areas that include high rock outcroppings or cliff areas adjacent to protected beaches. These areas may experience special rescue presentations involving people who fall or jump from these heights into the water. Such rescues can be complicated by difficult extrication routes and the possibility that the victims may be injured as the result of a fall or jump.

Sometimes, the best way to rescue a person trapped at the base of a cliff is to swim the victim to safety. In these cases, responses are initiated from adjacent, accessible beach areas or from rescue boats. If the victim is injured, a floating stretcher may be utilized.

Some lifeguard agencies are responsible for rescuing victims trapped on cliffs, or who fall from cliffs or rock outcroppings onto dry land. These agencies are outfitted with special extrication tools, equipment, and vehicles for such rescues. The San Diego Lifeguard Service, for example, handles 30 to 60 cliff rescues each year on cliffs up to 300 feet in height. This lifeguard service maintains a special rescue vehicle with a crane and mechanical cable to aid in cliff rescue. Coastal cliff rescue requires extensive training, which will not be covered in detail in this manual.

A lifeguard (below) assists a victim as they are hoisted by lifeguards at the top of the cliff.

[Photographic Credit: Paul Hansen]

The San Diego Lifeguard special rescue vehicle, with crane deployed, hoisting a victim.

[B. Chris Brewster]

Two lifeguards come to the aid of a victim trapped at the bottom of a cliff. One lifeguard swam to the victim, the other rappelled down the cliff. [Photographic Credit: Paul Hansen]

FLOOD RESCUES

Swiftwater rescue necessitated by flooding is extremely dangerous. Unlike surf, which allows for lulls between sets of waves, swiftwater is relentless. A person trapped against a stationary object by swiftwater can drown easily, and even the strongest swimming skills may be useless.

[Photographic Credit: Conrad Liberty]

One of the most dangerous hazards is the low head dam, which can be natural or manufactured. A low head dam is an obstruction across the path of a river which increases the upstream water level, but allows the river to flow over the top. In these cases, the water flowing over the dam can form a continual cyclical current back toward the dam itself. It thus becomes a self-perpetuating drowning machine. It creates a tremendous hazard because a person caught in this cyclical current, even with a personal flotation device, can be trapped and repeatedly recirculated under the water.

Lifeguards who lack special training in swiftwater rescue should make every effort to avoid making a rescue that requires use of a boat or actual entry into the swiftwater environment. Instead, consider methods that allow lifeguards to stay onshore.

One simple, but effective method for shore-based rescue is known as the pendulum technique. As the victim is swept along by swift moving floodwaters, the rescuer ashore uses a bag of line, known as a throw bag, to manually throw a line to the victim. The rescuer holds one end of the line while the weight of the line in the loosely open-ended bag causes it to play out toward the victim. The rescuer braces and when the victim grabs the line, the force of the current combined with the pull of the line causes the victim to swing to shore on the rescuer's side. If a victim is expected to be swept under an overhang, such as a bridge, netting may be lowered or rescue tubes snapped in the closed position may be dangled to allow the victim an easy purchase.

Other considerations, particularly for victims stranded on objects midstream, is use of a fire department ladder truck, with the ladder extended, or a helicopter. In any case, a highly buoyant personal floatation device should be worn at all times when working around floodwaters. Furthermore, it should be remembered that floodwaters are usually contaminated by sewage and other toxins. Rescuers involved in flood rescue should be inoculated against maladies such as hepatitis.

1   The word scuba was originally an acronym for *self-contained underwater breathing apparatus* and was therefore always capitalized (SCUBA). It is now commonly accepted as a word.

2   Statistical information in this section provided by the Diver Alert Network, Duke University Medical Center, Durham, North Carolina.

CHAPTER SIXTEEN

EMERGENCY PLANNING AND MANAGEMENT

CHAPTER HIGHLIGHTS

Emergency Operation Plan Development

The Incident Command System

IN THIS CHAPTER:

Even the best emergency operation plan will fail unless the emergency personnel devoted to the incident work in concert. The *incident command system* (ICS) was created to promote effective coordination of diverse emergency resources. A fundamental aspect of the incident command system is the *incident commander* (IC) — a single person ultimately responsible for overall management of all resources devoted to the emergency.

EMERGENCY OPERATION PLAN DEVELOPMENT

A vessel grounds on a rock off the beach with 23 victims aboard, some with serious injuries. Who will take charge of the response? A plane with three persons aboard loses power and the pilot ditches in the water 100 yards from on-duty lifeguards. What emergency responders should be summoned to help handle the incident? Five people are swept offshore in a rip current. They are rescued, but all aspirate significant quantities of water and need immediate advanced medical care. How will they be triaged and transported to the hospital?

Most emergency operations involving lifeguards are routine. In these cases, standard response methods should be very effective. In major emergencies, however, numerous responders from different agencies and specialized rescue equipment may be needed. These resources must be effectively coordinated and critical decisions must be made throughout the incident. Under the pressure of a major emergency, important considerations can be missed and valuable options ignored. For these reasons, professional emergency response agencies prepare *emergency operation plans* (EOPs).

EOPs are written guidelines to help emergency providers handle major emergencies in the best manner possible. Effective EOPs are prepared prior to an emergency, when there are ample opportunities to calmly consider all of the resources and courses of action that could be employed. They should include a menu of options to help ensure that no viable alternative is missed in the heat of the moment.

EOPs are based on worst case scenarios. They incorporate the emergency personnel whose availability can reasonably be expected. These plans should be designed to expand or contract, depending on the extent of the emergency. Some subjects of lifeguard Emergency Operation Plans are:
- Missing Persons
- Major Medical Emergencies
- Scuba Emergencies
- Fire
- Severe Weather
- High Surf
- Law Enforcement
- Dangerous Marine Life
- Environmental Disasters
- After Hours Emergencies
- Automobile/Aircraft Crashes

Preparation of an emergency plan usually begins with consultation among lifeguard staff members, particularly those with experience in major emergencies and/or special skills. Various emergency scenarios are considered and possible response modes suggested. The best modes of response are determined, including alternatives.

If it becomes clear that an emergency will require assistance from members of other agencies, they should be consulted and perhaps asked to provide a representative on the planning team. This not only provides expertise, but hopefully a buy-in to the plan which is ultimately devised.

Once the plan is complete and approved, a copy should be provided to all involved staff members for information. Any other agencies involved in or impacted by the plan should also receive a copy. Ideally, training of senior staff members likely to take charge should be initiated. Since the most senior staff members may be off duty the day of a major emergency, training should include any staff members likely to have a lead role.

One tremendous adjunct to an emergency plan is the checklist. Preparing such a list helps ensure that valuable options are not forgotten when an emergency occurs. Checklists should include all the likely steps to be taken in a given type of emergency. The incident commander can select the most appropriate options to take depending on the circumstances of the emergency, but a checklist helps to ensure that all major options are at least considered. An example checklist for a submerged swimmer scenario (Code X) can be found in Appendix B.

Checklists can help reduce unnecessary attention to the implementation of pre-planned emergency steps, making them almost automatic. In a scuba emergency, for example, the dispatcher can simply be advised via radio to follow the scuba emergency checklist, which may include summoning of an ambulance, notification of a local recompression chamber, and so on. In this way, the on-scene supervisor does not have to remember to advise the dispatcher of each step to take or tie up radio traffic. In addition, the task is accomplished sooner. Checklists for dispatchers can be written in such a way as to require clearance prior to taking a particular step, but they still help to remind all involved of the need to consider certain actions. The following sections include considerations which may be valuable in assembling emergency operation action plans for specific types of emergencies.

MISSING PERSONS

Large crowds and an abundance of activity make reports of missing persons very common in the beach environment. Once a person is discovered to be missing, the family or friends, particularly if a small child is involved, inevitably fear that the missing person has drowned. A crucial question in these cases is, *"Did you see the person submerge?"* In the vast majority of cases, a person reporting someone missing is simply fearful that the person has drowned, but in fact the missing person is found on the beach later.

If a credible person reports *witnessing* a submersion, a water search should be initiated immediately. Conversely, if a person is missing, but only believed to have been planning to swim, a full water search may well be inappropriate. In this case, there is no last seen point (datum) at which to initiate the search nor any certainty that the missing person is even in the water. Consideration should be given to the fact that committing lifeguard personnel to a search in this instance could unduly detract from safety protection provided to other water users.

The most difficult decision for a lifeguard in charge of a beach comes when the report of a missing person falls into the gray area between a witnessed submersion and a simple loss of a person on the beach. For example, how should the case be handled if a mother last saw her teenage son in the water, but turned away for 30 seconds and upon trying to locate him again, could not? In this case, the son may well have left the water or be lost in the swim crowd. On the other hand, he may have submerged.

It is essential that lifeguard agencies develop protocols for such cases to assist lifeguards in making the best possible decision and to protect the agency from criticism for a failed response to a legitimate emergency. Ultimately, judgment will have to be used based on the unique aspects of each case, but pre-planned procedures can give valuable guidance.

Procedures for conducting a search for a submerged swimmer are covered in the chapter entitled, *Search and Rescue.* The following steps should be employed when the victim is believed to be lost ashore.

1) Elicit a full description of the missing person including
   —name
   —age
   —height
   —weight
   —hair color
   —skin color
   —clothing description
   —swimming skills
   —medical problems
   —likely beach hang-outs
2) Find out the last seen location and direction of travel

3) Notify all agency staff in the area and consider notifying beach users with a public address system

4) Check likely locations, such as bathrooms, snack bars, arcades and so forth

5) If available, a public address system may be used to summon the missing person or to broadcast a description to elicit assistance in the search from beach patrons

6) Regularly check the "towel area" (i.e., where the group has located themselves on the beach)

7) Check the car if the group drove to the beach

8) Consider calling the home or hotel telephone number if nearby

During a check of beach facilities, the reporting person should be kept at the lifeguard facility until the incident is resolved and should be allowed to join in land-based searches only in the company of a lifeguard with communications gear. This policy ensures reunification once the lost person is located. It also prevents situations where the reporting party locates the lost person and disappears into the crowd without telling lifeguards that the problem has been resolved.

A lost child is found.
[Photographic Credit: Mike Hensler]

Local law enforcement personnel should be notified if a missing person is not located expeditiously. The actual time frame should be set by agency protocol. A missing person report form, which may be helpful in missing person cases, can be found in Appendix B.

MAJOR MEDICAL EMERGENCIES

Depending on beach activity, some lifeguard agencies need to summon an ambulance daily for transportation of injured persons to the hospital, whereas at others, this may happen only once or twice in a season. Regardless of volume, lifeguards should be prepared to summon needed assistance promptly in a medical emergency. This means having correct telephone numbers and radio frequencies readily available.

Depending on remoteness of the beach area and availability, helicopter evacuation may be necessary in some cases. Pre-planning will involve consultation with the helicopter provider to determine the cases to which they will respond. It will also involve considerations for appropriate landing areas.

Medical emergencies on the beach can draw crowds, which tend to obstruct efforts of emergency medical personnel and make the patient very anxious. Some agency protocols call for summoning police assistance for crowd control in any serious medical emergency.

Multiple trauma victims are a tremendous challenge to any medical aid provider. Boating accidents and car accidents are typical causes. Lifeguard agencies should be prepared to triage and treat several injured persons at the same incident. This includes knowing how to summon additional ambulances and other emergency resources for backup as necessary.

LAW ENFORCEMENT EMERGENCIES

Law enforcement EOPs may be initiated whenever the assistance of police is needed on the beach. In the case of a simple property crime, lifeguards may respond by calling for a police officer, while keeping the victim at the tower to await the officer's arrival. More serious incidents, however, may require additional emergency action.

Some lifeguards are trained and authorized to enforce the law. Some carry firearms or other weapons and are primary sources of law enforcement for the beaches they serve. Lifeguards without special training, authority, or equipment should avoid attempting to defuse or confront violent activity. Instead, the agencies they serve will usually advise them to react to violence by calling for emergency police assistance. All lifeguards should make reasonable attempts to protect beach visitors by helping to move them away from scenes of violent criminal activity, and to rescue and treat injured beach visitors if it can be done with a reasonable degree of safety.

Lifeguards should take reasonable steps to expeditiously inform the proper authorities of criminal activity and update them as the circumstances change. For example, police are understandably anxious to know if they are being summoned to an incident in which weapons are involved, as well as the type of weapons.

One area in which all lifeguards can provide valuable assistance to law enforcement is through observation and documentation. Criminals often forget that lifeguards have a commanding view of the beach and may attempt to hide in plain view of lifeguards.

An impediment to law enforcement is that witnesses often forget details of the description of those involved in criminal activity. This information can be critical to capture and ultimate prosecution of the suspect(s). Lifeguards should attempt to thoroughly document the descriptions and actions of those observed to be involved in criminal activity. Witnesses to a crime, or victims, should be contacted when it is safe to do so and asked to wait for police. Names and addresses should be documented so that, if they leave the scene, the information can be provided to police upon their arrival.

SEVERE WEATHER

As explained earlier in the chapter on weather, lifeguards assist beach visitors by monitoring weather conditions, by warning beach visitors of approaching severe weather conditions, and by assisting beach visitors in the event of sudden, severe weather. When such weather conditions approach beach areas, emergency operations plans for severe weather are initiated. At small beach facilities, this may be the responsibility of the tower lifeguard after recognizing threatening weather patterns. At larger facilities, EOPs may be initiated by a supervisor.

The goals of any severe weather EOP are to:
- Alert the public to threatening weather conditions
- Warn beach visitors who may be reacting to threatening weather conditions with unwise actions
- Ensure the safety of lifeguard staff
- Protect beach facilities
- Assist with protection of adjacent beach property

Severe weather warnings are best made using public address systems. Alerts can also be sounded using long blasts from whistles or other alarm devices, and gestures can be used to call people in from the water and warn them of weather conditions. Flags can be flown if their meaning is widely understood in the area.

Most people will recognize threatening weather and move toward reasonable shelter on their own. Some visitors, however, may react to threatening weather by attempting to wait the storm out on the beach or gather in the unsafe shelter of tree groves or other areas. Lifeguards can watch for this behavior and warn visitors to move to adequate shelter, offering suggestions as to areas or facilities that have been recognized or established as storm shelters (in electrical storms, automobiles and grounded buildings may be considered safe shelter areas).

Lifeguards should protect themselves, too. In many areas, lifeguards are ordered out of towers during lightning activity, since certain tower designs may not offer adequate protection from lightning strikes. These policies are to be taken seriously, since lifeguards have been killed during electrical storms at beach facilities.

At some agencies, lifeguards are recognized and trained as special rescue responders during times of severe weather incidents. Lifeguards may be called to stand by and respond to rescues in floods, hurricanes, tornadoes and other storms. This type of rescue response requires special training beyond the scope of this manual.

FIRE

Emergency plans for fire usually involve the summoning of fire services and the establishment of crowd control measures to protect beach visitors. Lifeguards can establish and maintain access for incoming fire fighting equipment and should be prepared to provide medical aid to persons injured by the fire.

At beaches in wooded areas, lifeguard EOPs should include evacuation procedures for personnel and the public if a wildfire threatens beach areas or public access routes.

THE INCIDENT COMMAND SYSTEM

Even the best emergency operation plan will fail unless emergency personnel devoted to the incident work in concert. Responses to major emergencies can involve large numbers of emergency personnel and related equipment, sometimes from different agencies with differing response protocols. The goal in these instances is to utilize all emergency resources in the most efficient manner possible to resolve the situation. Unfortunately, the actions of emergency personnel do not always complement each other.

The *incident command system* (ICS) was created to promote effective coordination of diverse emergency resources. A fundamental aspect of the incident command system is the *incident commander* (IC)—a single person ultimately responsible for overall management of all resources devoted to the emergency.

The IC is usually a member of the agency most directly responsible for the emergency. The incident commander could be the head lifeguard, a high ranking police officer, or a fire department supervisor, but the IC need not be the most senior member of a given agency. Regardless of who the IC may be, members from the IC's agency and all other responding agencies report to the IC for assignment. This requires that agency pride be put aside in favor of achieving a common goal. At major incidents, a liaison system should be arranged which allows a representative from each agency involved in the emergency to expeditiously communicate pertinent information to and from the IC.

Lifeguards and a paramedic load one of three victims of a cliff collapse into an IRB for transport to a waiting medical transport helicopter. [Photographic Credit: San Diego Union Tribune]

The incident command system is designed to develop from the time an incident occurs until the emergency is resolved. The incident command structure can be expanded or contracted depending upon the changing conditions of the incident. It can be seen as a pyramid with the IC at the top. In its most rudimentary form, if two lifeguards respond to a reported drowning, one will usually take charge and make the decisions. This person is in command of the incident — the IC. At more complex emergency incidents, the IC may be ultimately responsible for hundreds of emergency responders. As the incident expands in size, the responsibility for acting as IC is typically pushed higher up the chain of command.

The basic principles of the incident command system are easy to understand. Many agencies follow them naturally, without any specific training. Larger agencies likely to become involved with major emergencies should provide training to their supervisory personnel on detailed principles of the incident command system. An excellent source is the Federal Emergency Management Administration. Other sources include local firefighting organizations which may provide extensive training in the incident command system as it relates to the fire service. This training is easily adapted to lifeguard work.

INCIDENT COMMAND RESPONSIBILITIES[1]

An incident commander has several general responsibilities:
1) Assess incident priorities
2) Determine strategic goals and tactical objectives
3) Develop or approve and implement the incident action plan
4) Develop an incident command structure appropriate for the incident
5) Assess resource needs
6) Order, deploy, and release resources as appropriate
7) Coordinate overall emergency activities
8) Serve as the ultimate incident safety officer, responsible for preventing injuries
9) Coordinate activities of outside agencies
10) Direct information release to the media

1   The Incident Command System (NFA-ICS-SM), National Emergency Training Center, FEMA, Emmitsburg, MD 1992.

CHAPTER SEVENTEEN

AQUATIC SEARCH AND RECOVERY

Chapter Highlights

Initial Search

Full Search

Search Methods

Search Patterns

Recovery of a Viable Victim

Body Recovery

Debriefing and Counseling

In This Chapter:

Reports of missing persons do not always call for an in-water search, but a credible report of a submerged swimmer should immediately trigger a carefully pre-planned response. The most difficult decision in the case of a recovered, non-breathing victim is whether to first retrieve the victim to shore, where well managed medical support can be provided, or to initiate resuscitative efforts in the water.

When a swimmer submerges and is unable to return to the surface, the final stage of the drowning process begins. Oxygen is no longer available and death is imminent.

It is believed that brain death normally occurs within four to six minutes of the cessation of circulation. Since effective CPR requires a firm surface, a submersion victim whose heart has stopped must not only be found and brought to the surface, but also to shore or aboard a rescue boat with adequate deck space for CPR, before this lifesaving technique can be initiated. Submerged victims can be very hard to find in the open water environment, particularly when there is limited water clarity or there is current action. The last seen point can be quickly lost on a body of water with no landmarks. For these reasons, USLA believes that in open water, there is a brief *two minute window* of enhanced opportunity for successful recovery of a submerged victim.

During the initial two minutes, responding lifeguards may be able to make quick dives at the last seen point, bring the victim to the surface, perform initial in-water resuscitation, and retrieve the victim to shore for further medical assistance. The two minute window provides the potential for retrieving the victim to shore within four to six minutes of submersion for administration of CPR.

After the two minute window has closed, the chances of successful recovery and resuscitation decline rapidly. Water currents can quickly move the body, poor water visibility can begin to greatly deter the recovery attempt, and the last seen point of the victim can be easily misplaced.

USLA does not intend to suggest that extensive search and recovery procedures are pointless. There are recorded incidents of fully successful resuscitations of victims submerged for up to and exceeding one hour. Although most of these seemingly miraculous cases have occurred in very cold water, USLA recommends that the emergency portion of searches for submerged victims normally last one hour and that resuscitation attempts be initiated upon recovery of a victim during this period.

[Photographic Credit: Conrad Liberty]

Despite this recommendation, attention must be focused on the critical importance of the first minutes after a submersion occurs. This brief opportunity is yet another reason why prevention is such a critical aspect of open water lifesaving. Nonetheless, all lifeguards must be prepared to instantaneously and effectively conduct search and recovery procedures.

Reports of missing persons do not always call for an in-water search. Often the missing person is simply lost on the beach. The chapter entitled *Emergency Planning and Management* provides guidelines for determining the point at which an in-water search is appropriate. This chapter is intended to detail search and recovery procedures once it is determined that a full emergency search should be conducted for a submerged victim. The term *emergency search* refers to the period during which personnel and equipment are fully committed in an effort to recover a victim they believe they may be able to successfully resuscitate. After that time, the search becomes a non-emergency body recovery attempt.

SEARCH

INITIAL SEARCH

If a lifeguard onshore observes a submersion, or receives a credible report of a submersion, the alert to other personnel is essential. Extensive backup should be immediately responded. If a victim submerges as a lifeguard approaches in the water, lifeguards onshore can be alerted by using the USLA approved arm signal for a submerged victim. The lifeguard looks toward shore and crosses both arms overhead in the form of an X (the USLA Code X signal). As with all arm signals, lifeguards ashore should respond with the same signal to show that the signal has been received and understood.

Perhaps the most critical task in initiating a search for a submerged swimmer is to fix a *last seen point*. Open water can be very deceiving and even the best executed search pattern is likely to be unsuccessful if the starting point of the search is inaccurate. Currents may quickly move the searchers. If the submersion was witnessed by a non-lifeguard, the witness should be interviewed thoroughly, but quickly, in order to obtain an accurate last seen point. If the witness has left the scene of the submersion to report the incident to lifeguards, the witness should immediately be returned to the scene with responding lifeguards to help fix the last seen point, and a lifeguard should be placed in the water to assist the witness in visualizing that location.

Once a last seen point is determined, it should be fixed by use of a marker buoy or by lining up two stationary objects ashore that are one in front of the other. As long as these objects maintain the same position relative to each other, the lifeguard is staying on a consistent line. By taking two such sitings from different angles which intersect at the last seen point, the lifeguard in the water can help greatly in fixing the location until a buoy or boat can be placed there. This is known as using cross-bearing landmarks.

The first lifeguard arriving at the last seen point should make several immediate surface dives in an attempt to locate the victim. The RFD can be left floating on the surface if it will impede diving.

The second lifeguard in the water should carry a marker buoy, along with a mask, snorkel, and swim fins. The purpose of the buoy is to fix the last seen point as accurately as possible. USLA recommends that all beaches maintain inexpensive marker buoys as standard equipment readily available to all lifeguards at a beach. Masks, snorkels, and swim fins should also be immediately available for underwater searches. The second lifeguard drops the marker buoy at the last seen point and assists the first lifeguard in surface dives until the victim is found, or a more organized search can be mounted.

If a marker buoy or swim fins are not immediately available, response of the second lifeguard should not be delayed while waiting for this equipment. The clock in the two minute window is ticking.

If possible, at least one lifeguard should be left ashore to act as the incident commander (IC) and coordinate the search. Communication must be maintained with arriving lifeguards and other public safety agencies.

FULL SEARCH

A report of a submerged swimmer should immediately trigger pre-planned emergency operation procedures. This includes sending backup personnel to the scene to provide assistance, along with any available search equipment.

It is a good practice to devise and maintain pre-planned checklists for use in managing emergency searches. Checklists help to ensure that all normal steps are considered by the incident commander in a logical, priority order. A checklist for this purpose, which may be used or modified as required, can be found in Appendix B.

A priority concern in these cases is to maintain adequate levels of safety for the swimming crowd. If lifeguard resources on the beach are seriously depleted, a second drowning could occur. It is best to clear the swimming area completely to make room for the search and to free additional resources.

The estimated time of submersion should be established and documented as soon as possible. This information is critical in determining the time available to summon additional personnel for the search and, ultimately, when to conclude the emergency portion of the search.

It is good practice to summon ambulance personnel, if available, at the start of a search for a submerged victim. In this way, advanced life support will not be delayed upon recovery of a victim. In addition, police may be useful to provide crowd control.

SEARCH METHODS

There are three general search methods:
- *In-water Search*—Wading and swimming lifeguards search the water. In shallow water, lifeguards may systematically wade back and forth parallel to the beach, searching the water with eyes, legs, and arms. In deeper water, lifeguards use face masks and snorkels, along with swim fins, watching from the surface, and making surface dives when necessary.

Missing person line search.

- *Surface Search*—Lifeguards are deployed in boats or on paddleboards and use these craft as platforms from which the water is searched. Helicopters provide a superior platform for this purpose. Since submersion victims sink, the value of a surface search is dependent on water depth and clarity.
- *Underwater Search*—Lifeguards equipped with scuba gear can dive below depths of skin divers and can stay submerged much longer. Trained divers are extremely valuable during the emergency portion of a search but only if scuba equipment is readily available. Advanced lifeguard agencies maintain scuba equipment at their beaches for this purpose.

SEARCH PATTERNS

Prior to initiation of a full search, a search zone should be established. This provides search personnel with boundaries. Ideally, the search zone should be marked to give search teams a reference point during water searches. Markers may include range poles, buoys, or cross-bearing landmarks. Buoys are ideal in a flat water environment, but may be unusable in strong surf or heavy current conditions.

The IC should establish a search pattern to ensure systematic coverage of the search zone. The two most common search patterns are the parallel search (also known as the line search) and the circular search. Surface search teams may start in deeper water, working a pattern toward shore, while in-water search teams may work from shallow to deeper water. Grid lines may be used to delineate search zones and ensure search teams cover the area completely.

In the circular search, a buoy is placed at the last seen point and an anchor guard holds a line at that point. Lifeguards then space out an appropriate distance from the anchor guard, holding the line, and swim a circular pattern. Once a full circle has been turned, the searchers move down the line past the lifeguard farthest from the center buoy and swim another circle around the buoy. This is repeated until the area is thoroughly covered or the body is found. If the body is not found at first, the pattern may be started over again.

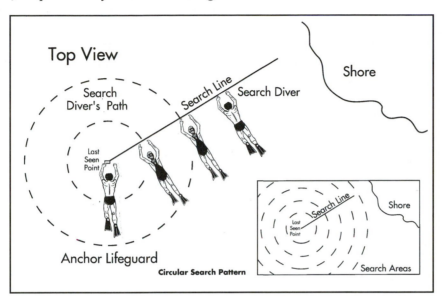

In the parallel search (also known as the line search or grid search), it is best to start by marking off a rectangular area using buoys. A line of lifeguards, spaced appropriately, swim parallel to each other along one end of the rectangle, from one side to the other. They then move sideways along the side of the rectangle and swim back to the other side. This back and forth pattern can be continued until the area is fully searched. At this point the IC can order that the area be searched again, or create a new area adjacent to the area searched. Once the second area has been thoroughly covered, a new one can be created and so forth.

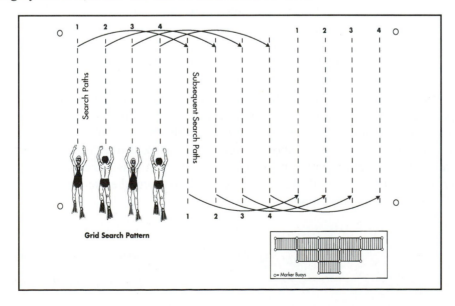

It is a good practice to designate one offshore lifeguard to take charge of the search line. This helps ensure that order is maintained. If possible, this lifeguard should be on a rescue board or rescue boat.

Rescue boats are extremely valuable in searches and should always be used if available. They allow on-scene supervision, support for the searchers, and facilitate communication to shore. If a victim is recovered, rescue boats provide a rapid method of retrieval to shore. Some include a platform large enough for CPR, along with advanced medical equipment. When rescue boats are used, caution must be employed to avoid running over a submerged searcher.

The potential for success of a search is largely dependent upon water clarity. In clear water, a few lifeguards can cover a large area in a short time. As water clarity decreases, the difficulty of mounting a successful search increases dramatically. In water with twenty foot visibility which is twenty feet deep, searchers can space themselves twenty feet or more apart. It is a good practice to keep searchers close enough together so that they can see each other underwater. This helps ensure that the searchers do not become spaced too far apart, and the victim is not missed between lifeguards in a search pattern.

If the body is not recovered within a one hour period, longer if so designated by the incident commander or agency protocol, the search may be changed from one of an emergency search to that of a body recovery. When the emergency portion of the search is terminated, lifeguard personnel can be returned to preventive lifeguarding duties, but it is a good practice to continue the search at a lower staffing level. While family members or friends of the missing victim may be able to understand the need to protect other swimmers, they are likely to view complete termination of the search as callous abandonment. A life has been lost and the shock can be profound for all involved. The investment of further time and resources is well justified if available.

RECOVERY

RECOVERY OF A VIABLE VICTIM

If a victim is recovered within an established time-frame after submersion (usually one hour) resuscitation efforts should be initiated. The most difficult decision in the case of a recovered, non-breathing victim is whether to first retrieve the victim to shore where well-managed medical support can be provided, or to initiate resuscitative efforts in the water.

USLA believes that, in most cases, an initial attempt at resuscitation should be initiated in the water by opening the airway, checking for breathing, and delivering the initial breaths recommended in current CPR protocol. If this fails to produce a response, transport to shore should be prioritized over further in-water resuscitation attempts. If both can be accomplished, lifeguards should do so, but in-water resuscitation is very difficult in most cases. Ashore, the victim can be provided with advanced life support.

Steps to Retrieval and Resuscitation of a Viable Victim

1) The victim is brought to the surface and the lifeguard signals to shore with the USLA approved arm signal for a resuscitation case—wave one arm back and forth several times.

2) The lifeguard turns the victim to a face-up position and thrusts one arm under both of the victim's armpits, behind the victim's back.

3) The lifeguard passes the RFD to the hand of the lifeguard's arm which is under the victim's armpits. The victim is now supported on one side by the lifeguard's body and on the other by the grasped RFD. The lifeguard's other hand is free.

4) The airway is opened and the lifeguard checks for breathing.

5) If there is no breathing, the lifeguard delivers initial breaths consistent with current CPR protocol.

6) Another check for breathing and a pulse is made.

7) a) *If there is a pulse but no breathing,* ventilatory support should be continued. The victim is moved to shore with assistance of other lifeguards.

   b) *If there is no pulse,* the victim is moved to shore or a rescue boat rapidly, with ventilatory support provided as effectively as possible during retrieval. The priority becomes evacuation to shore.

Note: In most cases, particularly late in the emergency search, in-water resuscitation attempts will not prove successful. Retrieval to shore is critical, particularly if advanced medical support is waiting.

BODY RECOVERY

Body recovery requires preparation and discretion. Corpses should be covered or placed in special bags designed for that purpose. Crowd control is important, as is the treatment of family members and other people close to the deceased person who may be present at the recovery.

Depending on local protocol, police, a coroner, or both should be summoned to accept custody of the body. Police officers often have experience in notifying and working with next of kin of deceased persons. They can be a helpful resource in this area. Since some water deaths are a result of foul play, lifeguards should be careful to preserve any evidence and should avoid moving a recovered body without permission from the proper authorities.

DEBRIEFING AND COUNSELING

Once search and rescue procedures are concluded, the incident commander should terminate command and return lifeguards to regular duty assignments as needed. Careful documentation of the event should be made for further investigation. In addition to standard incident reports, many agencies will require all involved lifeguards to prepare a narrative report and participate in a debriefing session or operational critique. A major emphasis of this process should be development of ideas that will help do an even better job in the future. Any drowning in a lifeguarded area should be fully investigated.

Like all emergency personnel, lifeguards are susceptible to psychological trauma related to witnessing death. Lifeguards are particularly likely to be affected considering their commitment to drowning prevention. Because of this commitment, a drowning may be perceived by as many as a terrible failure and the associated guilt may be overwhelming. Some agencies conduct a type of counseling called critical incident stress debriefing (CISD) as a routine following major incidents. Local crisis intervention services may also be a source of assistance. Supervisors should be prepared to offer support and carefully monitor their personnel for signs of stress. Sensitivity is essential in these cases.

CHAPTER EIGHTEEN

MEDICAL CARE IN THE AQUATIC ENVIRONMENT

Chapter Highlights

Standard of Care

Minor, Intermediate & Major Injuries

Spinal Injuries

Standing Backboard

In This Chapter

Many of the spinal injuries lifeguards encounter involve victims who walk up complaining of neck or back injury sustained during water recreation. Recognition and immobilization are of extreme importance to minimize further injury. Lifeguards should not assume that, because the victim is able to walk, there is no serious injury to the spinal column. There may well be injuries which could cause immediate, irreparable harm through one inadvertent movement.

The beach and open water compose a natural, ever-changing environment with many dynamic forces at work. These forces, combined with the wide variety of intensive physical recreational activities in which beach users participate, make injury and illness inevitable, even commonplace.

Injuries which happen away from the beach, such as traffic accidents or in-home accidents, typically result in the response of emergency medical aid providers to the scene, sometimes from significant distances. When people are injured at the beach, lifeguards are an immediate source of emergency medical attention. Lifeguards are almost always the *first responders* to medical aid needs at the beach. It is up to lifeguards to provide immediate medical aid and determine if further treatment is needed.

Because lifeguards are typically the first medical aid providers to respond to injury and illness at the beach, it has long been recognized that beach lifeguards must have adequate medical aid training to provide primary medical care, and to evaluate the need for further assistance. For minor injuries, the primary care rendered by lifeguards is usually adequate to fully resolve the problem without a higher level of care. These are the vast majority of cases handled by lifeguards. A number of recommended treatment protocols for injuries related to aquatic life can be found in the chapter entitled, *The Aquatic Environment.*

More serious conditions, such as difficulty breathing or loss of consciousness, require continued support of the victim until a higher medical authority can take over. This will typically involve transportation to a medical facility by an ambulance. However, lifeguards must be capable of supporting life, sometimes for an extended period of time, until a higher medical authority can take over.

To ensure that all beach lifeguards are prepared to assume these responsibilities, USLA sets minimum recommended standards for emergency medical training of lifeguards. They include full training in all levels of cardio-pulmonary resuscitation (CPR) and obstructed airway, as well as general training in emergency medical care at a level designed for those who will regularly practice in the field. The specific minimum recommended standards change from time to time and current information in this area is available from USLA. More advanced lifeguard agencies encourage or require their personnel to become qualified at the level of emergency medical technician (EMT) or Department of Transportation first responder. At some agencies, lifeguard paramedics are employed.

The information provided in this chapter, and elsewhere in this manual regarding the treatment of injury and illness, is intended to supplement approved courses in emergency medical aid. These courses usually do not go into great depth on issues specific to the beach environment. While lifeguards may find the information in this chapter a valuable supplement to other medical aid training they have received, no lifeguard should practice any emergency medical aid technique beyond the lifeguard's level of training and qualifications.

Lifeguard agencies should ensure that lifeguard personnel receive continuing, in-service emergency medical care training, regardless of the level of training that employees may have when joining the lifeguard service. Ongoing training ensures that all medical aid equipment is properly used, new up-to-date techniques are practiced, and all established local protocols are carefully followed. In-service training should also include topics relating to the local beach environment.

STANDARD OF CARE

Medical services use the term *standard of care* to define the minimal acceptable level of care provided to patients based on local laws, administrative orders, and agency protocols. Standard of care establishes the minimum training required of emergency medical providers and outlines the level of treatment and equipment required for emergency medical services. Standard of care may limit the treatment that may legally be provided, based on the training levels the provider has attained. For example, a basic emergency medical technician (EMT) is not authorized to use some of the treatment methods or equipment that a paramedic is permitted to use.

Most lifeguard agencies work closely with local emergency medical services and health care professionals in establishing a standard of care for medical services at the beach. This helps to determine the level of training and equipment needed for the employed lifeguards.

MINOR INJURIES

Minor injuries are conditions unlikely to require medical treatment beyond primary care. A vast majority of injuries sustained at beaches involve minor cuts and scrapes that can be quickly and effectively treated by lifeguards. Most lifeguard stations are equipped with a supply of items commonly used to treat minor injuries, including sterile gauze pads, antiseptic, and adhesive bandages.

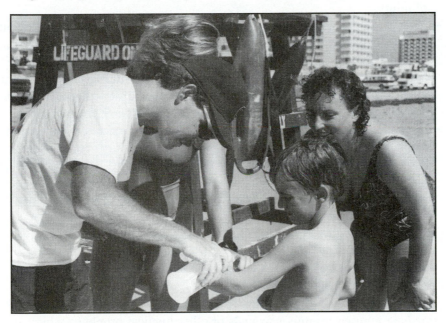

Lifeguard treats a jellyfish sting. **[Photographic Credit: Mike Hensler]**

Recommended Guidelines for Treatment of Minor Injuries

- *Lifeguards should inspect the injury*—Beach users occasionally request medical supplies for self-treatment without revealing the injury. Lifeguards should take reasonable steps to ensure that the injury is no more serious than the person believes. This demonstrates a concern for the person's injury and provides an opportunity to dispense useful advice.
- *Lifeguards should treat the injury*—People who request medical supplies usually plan to treat themselves or their children without further assistance. Lifeguards are usually better trained and qualified to provide this assistance. Furthermore, a request for supplies is often, in reality, a request for medical assistance. Therefore, lifeguards should offer to assist in treatment of an injury which is brought to their attention. Direct treatment by the lifeguard helps ensure that wounds are treated properly, and demonstrates the concern and capabilities of lifeguard personnel.

Treatment for minor injuries should never be forced on an adult. If the offer of assistance is declined, some agencies allow dispensing of minor medical supplies to persons requesting them. It is wise to note the name and other information of persons who insist upon self-treatment so that it is documented, in case of subsequent complaints about the quality of aid rendered.

It is not a good practice to dispense medical supplies to minors in lieu of treatment. If there is a parent or an adult supervisor of the minor, lifeguards should make sure that the adult knows of the injury, preferably before treatment. If the adult wishes to treat the child using lifeguard supplies, it may be allowed. If there is no adult accompanying the child, lifeguards may be required to treat the wound and take steps to make sure that a parent or legal guardian is notified before the child is released from treatment. In some areas, this is a requirement of law. Obviously, this is dependent upon the level of injury.

- *Lifeguards should treat minor wounds properly*—Whenever lifeguards initiate medical treatment for an injury, they assume a responsibility to treat it properly. A carelessly treated laceration, for example, may become infected later, resulting in serious complications well beyond the severity of the initial injury. It is always prudent to warn of the possibility of infection and to encourage a visit to the doctor in the case of any adverse changes.

- *Lifeguards should document treatment*—It is a good practice to document any medical treatment provided, even if minor. This can help greatly if the victim later comes to a belief that improper care was provided. Documentation provides a record of what was said and done. If the victim was advised to see a doctor, this can be noted. A brief report can also be used when generating annual statistics on workload. An example *Incident Report,* which can be used to document minor medical aid, can be found in Appendix B.

INTERMEDIATE INJURIES

Intermediate injuries are minor wounds or other medical problems which are not immediately life threatening, but which may require care at a medical facility. These are most typically lacerations that require stitches, minor puncture wounds to the extremities, and other similar injuries. In cases of intermediate injuries, lifeguards should stabilize the injury and advise the injured to seek treatment at a medical facility. It is good practice in these cases to offer or recommend transportation by ambulance.

The assessment of intermediate injuries requires good judgment and skills on the part of lifeguards who must take care not to release a person whose status may quickly deteriorate. A person with blood loss from a head cut, for example, might lose consciousness while driving to the hospital for stitches. It is prudent to establish guidelines to aid in this decision making. Some lifeguard agencies prefer to simply avoid such judgment calls, due to the level of responsibility placed on the lifeguard. At these agencies, a higher level of care is always sought before the patient is released.

All recommendations for further treatment of injuries should be carefully documented on medical reports. Pre-printed maps with directions to the nearest emergency facilities can be helpful.

As a general rule, minors with intermediate level injuries should not be treated and released. Either the parents should be summoned to the scene, or the minor should be turned over to an ambulance for transportation to the hospital. In many areas, this is a legal requirement. In most areas, civil liability increases dramatically if a minor with an intermediate injury is treated and released, particularly if any complications ensue. For the same reasons noted in the section on minor injuries, it is important to document treatment for intermediate injuries. Example reports for this purpose can be found in Appendix B.

MAJOR INJURIES

A major injury is defined as any injury or illness requiring immediate care at a medical facility. This includes injuries which are immediately life-threatening, such as uncontrolled bleeding. It can also include injuries which are not immediately life-threatening, such as a simple, closed fracture. The recognition and assessment of major injuries will indicate the need to activate an emergency operation plan.

The first step when encountering a person in need of emergency medical care is to determine the exact nature of the problem. The general examination procedure is as follows:

1) Determine that the area is safe to enter without further risk to lifeguards or the victim and mitigate any continuing threat to the safety of the victim or lifeguards.
2) Summon necessary backup.
3) Treat immediate problems according to level of medical training, including:
   A. Airway (ensure spinal protection precautions);
   B. Breathing;
   C. Circulation (CPR if needed);
   D. Bleeding.
4) Determine mechanism of injury.
5) Conduct a full patient assessment for any and all injuries including those to the head, spine, body cavities, and extremities, as well as shock.
6) Stabilize injures according to medical protocol and level of training.
7) Avoid moving the victim until the full extent of injury is determined.
8) Monitor and *record* vital signs.
9) Protect body heat.
10) Discourage onlookers who may make the patient anxious or obstruct rescue personnel.
11) Make the patient as comfortable as possible.

Additional Guidelines for Major Medical Aids

- *Keep bystanders back and maintain order*—A pushing crowd can aggravate the fear and anxiety of an injured person. Keeping onlookers away and calming bystanders can greatly assist the patient. In this effort, a courteous but firm approach is best. Police officers may be helpful in some cases.

- *Maintain control of the situation*—In a medical emergency, other beach visitors may offer assistance, suggest treatment, and try to take over care. It is not rare to have bystanders state, "I am a nurse," or "I am an EMT." These cases can be difficult. Lifeguards do not know the person or their level of training, but do not want to prevent care from a qualified medical provider with a higher level of training. Unfortunately, there are many examples of individuals professing to have high levels of medical qualifications who are later found to be impostors. While trained bystanders often can assist with stabilizing the patient, it is important for lifeguards to maintain control of the situation and keep treatment within the lines of established protocols.
- *Use discretion in treating injuries to persons' private areas*—The beach is a very public place. If treatment of an injury will require removal of clothing, it may be best to bring the patient inside, if possible. Privacy is a secondary issue in the case of a life-threatening injury, but it should be considered. When clothing must be removed, or private areas of the body treated, it is best to have a lifeguard of the same sex as the victim handle treatment. If this is not possible, another lifeguard should be present. While this may seem to create an additional violation of the person's privacy, it may be prudent in order to avoid a later complaint that liberties were taken.
- *Recommend further treatment*—In all cases where a victim is not transported directly to a hospital, it is prudent to recommend further treatment as appropriate.
- *Document treatment and advice*—Documentation of treatment is most important when treating major injuries. The long-term complications of these injuries and the potential for serious consequences make it increasingly likely that someone will later question the quality of care provided. It is also very important to document any refusal of recommended treatment.

SPINAL INJURIES

The spinal cord is surrounded by a flexible column of bones (vertebrae). Injury to this column usually results from a sudden severe blow or twist to the head, neck, or back. The cervical spine (neck) is the most commonly injured area. Spinal injuries are not at all uncommon at the beach. Diving, body surfing, and falls are some of the causes. Injury usually occurs when the victim's head strikes an object such as the sand bottom and is hyperextended backward or forward.

The initial trauma may cause a very serious and evident injury, or one that is subtle and hard to recognize. Any movement, however minor, can result in serious irreversible injury. Spinal injuries, therefore, require extraordinarily cautious handling. This can be a major challenge at the beach for several reasons. The victim may be further traumatized by moving water. The victim may be in a position which makes access and extrication very difficult. Water on a backboard can cause the victim to inadvertently slip out of position or completely off the backboard. For reasons such as these, all lifeguards should be fully trained in the necessary techniques for treating spinal injuries. Spinal stabilization devices are basic equipment which should be readily available for use on all lifeguarded beaches. This equipment is discussed in the chapter entitled, *Standard Rescue Equipment.*

This section highlights several techniques for treating spinal injuries in the open water environment. It is not meant to serve as a substitute for thorough training in the care and prevention of spinal injuries. Lifeguards should always follow the treatment protocols in their medical aid training and agency guidelines.

RECOGNITION OF SPINAL INJURIES

Severe injuries to the spinal cord can immediately affect the injured person's ability to move or feel below the level of injury. The single most obvious sign of a spinal injury may be sudden inactivity following activity in the water. A lifeguard is observing people in the water, with all the activity accompanying regular water sports, when suddenly a person is observed to be immobile for an inexplicable reason. This observation alone may trigger a response based on a suspected spinal injury.

Another presentation that should raise suspicion of a possible spinal injury is a person who is floating face down in the water. Face down presentations are extremely unusual because the bodies of victims who stop swimming usually sink rapidly, particularly in fresh water. If a person is observed lying face down in the water, the person may be able to float but unable to move due to paralysis. The lifeguard may have a very brief opportunity to respond before submersion.

Signs (clues noticed by the lifeguard) and symptoms (clues given by the injured person) of spinal injuries include facial lacerations or abrasion, bleeding or fluid emanating from the nose, ears, or mouth, inability to speak, altered level of consciousness, neck or back pain, loss of motor function, tingling or loss of sensation, spinal deformity, cessation of breathing, and any history of trauma. A history of trauma likely to produce spinal injury is often the primary indication of spinal injury.

Water masks many signs of injury. For example, bleeding wounds often do not show well when a person is in the water. The absence of signs or symptoms does not eliminate the possibility of spinal injury. When in doubt, lifeguards should treat for spinal injury. Although the use of spinal immobilization equipment is cumbersome and time consuming, it is well worth the effort to protect the victim from a lifetime of paralysis or other serious problem.

RESPONSE TO SUSPECTED SPINAL INJURY

When a possible spinal injury has been detected by lifeguards, a special rescue response is necessary. The objectives of response to this type of injury include:
- minimize movement of the head, neck, and back to prevent further injury to the spinal column
- establish and maintain an open airway using an approved technique
- maintain the victim's buoyancy while stabilizing
- ensure that the victim is extricated from the water safely for further medical treatment

Treatment for spinal injuries includes assessment and support of airway, breathing, and circulation (ABCs). The airway should be opened using a modified jaw thrust maneuver without head tilt. The patient should be provided 100% oxygen as appropriate. CPR should be commenced if needed.

Response to spinal injuries includes the three components of a rescue: recognize and respond, contact and control, signal and save. However, specific techniques differ in flat water and surf conditions. Under either circumstance, normal protocol calls for the lifeguard at the head of the victim, who is responsible for immobilizing the head and neck, to direct movement of the victim.

FLAT WATER RESPONSE

When approaching a possible victim of spinal injury, the lifeguard should avoid disturbing the water surface, which could cause further injury. Upon reaching the victim, the lifeguard should move to a position facing the victim's side. Whether the victim is face down or face up, the first action should be to place one forearm along the sternum of the victim so that the rescuer's hand will be at the victim's jaw and the rescuer's other arm along the victim's spine so that the hand will be at the base of the base of the victim's skull. When the arms are in place, the hands are positioned on the jaw and head creating a firm hold that will maintain the head in a neutral position (neither flexed nor extended). This position, known as the vice-grip, should then be maintained throughout the rescue. If the victim is face down in the water, the lifeguard submerges and rolls the victim to a face up position, surfacing on the other side, maintaining the vice-grip during the entire maneuver.

Maintaining breathing and circulation is the primary goal, even in cases of serious and obvious spinal injury. There are two alternative ways to proceed in cases where rescue breathing is needed. The first is to provide the best possible spinal stabilization in the water while providing rescue breathing. The second is to carefully, but quickly, remove the victim from the water while utilizing full spinal stabilization. The latter should be used only when it can be accomplished quickly enough to ensure that rescue breathing can be initiated expeditiously.

Since the goal is to maintain the victim in a secure and neutral position, the lifeguard's arms will not be free. If the victim is in deep water, the RFD can be left to trail behind as the lifeguard kicks toward shallow water. Movements should be slow and deliberate. Backup is always required in the case of any spinal injury. Once shallow water is reached, the victim can be maintained in position until a spinal immobilization device can be utilized and the victim extricated to dry land.

If the ABCs are intact, the backup will apply an appropriate sized, rigid collar and then the victim will be carefully placed on a backboard. Head immobilization is applied once the victim is on the backboard and the victim is secured to the board according to current medical protocol. In some cases, it may be appropriate to remove the victim from the water prior to fastening all straps. In these cases, great care must be taken to ensure that the victim does not slip off the backboard. A properly executed lift in this case normally requires at least four people.

Once a spinal injury has been sustained, there is a great potential for further injury during transportation of the victim. In flat water, there is usually little need to remove the victim rapidly because there is no immediate source of further injury (such as a wave in the surf environment). Therefore, unless an immediate life-threatening injury necessitates faster action, it is well worth the time to take it very slow and easy, reassuring the victim all the way.

SURF RESPONSE

In surf conditions, the problems of spinal injuries can be compounded by the problems of extricating victims through the surf and maintaining spinal stabilization in forceful water conditions. This problem is accentuated by the fact that many spinal injuries take place in the surfline due to body surfing and similar activities. It is very difficult to fully immobilize a victim in surf conditions or moving water. USLA believes that the best technique is the *underarm spinal stabilization technique.*

To employ the underarm stabilization technique on a face down victim, the lifeguard places both arms under the victim's armpits then, bending the elbows, places the hands, palms in, on opposite sides of the victim's head. The hands maintain the head in a neutral position while the arms stabilize the victim's shoulders against the lifeguard's chest. The lifeguard then rolls the victim laterally into a face-up position.

If the victim is already face up, the lifeguard submerges behind and underneath the victim to apply the underarm spinal stabilization technique. The lifeguard then moves backward, while surfacing, maintaining in-line stabilization.

Lifeguards should determine if water conditions are favorable for securing the victim onto a backboard while in the water. To do so requires at least two lifeguards. In-line stabilization should be maintained at all times. The second lifeguard (the assistant) first applies a cervical collar as per medical protocol. Next, the backboard is submerged and placed under the victim, gently allowing it to rise and support the victim's back. A floating backboard is particularly useful in these cases. The victim is then fastened to the board according to current medical protocol. Finally, the head immobilizer is applied and the victim is removed from the water on the backboard.

If the victim must be removed from the water prior to applying the backboard, due to surf conditions or other immediate problems, the initial rescuer maintains in-line stabilization using the underarm spinal stabilization method. The assisting rescuer then faces the victim and primary rescuer while taking a position at the victim's feet. The assisting rescuer gently but firmly grasps the victim under both knees while maintaining a position between the victim's legs. Both rescuers then stand, lift the victim, and carry the victim to dry sand. Extreme caution must be exercised in breaking surf. The assisting rescuer must maintain a position close to the primary rescuer to help keep the spine of the victim in a secure position along the primary rescuer's sternum and abdomen.

If possible, the victim should be placed directly on a spine board after removal from the water. If there is insufficient staff or equipment to accomplish this, the victim can be placed on reasonably flat sand. In either case, the following maneuver should be used:

1) On the count of three, both lifeguards slowly kneel down on the sand or over the backboard keeping the relative position of the victim secure. The assistant straightens the victim's legs on the sand or board.

2) The assistant then stands or kneels *very carefully* over the victim with one foot or knee on each side near the victim's waist. When ready, the assistant then takes over stabilization of the victim's head, with one hand on either side to hold it in a neutral position.

3) Once the initial lifeguard's hands are free, this lifeguard slowly slides the hands down to the armpits of the victim, avoiding any movement of the victim's shoulders.

4) On the count of three, the victim's upper body is gradually lowered to the backboard or the sand, while keeping the head in a neutral position.

SINGLE LIFEGUARD HEAD SPLINT ROLL

When a solo lifeguard is confronted with a possible spinal injury victim lying face down (prone) in shallow water, the victim will have to be rolled into a supine position. How this is done depends on the victim's physical condition and local environmental factors, such as water depth. One of the best methods to accomplish this is the single rescuer head splint roll.

To execute this roll, the lifeguard first extends the victim's arms over the victim's head. The victim's upper arms provide longitudinal stability to the head and neck with gently sideward pressure. Thus the term head splint. Next, while grasping the victim's wrist in one hand and maintaining upward overhead pressure, the lifeguard's other hand is placed on the victim's hip. With extreme care, the victim can now be gently rolled toward the lifeguard in a supine position.

Having successfully accomplished the head splint roll, the lifeguard moves to the head of the patient and maintains the head and neck in-line, while monitoring ABCs. Barring any further complications, the lifeguard remains in this position until additional assistance arrives.

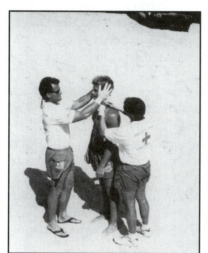

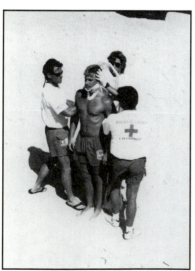

STANDING BACKBOARD

Many of the spinal injuries lifeguards encounter involve victims who walk up complaining of neck or back injury sustained during water recreation. Recognition and immobilization are of extreme importance to minimize further injury. Lifeguards should not assume that, because the victim is able to walk, there is no serious injury to the spinal column. There may well be injuries which could cause immediate, irreparable harm through one inadvertent movement. The victim should not be allowed to lie down or sit. The lifeguard moves to the rear of the victim and uses the hands to stabilize the head and neck, meanwhile reassuring the victim that this is a necessary procedure and possible catastrophic injury could occur if proper neck and back precautions are not taken.

An assistant is summoned to apply a properly fitted cervical stabilization collar while the head and neck are immobilized. The assistant then slides a backboard between the victim and the initial responder. The initial responder's elbows must be raised to approximately shoulder height to allow positioning of the backboard, while stabilization is maintained on the head and neck. A second assistant is then utilized. The two assistants stand facing the victim on opposite sides. They grasp opposite sides of the backboard with one hand by reaching under and through the victim's armpit area. The outside hand of each assistant holds one of the victim's arms. The victim is then lowered toward the lifeguard at the victim's head, while that lifeguard pivots the hands to maintain head and neck stabilization throughout the lowering process. Once the victim

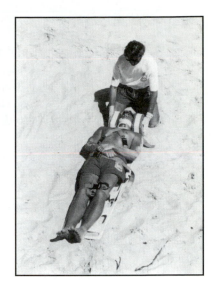

Photographic credit: Mike Hensler

has been lowered to the ground, normal backboard protocol is implemented.

SPECIAL CONSIDERATIONS

In developing a standard of care for emergency medical treatment, lifeguard agencies must consider several factors that may have a legal bearing on care provided by lifeguards.

CARE BEYOND TRAINING

Each lifeguard agency should set limits on the emergency medical care that lifeguards are authorized to provide depending on local laws and policies. The provision and use of any medical or rescue equipment should be restricted to those lifeguards who have received training in its use and who are specifically authorized to do so.

DUTY TO ACT AND ABANDONMENT

Because lifeguards are appropriately considered by the public to be knowledgeable in emergency medical care, visitors will look to lifeguards for advice and treatment. Lifeguards are considered to have a duty to act. Even when the lifeguard is confused or unsure about a particularly complicated injury or illness, it is important to follow through by carrying out the basic steps of care based on the lifeguard's level of training. In such situations, lifeguards should remember the medical credo, "do no harm," as a reminder to be conservative and deliberate.

Once treatment for an injury has begun, it should not be stopped until the situation is controlled, the patient is turned over to a higher medical authority, or consent to treat further is denied. Once CPR has begun, for example, it should not be stopped until the patient is revived or an authorized medical authority has determined that further attempts should be terminated.

A charge of *abandonment* may be made if a bystander takes over patient care and a lifeguard acquiesces, leaving the patient in the hands of the bystander. In a major medical emergency, lifeguard personnel should maintain control of the situation until it can be turned over to the responding emergency medical service. Bystanders should be permitted to assist in providing medical aid only if qualified to do so and only under oversight of the lifeguard.

TREATING MINORS

When treating minors, the most significant concern beyond treatment is the importance of gaining parental consent. Most lifeguard agencies establish strict policies regarding notification of parents before, during, or after medical treatment. Care should not be delayed for this purpose in cases of life-threatening injuries, but parents should be contacted as soon as reasonably possible.

Release of a minor from treatment without prior notification of a parent or guardian should be avoided. This must also take into account the extent of injury. For example, if lifeguards were required to notify a parent for every stubbed toe treated, lifeguard stations would be full of minors waiting for parents. On the other hand, any intermediate level injury or above would normally necessitate parental notification prior to release of the minor to anyone other than a higher medical authority.

CONSENT

An adult has the right to refuse treatment. Exceptions may include persons who are obviously delirious or otherwise unable to make reasonable decisions. In general, an unconscious person is considered to have given *implied consent* for emergency treatment. If an apparently coherent adult declines treatment, it is best to ask the person to sign a waiver of treatment to help indemnify the lifeguard and lifeguard agency. Witness names should also be included. Most emergency medical services have special release forms that can help to absolve agencies of responsibility for refused treatment.

Parents and legal guardians can generally refuse treatment on behalf of minors, but at a certain point this may border on child abuse or negligent care. If a parent refuses treatment for a minor in obvious and serious need, it may be prudent to contact the proper authorities.

MEDICATIONS

Most lifeguard agencies have established policies prohibiting lifeguards from dispensing medications, including non-prescription remedies, even aspirin and aspirin substitutes.

MEDICAL AID EQUIPMENT

Every station where a lifeguard will be posted should have a medical aid kit containing supplies necessary for the treatment of minor wounds and injuries, as well as initial treatment of intermediate and major injuries. Such kits are usually developed and stocked based on past experience of the types of injuries which are likely

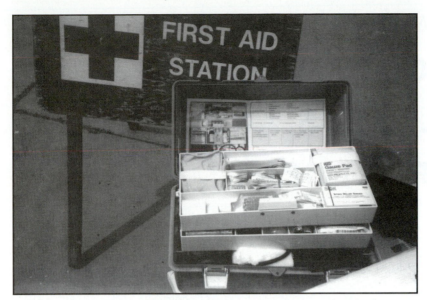

[Photographic Credit: Dan McCormick]

to be treated and the level of training of lifeguards who will use them. Pre-packaged, component type first-aid kits do not meet the needs of most lifeguard agencies, since supplies in those kits are inadequate to provide care to large numbers of beach visitors. In all first aid kits, items used in taking universal precaution should be included. For further information on universal precaution, see the chapter entitled, *Lifeguard Health and Safety*.

First aid supplies and each first aid kit should be cleaned and properly stocked at all times. It is the responsibility of the lifeguard in charge of a station to ensure that this is done at the beginning of each shift. As supplies are depleted during the day, they should be immediately restocked as necessary.

CHAPTER NINETEEN

SCUBA RELATED ILLNESS AND TREATMENT

CHAPTER HIGHLIGHTS

How Scuba Works

Decompression Illness

Symptoms of Decompression Illness

Treatment of Decompression Illness

Reporting Diving Accidents

IN THIS CHAPTER

Some very important information to convey to the receiving emergency room is the patient's dive profile. How deep and for how long? How many dives in the last 24-hours? Was there a rapid ascent? If the diver is unable to provide this information, the depth gauge on the tank or computerized dive recorder may provide it. The dive buddy is another excellent source. The lifeguard can then call the emergency room physician with this information. Since many doctors are unfamiliar with the Divers Alert Network, the lifeguard should advise the medical staff of DAN's free medical consultation services and *provide the DAN emergency telephone number.*

Divers Alert Network (DAN) 24-hour emergency hotline: (919) 684-8111

The development of modern scuba equipment has helped diving grow into one of the more widely practiced aquatic sports. Exploring the underwater environment, however, is not without risk. It is difficult to judge the actual rate of injury associated with diving because the number of participants is unknown. Estimates of the number of active scuba divers in the United States range between 1.5 and 3.5 million.[1]

The Divers Alert Network (DAN), a non-profit, membership association dedicated to the safety of recreational scuba diving, provides annual statistics based on the number of reported injuries and deaths associated with scuba diving. DAN, which is affiliated with Duke University Medical Center, collects this information primarily from hyperbaric chambers used to treat scuba-related illness. Most of the statistical information in this chapter is provided by DAN.

DAN estimates that there are over 900 cases of decompression illness suffered by U.S. scuba divers each year. In recent years, about 90 recreational scuba diving deaths per year have been reported to DAN. The annual incidence of reported recreational diving deaths appears to be holding steady but the number of decompression illness cases treated each year is rising.[2] This may be due to a higher frequency of decompression illness or increased awareness about the disease and resultant tendency to seek treatment.

Most injured divers fall between the ages of 25 and 44. Male and female risk factors appear roughly equal. Divers with less than two years experience or 20 dives make up about 40% of reported decompression illness cases.

HOW SCUBA WORKS

Scuba divers breath air which is compressed in two different ways. First, large amounts of air (not pure oxygen) are pushed into a scuba tank by a mechanical air compressor. This increases the air capacity of the tank. A regulator with a hose and mouthpiece attached is then used to breathe air from the tank. The regulator reduces the pressure of the compressed air in the tank to a safe level that will not damage the lungs.

When air is made available through the regulator during a dive, it is inhaled at a pressure consistent with the depth of the dive. This is because as a diver descends,

A regular scuba tank with regulator, and a smaller tank used by lifeguards for rapid search and recovery in shallow water. [Photographic Credit: Mike Hensler]

the ambient (surrounding) atmospheric pressure becomes greater due to the increasing pressure of the water above. This pressure is expressed in *atmospheres.* Surface atmospheric pressure is 14.7 pounds per square inch (psi). This is known as one atmosphere of pressure. For every 33 feet a diver descends, an additional atmosphere of pressure is added. Therefore, a diver at 33 feet experiences two atmospheres of pressure, at 66 feet three atmospheres, at 99 feet four atmospheres, and so on.

As pressure increases, the volume of a given quantity of air decreases. For example, if a bubble of air at the water's surface were taken to two atmospheres (33 feet in depth), it would be reduced to one half its surface volume; at three atmospheres, one third its surface volume; at four atmospheres, one quarter its surface volume; and so on.[3]

A diver at a depth of 33 feet can inflate the lungs normally by breathing through a properly functioning regulator, but the air is still compressed to one half the volume it would have on the surface. If this diver were to hold a breath while rapidly ascending to the surface, the volume of air in the lungs would double.[4] Therefore, while the regulator reduces the pressure of air from the scuba tank to a comfortable, breathable level, air breathed below the surface remains compressed compared to what its volume would be on the surface.

DECOMPRESSION ILLNESS

Decompression illness occurs when gases dissolved in body tissues produce bubbles as the diver ascends to the surface, or at some point in time after the dive. There are two types of decompression illness: decompression sickness (DCS) and arterial gas embolism (AGE). Decompression sickness comprises about 90% of reported diver illness cases, with the remaining 10% involving AGE.

Decompression sickness, often called *the bends,* involves changes to nitrogen in the body. Nitrogen makes up about 79% of the air we breathe and is carried through the bloodstream as a normal process of circulation. The increased pressure during diving causes an increase in nitrogen content of body tissues. If a diver ascends too rapidly to allow for the gradual release of nitrogen, gas bubbles can form in the bloodstream and body tissues which can then inhibit normal circulation. Decompression sickness most often occurs in dives below 80 feet and is strongly associated with repetitive, deep, and prolonged dives.

Dive tables were created many years ago by the U.S. government to help scuba divers avoid decompression sickness. Through calculations based on these tables, divers can determine the number of dives they can make safely in a day, or if in-water decompression stops must be made while ascending from various depths. These stops are intended to allow the release of nitrogen from the tissues before it produces bubbles. This is known as off-gassing. Many divers now use small computerized gauges which make the dive table calculations automatically and more accurately. Over half of the diving accident cases reported to the Divers Alert Network involve dives which did not follow the dive tables.

Arterial gas embolism (AGE), also known as air embolism, occurs when compressed air is trapped in the alveoli—the small sacs in the lungs where exchange of carbon dioxide and oxygen take place. AGE most often results from a rapid ascent when the diver runs low on air or out of air.[5] In a panicked ascent, divers sometimes hold their breath, which closes the airway and allows expanding gas to over-inflate lung tissue. The expanding gas causes rupture of the alveoli, forcing air bubbles into the lung tissue and the arterial bloodstream.

AGE cases can happen at any depth. Cases have been reported in as shallow as four feet of water. In recent years, the percentage of AGE cases have been declining. DAN believes that this is due to slower ascent rates, better training, safety stops near the surface before exiting the water, and possibly the practice of spending the last minutes of the dive near the surface where divers are less likely to run out of air.[6]

SYMPTOMS OF DECOMPRESSION ILLNESS

Onset of symptoms of decompression sickness (DCS) is usually somewhat gradual, although they may be present immediately upon surfacing. They include, in particular, pain in the joints and numbness. This is often described as a dull ache, perhaps slowly getting worse. Pain is most often felt first in the joints, such as elbows and knees. Other frequently reported symptoms are dizziness, headache, extreme fatigue, weakness, nausea, visual disturbance, and difficulty in walking.

Divers tend to deny symptoms of DCS, which delays treatment. DAN reports that only 25% to 30% request assistance within four hours after symptom onset. This is a critical issue in treatment of decompression sickness because the longer the delay in providing proper treatment, the greater the likelihood of long-term complications which are not fully resolved.[7] For this reason, even a slight hint of decompression illness symptoms should be taken very seriously by the lifeguard, and transport to the hospital should be strongly encouraged.

Onset of symptoms of AGE is typically more rapid than those of DCS. They can be immediate and extreme. A diver who suddenly loses consciousness upon surfacing should be assumed to have AGE.[8] Symptoms similar to an acute stroke can be one of the most serious results of AGE.[9] These cases usually involve a dive profile with a very rapid ascent. DAN reports that 50% or more of AGE cases requested assistance within four hours.

TREATMENT OF DECOMPRESSION ILLNESS

Lifeguards need not spend extensive amounts of time deciding whether a diving case involves DCS or AGE. Both can be very serious. If either are suspected, the victim should be treated for ABCs, given *high flow oxygen,* and transported to an emergency room under the care of trained ambulance personnel.

At one time, emergency responders were taught to place divers in a radical head down position, perhaps on their side. *This is no longer recommended* and may actually worsen the problem.[10] Instead the patient should be transported supine.

Full resolution of a decompression illness generally requires treatment in a recompression chamber. The recompression chamber allows the patient to be artificially returned to an atmospheric pressure consistent with the dive profile, which facilitates a reversal of the problems associated with rapid ascent. The patient is then slowly reintroduced to normal surface air pressure.

Recompression chambers are not always readily available near a diving accident site. Even if a recompression chamber is nearby, it may be in use for other medical reasons. Therefore, it is important to notify the nearest recompression chamber as early as possible when a diver presents symptoms of a decompression illness. In addition, transport by helicopter may be necessary, depending on proximity of the recompression chamber. The aircraft should be pressurized or kept below 1,000 feet.[11]

Some very important information to convey to the receiving emergency room is the patient's dive profile. How deep and for how long? How many dives in the last 24-hours? Was there a rapid ascent? If the diver is unable to provide this information, the depth gauge on the tank or computerized dive recorder may provide it. The dive buddy is another excellent source. The lifeguard can then call the emergency room physician with this information. Since many doctors are unfamiliar with the Divers Alert Network, the lifeguard should advise the medical staff of DAN's free medical consultation services and *provide the DAN emergency telephone number.*

A diver with decompression illness symptoms who refuses treatment should be advised to seek further medical assistance if there is any worsening of symptoms. One other important consideration in a decompression illness case is the dive buddy. If two divers have followed similar dive profiles and one exhibits complications, the other should be carefully checked. Even if symptoms are not readily apparent, they may appear within a short period of time.

REPORTING DIVING ACCIDENTS

The Divers Alert Network maintains a 24-hour medical emergency hotline. This hotline provides injured divers and medical aid providers with expert consultation and referrals. The DAN emergency hotline number is (919) 684-8111. DAN also maintains an information hotline to provide answers to commonly asked questions about scuba diving medicine and safety. This number, (919) 684-2948, is answered 9 a.m. to 5 p.m. Eastern Time on regular business days.

All scuba diving accidents should be reported to DAN. This allows DAN to produce information aimed at increasing diver safety. A report form is included in Appendix C.

Lifeguards and lifeguard agencies are encouraged to join DAN and help support this organization. Oxygen training courses are also available through DAN for emergency medical personnel. Membership and training information is available by writing to Divers Alert Network, Box 3823, Duke University Medical Center, Durham, North Carolina 27710.

1   Dovenbarger, J.A., ed; *1992 Report on Diving Accidents and Fatalities,* Divers Alert Network, Duke University Medical Center, Durham, North Carolina

2   Ibid.

3   *PADI Open Water Dive Manual,* 1988, PADI, Santa Ana, California

4   Ibid.

5   Dovenbarger, J.A., ed; *1992 Report on Diving Accidents and Fatalities,* Divers Alert Network, Duke University Medical Center, Durham, North Carolina

6   Dovenbarger, J.A., Director of Medical Services, Divers Alert Network. Personal communication to the Editor dated September 9, 1994 (cover letter from Donna Uguccioni, M.S.)

7   Dovenbarger, J.A., ed; *1992 Report on Diving Accidents and Fatalities,* Divers Alert Network, Duke University Medical Center, Durham, North Carolina

8   Kizer, Kenneth W., Undersea Emergencies: Treating Barotrauma and the Bends, *The Physician and Sportsmedicine,* August 1992, 20, 8

9   Ibid.

10 Ibid.

11 Ibid.

CHAPTER TWENTY

LIFEGUARD HEALTH AND SAFETY

Chapter Highlights

Skin Protection

Eye Protection

Selecting Sunglasses

Ear Protection

Infection Control

Physical Conditioning

In This Chapter

Skin cancer can kill, and has killed lifeguards, *even at a young age.* If caught early enough, the deadly forms of skin cancer usually can be removed and their spread often stopped, so lifeguards should have regular screenings for skin cancer, at least once a year.

SKIN PROTECTION

The warm rays of the sun serve as a major attraction to beach users, but the sun's rays can be dangerous, even life threatening. Every year tens of thousands of people contract skin cancer. Sometimes, surgical procedures can be employed to remove the growths but in other cases, medical procedures are unsuccessful and death eventually results. Skin cancer can kill, and has killed lifeguards, *even at a young age.*

Lifeguards are particularly vulnerable to sun related problems because of the high levels of exposure they sustain and because of the strength of the suns rays at the beach. Reflection off the water and sand can triple the intensity of the sun's rays. The most serious threat to both the skin and eyes comes from the ultraviolet (UV) component of sunlight. There are two types of UV light which normally reach the earth—UV-A and UV-B. UV-B has a shorter wavelength and appears to be the primary cause of sunburn. Most of the early sunscreens were aimed solely at UV-B protection. UV-A, long thought to be the harmless tanning rays, is now recognized as presenting hazards similar to UV-B, although the effects may be realized more gradually.[1]

Despite claims to the contrary by some sunscreen manufacturers, there is no such thing as a safe tan. Even gradual tanning damages the skin. Exposure to UV rays adequate to produce tanning or burning actually harms the skin at the cellular level, causing direct injury to DNA. As the body begins a process of trying to repair the damage, it produces melanin, a protective pigment which darkens (tans) the skin.[2] Most people's bodies can partially repair the damage; but the repair is never complete and long term injury accumulates over the years.[3] Skin exposed to the sun ages at a significantly accelerated rate.

Generally, people with darker skin pigmentation are better protected from sunburn than those with lighter skin. Darker skin, however, only provides increased protection, not complete immunity from sun related skin damage.[4]

Skin cancer, the most common of all cancers, is widely believed to be associated with sun exposure and the damage to DNA. The number of office visits to physicians for skin cancer has increased by more than 50% since 1970.[5] There are three main types — melanoma, squamous-cell carcinoma, and basal-cell carcinoma.

Melanoma is the deadliest form of skin cancer and one of the most deadly of all cancers. If left untreated for an extended period, the cure rate is very low. Squamous-cell carcinoma can also kill. Basal-cell carcinoma is the least threatening of the three and usually can be removed during an office visit to a physician. If caught early enough, the deadly forms of skin cancer usually can be removed and their spread often stopped, so lifeguards should have regular screenings for skin cancer, at least once a year.

SKIN CANCER SYMPTOMS

The following are some symptoms of skin cancer which should be evaluated by a physician:
• An existing mole which enlarges irregularly or takes on a notched border
• Red, blue, or white areas in a mole
• Itching or bleeding in a mole
• The appearance of a new mole in an adult
• A scaly or crusty raised area
• Raised hard red bumps with a translucent quality to their surface

Many experts believe that sunscreen, if properly applied, helps to prevent skin cancer. Whether or not sunscreen helps prevent cancer, sunscreen can clearly help to *avoid* sunburn and *reduce* the damage caused by exposure to the sun.

In an effort to describe the level of protection offered by different sunscreens, the *sun protection factor* (SPF) was developed. The theory of SPF is that a person who properly applies a sunscreen with an SPF of 15, for example, should be able to stay in the sun 15 times as long as if no sunscreen is worn and still receive about the same amount of skin damage. Lifeguards of all skin types should use a sunscreen with an SPF of at least 15. Beyond SPF 30, however, the value of increasing SPFs appears to be negligible.[6]

While most sunscreens are aimed at UV-B protection, some claim to provide UV-A protection also, and it appears that most will do so soon. Lifeguards would be wise to select a sunscreen with both UV-A and UV-B protection.

A concern of some dermatologists is that sunscreen may create an air of permissiveness about sun exposure. By using sunscreen, many people seem to believe they eliminate damage from the sun's rays and therefore do not have to worry about sun exposure. This may make them more likely to stay out in the sun. The reality is that there is damage to the skin even with sunscreen. The damage is simply less than it would be without any sunscreen.

An excellent protection from the sun is the wearing of tightly knit, opaque clothing and wide brimmed hats. More advanced lifeguard agencies require their lifeguards to wear shirts and hats to help protect them from the sun.

Choosing a waterproof sunscreen is highly recommended for lifeguards. These sunscreens are formulated to stay on after repeated submersion in the water. Even so, lifeguards should reapply sunscreen several times each day.

Sunscreen should be applied to dry skin 15 to 30 minutes before sun exposure. It should be used even on cloudy days because up to 80% of UV rays penetrate clouds. Attention should be paid to ensuring an even distribution over all exposed areas. Particular heed should be paid to the lips, ears, nose, shoulders, and head, since these areas are highly susceptible to burning.

EYE PROTECTION

Keen eyesight is essential to lifeguards and the swimmers they watch over. Unfortunately, eyesight can be seriously damaged by sun exposure. With proper protective steps however, the chances of eye damage can be significantly reduced. Serious eye problems associated with sun exposure include:
- *Cataracts*—A clouding of the lens of the eye
- *Macular Degeneration*—Loss of central vision
- *Photokeratitis*—Damage to the cornea of the eye from exposure to intense light
- *Pterygium*—A callous-like growth that can spread over the white of the eye

Cataracts and macular degeneration generally occur over a period of years and primarily affect people later in life. They can cause full or partial blindness and require surgery. Pterygiums, caused by exposure to sun, wind, and dust, occur over a period of years and are often sustained by lifeguards. These three conditions typically require surgery. Photokeratitis can develop shortly after overexposure to intense UV light and can be very painful. Recovery occurs over several days and sometimes requires bandaging the eyes.[7]

One study has found that those who do not protect their eyes from the sun triple the risk of developing cataracts. Therefore it is clearly important to protect the eyes at all times. The best way to do so is through use of good quality (not necessarily high cost) sunglasses. The use of umbrellas, hats, and visors can also be of help. A wide brimmed hat reduces the amount of UV rays reaching the eyes by as much as 50%.[8]

SELECTING SUNGLASSES

Lifeguards need not pay high prices to purchase good quality sunglasses. Many inexpensive sunglasses offer very high quality protection. Price appears to be more directly related to marketing decisions and style considerations. In selecting sunglasses, lifeguards would be well advised to discount claims indicating that the product meets some sort of national standard. Federal and industry standards have been criticized over the years as being too low.

USLA Buying Guide for Sunglasses

Feature	Recommendation
UVA Protection	99–100%
UVB Protection	99–100%
Blue Light Spectrum Protection	Highly recommended
Optical Material	Optical Quality Glass or Polycarbonate
Lens Color	Brown, Grey, or Amber Recommended
Screening of Visible Light	75–95%
Meets FDA Breakage Requirement	Required
Polarized	Highly recommended
Wrap Around Style	Highly recommended

The most important thing to look for in sunglasses is protection from UV-A and UV-B rays. Considering the high exposure of the lifeguard's eyes to intense sunlight, lifeguards should insist on sunglasses which filter out 99 to 100 percent of both UV-A and UV-B light.

UV protection is unrelated to darkness (tint) of the glasses. Even eye glasses with no tint can be manufactured to provide full protection from UV light. However, wearing dark glasses that do not screen UV rays can actually cause more damage than not wearing glasses at all, since the screening of visible light causes the pupils to dilate, letting in more UV rays.

Another part of the light spectrum, blue light, has also been associated with some forms of eye injury. Sunglasses which block blue light would be a good choice. The best lens colors for blocking blue light are believed to be gray, brown, or amber.[9] Blue lenses should be avoided.[10]

Choose sunglasses of an adequate tint to allow observation of the water and sand without squinting on days with bright sunlight. Those that block between 75 and 95% of visible light are probably a good choice. One rule of thumb is that if the eyes can be seen when looking in a mirror, the glasses are probably not dark enough. Obviously though, this can be taken to extremes. There is a need to be able to see clearly and if the glasses are too dark, vision may be inhibited.

Good quality lenses are generally made of high quality optical glass or polycarbonate. Optical glass is more distortion free and resistant to scratching than polycarbonate, but glass is heavier and usually more costly. Choose a design that covers as much of the area around the eyes as possible without affecting peripheral vision. This helps protect from side light, as well as from the blowing sand that contributes to formation of pterygiums. Make sure the lenses pass the FDA requirement for breakage.

Polarized sunglasses dramatically reduce reflected glare—a major problem for lifeguards trying to watch a swim crowd. Lifeguards are well advised to select polarized sunglasses to help reduce eye fatigue and improve observation.

EAR PROTECTION

Chronic irritation and inflammation of the external ear is a frequent problem for lifeguards and other swimmers. The most common afflictions are known as swimmer's ear and surfer's ear. The causes are similar. In both cases, the inner ear becomes infected.

A healthy external ear canal is coated with earwax. This wax not only forms a water-repellent coating, it also contains antimicrobial substances. Unfortunately, continual contact with the water washes earwax away, removing the protection. This problem is exacerbated when people stick fingers or other items in the ear to remove water, scraping away the earwax.

Ocean swimmers, particularly surfers, are believed to have twice the ear problems of pool swimmers.[11] This is because the roiling ocean environment can cause sand and other debris to enter the ear canal. Bony growths (exostoses) within the ear canal can develop from prolonged exposure to cold water and wind. These further trap debris. In attempting to remove this debris, the lifeguard can traumatize the ear canal.

The most common symptoms of these afflictions are pain, inflammation, and itching. Hearing loss may be experienced in some cases and there can be discharge from the ear.[12] Lifeguards with these symptoms should see a doctor.

Prevention of ear problems primarily involves keeping the ear canal dry and clean. Standard wax earplugs are not a good choice. Instead, use silicone earplugs.[13] Wearing tight fitting swim caps and wetsuit hoods can help reduce cold water-induced injury and debris impaction. After swimming, tilting the head and jumping vigorously, as well as gently drying the outer ear with a towel are helpful. Lifeguards should make every effort to avoid reaching into the ear with anything. Physicians can recommend drying agents, as well as cleaning agents that help remove impacted debris.

INFECTION CONTROL

Infection of a health care worker through exposure to the body fluids of another person (known as cross-infection) is very rare. Nonetheless, it can occur, particularly through exposure to blood and oral secretions. These secretions can carry pathogens—agents, particularly living microorganisms, which cause disease. Whenever medical aid is rendered by a lifeguard, contact with the victim's bodily fluids is possible and in some cases it is likely. The best way to avoid infection from bloodborne pathogens that the victim may be carrying is to employ universal precaution.

A lifeguard wearing universal protection including eye protection, gown, mask, and gloves. [Photographic Credit: William McNeely, Jr.]

Universal precaution is an approach to infection control. According to the concept of universal precaution, all human blood and certain human bodily fluids are treated as if known to be infectious for human immunodeficiency virus (HIV), hepatitis B virus (HBV), and other bloodborne pathogens.[14]

Lifeguard exposure is most likely during treatment of open, bleeding wounds and during resuscitation attempts using mouth-to-mouth techniques. Mouth-to-mouth resuscitation provides an enhanced exposure to bodily fluids and sometimes blood. The most effective way to avoid this exposure and to provide the best possible resuscitation is through use of a mechanical resuscitator or a bag-valve-mask (BVM) device. Unfortunately, such equipment is not always available at the moment a drowning victim is recovered or a person collapses from a heart attack. For these circumstances, the so-called one-way mask is an alternative.

The one-way mask is placed over a non-breathing patient's breathing passage, allowing the lifeguard to perform resuscitation while avoiding contact with the patient's breathing passage, saliva, regurgitant, or blood. Many such masks are equipped with special ports to allow resuscitation supported by supplemental oxygen. At some agencies, masks are issued to all lifeguards. They are required to have these items with them at all times while on duty. Special cases have been developed which allow attachment of resuscitation masks to RFDs.

GENERAL RECOMMENDATIONS ON EXPOSURE

During Water Rescue Of a Bleeding Victim
- Avoid contact with the victim if possible.
- Avoid contact with bleeding areas when removing the victim from the water.
- Wash off any blood as soon as possible.
- During in-water resuscitation attempts, wash any blood or body fluids away from the victim's mouth before contact. The rescuers mouth should be washed out after contact.
- If possible, move the victim to dry sand to prevent further in-water exposure.

During Medical Treatment Of a Victim Ashore
- Assume that all blood and bodily fluid is infected and treat it as such.
- Use mechanical ventilation whenever possible.
- Use disposable resuscitation masks with a system that prevents body fluids from passing through the mask.
- Use oxygen delivery systems with disposable masks whenever possible.
- Wear occlusive gloves for handling bleeding victims.
- If the victim is bleeding profusely, especially from an artery, wear a mask, goggles, and an occlusive gown in addition to occlusive gloves.
- Wash the hands with soap and water after contacting blood, even if gloves are worn.
- Clean up blood and body fluids on equipment with a germicide containing household bleach and then air dry. Wear gloves while performing this task. Place used blades and needles in a disposable, puncture-proof container.
- A course of hepatitis B vaccine is recommended for all health care providers who may be at risk for exposure. Hepatitis B immune globulin may be indicated after a documented exposure.

When Infected Items Are Found On The Beach
- Remove the items using universal precaution.
- Dispose of the items in a manner which avoids exposure to others, consistent with agency and regulatory protocol.

In Case Of Possible Infection
- Lifeguards who are involved in contact with potentially infectious material should follow agency protocol. If no protocol exists, the lifeguard should contact a physician.
- Lifeguards exposed in a blood-to-blood inoculation with known or suspected fluids should follow agency protocol, which should include contact with a physician.

OSHA REQUIREMENTS

Under an employment rule established by the Occupational Safety and Health Administration (OSHA) in 1991, certain steps must be taken by all employers to help employees avoid cross-infection. The OSHA rule specifically states, "This section applies to all occupational exposure to blood or other potentially infectious materials... Occupational exposure means reasonably anticipated skin, eye, mucous membrane, or parenteral contact with blood or other potentially infectious materials that may result from the performance of an employee's duties."[15] Lifeguards clearly fall under the requirements of this rule. The following are some selected OSHA requirements:

- *Hepatitis B Vaccine*—The employer shall make available the hepatitis B vaccine and vaccination series to all employees who have occupational exposure. There will be no cost to the employee.
- *Protective Equipment*—The employer shall provide at no cost to the employee and make readily accessible to the employee appropriate personal protective equipment.
- *Use of Protective Equipment*—The employer shall ensure that the employee uses appropriate personal protective equipment unless the employer shows that the employee temporarily and briefly declined to use personal protective equipment due to unusual circumstances.
- *Exposure Control Plan*—Employers must establish a written Exposure Control Plan designed to eliminate or minimize employee exposure.

Copies of the most current OSHA standard on occupational exposure to bloodborne pathogens are available by contacting:

OSHA Office of Publications
U.S. Department of Labor
Room N3101
200 Constitution Avenue NW
Washington, DC 20210

The United States Lifesaving Association is closely monitoring development of procedures and techniques that can be used to minimize lifeguard exposure to bloodborne pathogens. New developments in this area are frequently described in the USLA publication, *American Lifeguard Magazine*.

PHYSICAL CONDITIONING

Lifeguarding is perhaps the most physically demanding of the emergency services. At any moment, open water lifeguards may be called on to respond over long distances and in challenging conditions, to rescue and retrieve swimmers in distress. Although equipment has been developed to assist lifeguards on these responses, superior swimming skills, sheer physical strength, and endurance can make the difference between life and death for a victim. For these reasons, the maintenance of top physical conditioning is a very important aspect of every lifeguard's responsibilities.

Advanced lifeguard agencies encourage lifeguards to maintain their physical conditioning by providing opportunities to engage in physical exercise during the

[Photographic Credit: Chris Gierlich]

working day. This, combined with the provision of workout facilities and equipment, is highly recommended as it helps foster an emphasis on the need for lifeguards to maintain high levels of conditioning. Some lifeguard agencies require participation in routine workouts. Many agencies encourage lifeguards to participate in lifeguard competitions as motivation toward maintaining physical fitness and improving rescue skills, also. Lifeguard workouts should include the following considerations:

- Lifeguards, like all athletes, should stretch muscles before using them. Proper stretching techniques include all major muscle groups in the body and should be accomplished slowly, avoiding jerking movements. Since lifeguards must be prepared for immediate response at any time, it is a good practice to stretch each morning prior to beginning work.

- Workouts should include in-water conditioning. Lifeguards cannot maintain fitness for water rescue exclusively through dry land training. Regular swimming workouts should be performed in conditions similar to those in which rescues will take place.

- Swimming rescues involve running, entry, and approach swimming. Workouts should include these skills.

- Workouts should include drills using various pieces of rescue equipment, including RFDs and rescue boards. This produces the combined benefit of physical conditioning and skill building. Rescue board launches and paddling drills should be included. If swim fins are used in rescue, they should be used in some workouts. Coaching and proper technique instruction should be emphasized in regular workouts.

- Achieving and maintaining fitness goals requires that intensity of the workout progressively increase until the goal is reached. This can be accomplished by

[Photographic Credit: Mike Hensler]

increasing the total work (swim farther) or the work rate (swim faster). Increasing intensity or distance in workouts must be done gradually as progressing too quickly can lead to overuse injuries.

• Lifeguarding requires both speed and stamina. Sprint type workouts should be combined with those designed to promote endurance.

• Lifeguard physical training should be aerobic in nature, with the emphasis on exercising the cardiovascular system.

1   Pine, Devera, FDA Consumer; *Cool Tips for a Hot Season,* June 1992, 26, 5, p20

2   Eller, Mark S. et al; Nature, December 1994, 372, 6505, p413

3   Greeley, Alexandra, Nutrition Health Review, Summer 1991, 59, p14

4   HealthFacts, *Sunscreens and Sunglasses: A Consumer's Guide,* June 1990, 15, 133, p1

5   Nightingale, Stuart L., The Journal of the American Medical Association, July 21, 1993, 270, 3, p302

6   Ibid.

7   Auerbach, Jessica, FDA Consumer, *Protecting Your Eyes from Everyday Hazards,* June 1990, 24, 5, p28

8   HealthFacts, *Sunscreens and Sunglasses: A Consumer's Guide,* June 1990, 15, 133, p1

9   Ibid.

10 Wischnia, Bob, Runner's World, *Don't Be Blinded by the Light,* June 1991, 26, 6, p74

11 Schelkun, Patrice Heinz, The Physician and Sportsmedicine, *Swimmer's Ear: Getting Patients Back in the Water,* July 1991, 19, 7, p85

12 Ibid.

13 Ibid.

14 Occupational Safety and Health Administration (OSHA), (1991), *Occupational Exposure to Bloodborne Pathogens,* 29 CFR Part 1910.1030

15 Ibid.

CHAPTER TWENTY ONE

LIFEGUARD FACILITIES AND EQUIPMENT

CHAPTER HIGHLIGHTS

Lifeguard Towers

Main Lifeguard Stations

Lifeguard Tower Equipment

Tower Preparation

Tower Maintenance

IN THIS CHAPTER

Like all emergency services, lifeguard agencies should have equipment available at an adequate level to allow a professional response to both the routine and major emergencies which can be reasonably anticipated.

Most emergency services operate from central stations—facilities designed to house the operations and equipment of the agency. This is true of police, fire fighting, and emergency medical services. Depending on their size, some agencies also maintain satellite stations. Along with providing a gathering point for personnel and material, these stations serve as contact points for people requesting service, whether in person or by telephone.

Like other emergency services, lifeguard agencies operate on the station concept by erecting lifeguard towers on beaches. Lifeguard towers serve as central points where lifeguard equipment is positioned for immediate use. Lifeguard towers are typically the most highly recognized features on a beach, often used by beach patrons as landmarks to meet each other. Beach patrons also look to the lifeguard tower for assistance, making it the focal point for summoning help.

Two veteran lifeguards watch the water from a stand on a slow day in Avon-by-the-Sea, New Jersey.

LIFEGUARD TOWERS

Lifeguard tower design varies tremendously across the United States, from small portable chairs to large, enclosed units. They may be known as stands, chairs, bird-cages, or perches. Certain features however, are common:

In Daytona Beach, Florida, lifeguard stands have wheels at the base to allow them to be continually moved in response to the wide tidal variation on this beach. **[Photographic Credit: Mike Hensler]**

- *Elevation*—Towers give lifeguards an elevated position from which they can observe their entire area of responsibility, from the water to the beach. This elevation allows the lifeguard to look down on the water, which aids in recognizing hazardous conditions, and facilitates observation of swimmers in heavily crowded swimming areas. Elevation of the tower also helps to make the station highly recognizable to beach users, should they need the assistance of a lifeguard.

- *Identification*—To assist the public in determining the status of lifeguard protection, many agencies have developed signs or symbols that are attached to lifeguard towers, indicating whether lifeguards are on duty. These signs may be locked into place when towers are closed, and include instructions for how emergency help can be summoned. It is a wise practice to devise and follow a system of notification to let beach users know when a tower is open and staffed, and when it is closed.

- *Numbering*—If there are several towers on a beach, it is recommended that they be numbered with large, easily readable numbers on all sides. This helps to pinpoint reports of emergencies, particularly those received by telephone. Offshore rescue boats or helicopters responding to an emergency can be advised to work off a tower with a certain number. If helicopters are regularly used by police or other rescue agencies in the area, the tops of the towers should also be numbered.

   Numbering can greatly reduce the number of lost children at a beach. Since most towers on a beach look alike, visitors, particularly children, can easily become confused. By numbering the towers, parents can advise their children to "meet at Tower 5" if they become separated, for example. When lost children are found on a beach equipped with a public address system, parents can be advised to claim their children at a tower of a certain number.

- *Equipment Storage*—Lifeguard equipment is normally kept at the lifeguard tower during duty hours. Tower design should, therefore, include places where equipment can be mounted or placed for immediate retrieval. While some towers require that lifeguards remove equipment for secure storage elsewhere at the end of the day, other tower designs provide secure storage within.

- *Safety*—Until recently, many agencies designed lifeguard towers thinking only of economy of construction and resistance to vandalism. Today, however, more progressive lifeguard agencies design towers with features to protect lifeguards and beach visitors from possible injury. In many areas, ramps or stairs are replacing ladders leading to observation decks, since experience has shown that lifeguards have been injured on the job by climbing up on or

A Los Angeles County lifeguard tower. [Photographic Credit: Rob McGowan]

jumping down from towers. Enclosed towers offer protection from the sun and weather while providing unobstructed views. This is extremely important for two reasons. First, lifeguards exposed to the elements for long periods of time experience a reduction in their level of alertness that can adversely impact on safety. Second, as the chapter on *Lifeguard Health and Safety* shows, sun and wind exposure is a very real physical hazard for lifeguards.

- *Color*—Lifeguard towers should be of a color that is immediately recognizable to the public as a lifeguard facility. Consistent coloring is best. This is particularly important in an urban environment where the lifeguard station may tend to blend in with other buildings. Lifeguards sometimes forget that many beach visitors are there for the first time and, in an emergency, need to know immediately where to go. Some agencies mark their towers with the simple words, "Lifeguard Tower."

MAIN LIFEGUARD STATIONS

While many smaller lifeguard agencies operate exclusively from moveable towers or stands, larger lifeguard agencies typically utilize permanent towers on their beaches, often referred to as main stations. These large, multi-story structures are usually located at the beach or bay front, with direct access to the water area they serve. They may incorporate administrative staff offices, central communication and reception areas, first aid and recovery rooms, locker and shower facilities, training rooms, maintenance shops, vehicle and equipment storage areas, meeting and training rooms, and kitchen facilities.

A main lifeguard station with offices, locker rooms, and an observation deck.
[Photographic Credit: Rob McGowan]

Under the Tower Zero system of water surveillance (see the description of coverage systems in the chapter entitled *Water Surveillance*), the main station includes an observation deck which is the first observation point staffed on the beach and the last to close. This system provides considerable operational efficiency, since the Tower Zero station can have telephone or radio contact with other towers, vehicles, and boats, while the lofty observation platform allows a commanding view of the entire beach area.

LIFEGUARD TOWER EQUIPMENT

At each beach where lifeguards will be assigned to the protection of swimmers, emergency equipment must be readily available. Like all emergency services, lifeguard agencies must provide emergency equipment at an adequate level to allow a professional response to both the routine and major emergencies which can be reasonably anticipated. The items listed below should normally be provided at all beaches. Lifeguard agencies with advanced responsibilities will need additional equipment.

- RFDs for all assigned personnel
- Mask, snorkel, and swim fins
- Rescue board
- Rescue boat
- Boat tow
- Basic medical aid equipment
- Spinal immobilization device
- Oxygen
- Positive pressure resuscitation device
- Posted hours of operation
- Clipboard and report forms
- Logbook
- Communication equipment for outside assistance
- Equipment for lifeguard to lifeguard communication
- Equipment for signaling the public
- Binoculars
- Marker buoy—used for a missing swimmer
- Medical waste and sharps container
- Equipment for universal precaution

TOWER PREPARATION

At the beginning of each workday or shift, it is important that lifeguards make a thorough check of all equipment. Each agency should develop its own checklist for setting up the tower, including the following recommended points:

- As the lifeguard enters the beach area, an immediate scan of the water is made for any signs of trouble. This scan is repeated once the tower is staffed.
- The tower is checked for any damage or vandalism, which is reported immediately.
- The tower is unlocked and equipment is readied. The first piece of equipment prepared for use is the lifeguard's RFD.
- The tower is opened for service. Shutters may be removed or raised. Flags may be raised or changed. Any "Off-Duty" signs are secured or stowed.
- Communication equipment is checked to see that it is functioning properly. Radio checks are made. If telephones are installed, checks include calls to dispatch centers followed by a call-back to ensure that the telephone works in both directions.
- Lifeguard equipment is carefully checked and deployed. Each piece of equipment should be inspected for damage, wear, or improper maintenance. Once

Lifeguard station with off-duty sign on shuttered windows. [Photographic Credit: Paul Drucker]

Lifeguard station with shutters removed, prepared for the day. [Photographic Credit: Paul Drucker]

inspected, equipment is placed in pre-determined positions for immediate retrieval and use, if needed.

- Medical aid gear and supplies are checked and deployed. Shortages of supplies are reported immediately so that they can be replaced. Oxygen tank pressure must be checked.

- Supplies of report forms are checked. Completed forms that have not been turned in are submitted. Lifeguards ensure that there are suitable writing implements available. The lifeguard log is started for the day. This includes a record of the time the station is opened and closed and the personnel on duty.

- If provided, tower bulletin boards are checked and brought up-to-date with information that may include tide times and water/air temperature. Supplies of public education materials are checked.

- If boats or vehicles are used, they are thoroughly inspected. Motorboats and vehicles are checked for gas, oil, and other fluids as well as any unusual wear and tear.

[Photographic Credit: Dave Foxwell]

- Finally, the tower is checked for cleanliness. Personal gear is neatly stowed. If necessary, runways formed of cones or rope may be placed to dissuade beach visitors from settling immediately in front of the tower.

At some agencies, checklists for setting up the station must be followed by each lifeguard, regardless of the number of employees assigned to a station. In areas where lifeguards work in shifts, agencies may require that second shift employees complete the checklist even though the same checklist was completed by a lifeguard on a previous shift. This ensures that in an emergency, all necessary equipment is fully prepared and readily available. There is nothing worse than needing oxygen for a critically injured patient, for example, and finding that all oxygen cylinders are empty.

TOWER MAINTENANCE

During the workday, lifeguards must remember that the lifeguard tower is a public safety facility and treat it as such. The maintenance of a lifeguard tower will reflect on the quality of service provided by the lifeguard agency. An agency that keeps well-organized and clean stations will be perceived by the public as an efficient, professional organization. Dirty, cluttered, and disorganized stations will have the opposite effect.

Lifeguards must work to keep their stations tidy throughout the workday. This may include sweeping or washing the tower at regular intervals. Clothes and other personal items should not be hung or draped on or about the tower. During periods of low beach attendance, maintenance may include minor repairs to towers and rescue equipment.

CHAPTER TWENTY TWO

COMMUNICATION METHODS

CHAPTER HIGHLIGHTS

Communication Goals

Electronic Communication

The 9-1-1 System

IN THIS CHAPTER

Electronic communication has become a standard for professional lifeguard services in the United States. As the cost of portable, two-way radios has dropped, most lifeguard services have acquired these tools, or have plans to do so.

A fundamental measure of any emergency service is its ability to communicate quickly, efficiently, and effectively in a wide variety of conditions. It is the nature of lifeguard services that personnel are spread over large areas as they monitor and respond to problems in the beach environment. This creates a challenge for communication which must be met.

COMMUNICATION GOALS

All lifeguard services should have the capability of communicating effectively in the following three areas:
- *Communication among lifeguards*—Communication among lifeguards is an integral aspect of two of the three points of a rescue. During the *recognize and respond* portion of a rescue, the alert to others requires immediate, effective communication. During the *signal and save* portion, the first step is a signal to other lifeguards indicating if further assistance will be needed. Effective communication is essential during periods of emergency response, for maintaining

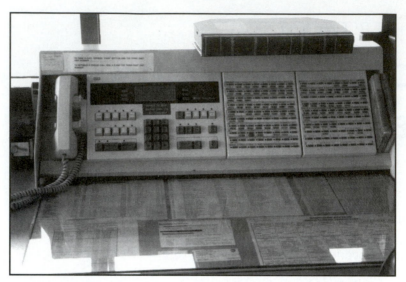

Main switchboard for incoming calls in Los Angeles County. [Photographic Credit: Rob McGowan]

effective coverage of supervised areas during normal operations, and for routine business in a work environment where lifeguards must be constantly spread out.

- *Communication with the public*—Lifeguards must have the ability to pass information efficiently and understandably to beach visitors in order to provide directions during emergencies or approaching bad weather, to move people out of dangerous areas (preventive lifeguarding), to help locate missing persons, and to provide important information about general beach conditions.

- *Communication with outside agencies*—Each lifeguard service must be able to communicate effectively with other emergency services, including neighboring lifeguard agencies, police, fire, rescue, and emergency medical services. In some areas, other services may be of use, such as the U.S. Coast Guard and any other source of rescue helicopters. For routine communication, lifeguards may need to contact animal control providers, tow trucks, child welfare workers, and so on.

COMMUNICATION TOOLS

There are three basic types of communication systems used by lifeguard agencies across the United States. The type of communication systems in use depends largely on available funds for communication equipment and conditions under which communication is necessary. Many agencies incorporate more than one of the following system types.

ELECTRONIC COMMUNICATION

The most effective form of routine and emergency communication is electronic communication. Electronic communication systems include two-way radio systems, telephones, and public address systems. Effective electronic communication systems allow for the transmission of a message over long distances with full clarity.

Two-Way Radio Systems

Two-way radios are rapidly replacing whistles, flags, and other traditional forms of lifeguard communication. As the cost of portable, two-way radios has dropped, most lifeguard services have acquired these tools, or have plans to do so. There are several reasons why two-way radios are a highly desirable tool for lifeguard communications. Like the telephone, the two-way radio allows for normal conversation to take place over a long distance. While flags or whistles may allow some limited

Lifeguard uses a portable radio for communication.
[Photographic Credit: Mike Hensler]

information to be transmitted over line of sight or audible range, the two-way radio can normally transmit well beyond this range and lifeguards using a two-way radio system can be very specific about their needs.

Unlike the telephone, when a lifeguard must leave the stand to provide a medical aid or warning to a beach visitor, the two-way radio allows a lifeguard to stay in communication at all times, and able to request specific forms of backup if a problem develops. Mobile communication is also helpful for supervisory personnel who can direct operations from a distance based on information provided.

A radio frequency serves as a constant conference call whereby all members of the organization are immediately made aware of a message and can respond at will. For example, if a lifeguard sends a rescue alert, all adjacent lifeguards with radios are immediately made aware of this, as are backup resources. Attention is immediately directed to the area of need.

Larger lifeguard agencies have several radio channels available, allowing for routine business level communication which does not impact adversely on the main, emergency channel. In major emergencies, communication can be shifted to a side or "tactical" channel so that the main channel is not tied up with radio traffic that prevents routine backup.

The most effective radio systems include the ability to converse with other local emergency service providers. This can be of tremendous benefit in emergencies, allowing direct communication with responding resources and continual updates. It is particularly useful when the incident command system is invoked. Very inexpensive radios are available which allow direct communication with Coast Guard resources and private vessels.

The effective use of lifeguard rescue boats requires accessibility to direct communication with lifeguards ashore. Equipment has been developed which allows hand-held radios to be placed in watertight pouches for use on smaller boats. Some of these pouches even allow submersion of the radio without damage. Larger boats are normally outfitted with mobile radios designed for vehicles.

Some lifeguards use "codes" while speaking on the radio. Many people are aware of the radio code "10-4," which generally means an acknowledgment of a message received. This is one of the 10 codes, so-called because they start with the number 10. There are many others which vary from agency to agency and from state to state.

The concept of codes is two-fold. First, they can replace oft used phrases, thereby reducing the amount of time spent transmitting a message. This is particularly valuable in an emergency when seconds count. The second major value of codes is that they can help mask the meaning of transmissions to prying ears.

While these are valuable reasons to use radio codes, a downside is that they can be difficult to learn and remember. In addition, for lifeguard agencies that often communicate on the radio with other agencies, codes can be confusing. The U.S. Coast Guard, for example, does not use codes. Lifeguards used to codes may have a difficult time transitioning between a conversation with an agency which uses codes and one which does not.

The alternative to codes is known as *clear text,* i.e. simple language. Effective clear text requires that lifeguards carefully consider their words before transmitting, and use the fewest words possible to get the message across as clearly as possible.

Two-way radios can only do one or the other (send or receive) at once. When one person is speaking, others normally cannot do so. Therefore, it is important that before a lifeguard transmits, it must be first confirmed that another conversation is not already taking place. Furthermore, the lifeguard should take great care to make transmissions brief and to the point so that if a more urgent message must be broadcast by someone else, that person can break in and use the radio for the higher priority message.

Telephones

The first electronic communication method acquired by most lifeguard agencies is the telephone. All lifeguard agencies should have access to telephones for communication with outside resources, and to allow the public to call for assistance or with questions. Many lifeguard agencies also use telephones for communication among towers or stands. While it can be difficult to extend and maintain wiring to temporary stands, this is a better form of communication than flags or whistles because a full explanation of a particular need can be transmitted using normal conversation, and reception of the message is certain.

Cellular telephones allow for telephonic communication without the need for wiring. They can be a very useful tool for lifeguards, particularly in major emergencies and in areas where a wired telephone is prohibitively costly. As costs decline and service areas expand, this technology will be increasingly valuable for

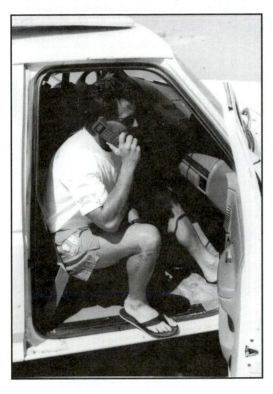

Cellular telephones can be a useful tool for lifeguards. [Photographic Credit: Mike Hensler]

lifeguards. In most communication among lifeguards, however, the two-way radio is probably a better alternative because of the open broadcast of messages it provides.

Many lifeguard agencies serve wide areas, which are under direct observation by the public who will sometimes observe emergencies or other incidents requiring lifeguard response. All lifeguard agencies serving public swimming areas should have a published emergency telephone number to allow contact by the general public. This telephone number should be answered whenever lifeguards are on duty.

It is good practice to arrange for emergency phone lines to be answered 24 hours a day. People reporting an emergency may have no idea of the hours of operation of the lifeguard agency they are calling, and precious time can be wasted as they fruitlessly try to summon help for an emergency. Several major lifeguard agencies in the United States maintain 24-hour lifeguard response, along with 24-hour communications. Others use pager systems to allow them to be notified in after hours emergencies. At a minimum, lifeguard agencies should arrange to transfer emergency telephone lines to another public safety provider which can ensure an emergency response, or provide a recording explaining how to get help in an after hours emergency.

The 9-1-1 system has had a profound impact on the reporting of emergencies by the public. For a discussion of this system and its impact on lifeguard services, refer to the section on the 9-1-1 system later in this chapter.

Public Address Systems

Public address (PA) systems are electronic voice amplification devices used primarily to provide information or direction to beach visitors. PA systems can be installed along beaches, on towers, on vehicles or vessels, or can be carried as portable megaphones. Public address systems can be of great value in preventive lifeguarding. Persons in a rip current, even far offshore, can be advised of how to extricate themselves. Lifeguards involved in rescue activity offshore can be updated and directed. Beachgoers can be advised of approaching bad weather.

A lifeguard holds a portable bullhorn.
[Photographic Credit: Mike Hensler]

In searches for lost persons, the PA can be invaluable. A single broadcast of the description of a small child can immediately turn the entire beach crowd into a search team. If an area must be closed suddenly to conduct an emergency search or because of water contamination, the public address system is certain to convey the message. Public address systems are also used in some areas to remind beach users of general regulations in an effort to gain compliance without personal contact. At the end of the day, the PA system can be utilized to advise beach users, even those swimming offshore, of the departure of lifeguards.

One pitfall to avoid with the PA is overuse. People visiting the beach are trying to relax. They want to avoid some of the stresses of everyday life. Constant use of a public address system can be very annoying and can ultimately cause beach users to "tune out" the broadcasts, so that when a truly important message is sent, it is ignored. Lifeguard services with a PA system are wise to develop guidelines aimed at moderating use.

VISUAL COMMUNICATION

Arm Signals

The use of arm signals among lifeguards provides an essential form of backup communication when electronic communication is impractical. For example, a lifeguard swimming offshore usually lacks access to a two-way radio and certainly to a telephone. Basic arm signals, such as those approved by USLA, are an essential component of a backup communication system. The very concept of the *signal and save* component of every rescue is that the swimming lifeguard will signal to other lifeguards whether the rescue is under control or further assistance is needed. The simple Code X signal can cause an entire search procedure to be commenced. USLA approved arm signals are covered in Appendix A.

Signs

Signs are used at many beaches to communicate with the public. Signs can explain rules and regulations, mark areas for special activities like surfing or boating, or explain the status of lifeguard protection, along with instructions for summoning assistance when lifeguards are off duty. The use of signs should not be discounted. If placed strategically, they can disseminate messages to large numbers of beach users. Persons visiting an unfamiliar beach are particularly likely to check signs to learn of unusual regulations with which they may be unaquainted. Signs are very valuable in informing beach visitors of hazards. All lifeguard agencies should maintain inexpensive chalkboards or dry erase boards which can be updated daily with pertinent weather and safety information. Signs and bulletin boards are also used to provide beach visitors with general public education materials.

A lifeguard tide board with updated conditions and a safety message.
[Photographic Credit: William McNeely, Jr.]

Flags

Like signs, flags are often used to communicate with the public. Flags may indicate the status of lifeguard protection, current water conditions, prohibited activities, or areas for special activities. In some areas, flags may be used by lifeguards to gain the attention of visitors for other communication purposes. Many agencies which use flags also provide signs that serve as a key for explaining flag use. This is an excellent practice as it greatly reduces public confusion.

Lifeguard attracts the attention of swimmers with a whistle and gestures using a hand-held flag. Note that the lifeguard's patch indicates he is an EMT.
[Photographic Credit: William McNeely, Jr.]

Some agencies also use flags to communicate among lifeguard towers. This is no longer a preferred method of communication because of its uncertainty. A lifeguard who drops a flag or changes flags cannot be sure that other lifeguards have noticed. A flag system which depends on others to spot a flag change before back-up will be sent may leave the lifeguard on the rescue alone and without assistance, due to lack of recognition of the signal.

AUDIBLE SIGNALING

Whistles

For years, whistles have been identified as communication equipment used by lifeguards. In many areas, whistles are used as attention-getting devices, followed by hand signals or other types of communication to impart messages or directions. Some agencies have developed complex whistle codes used for communication among lifeguards. Depending on the proximity of lifeguard towers, whistles may be a more certain method of communication among lifeguards than flags, in that the receiving lifeguard is alerted to the signal and can respond in kind.

Nonetheless, the use of whistles should be seen as an ancillary form of communication which has limited application in the beach environment, due to the restricted ability of whistle systems to convey complete messages with certainty.

Alarms

Audible alarms include air horns, bells, and buzzers installed at lifeguard towers. Like whistles, audible alarms are utilized in some areas as attention-getting devices to alert the public or other staff, and prepare them to receive directions or messages. In some areas, alarm codes are developed for communication among lifeguards. Other agencies have installed alarms that automatically ring in different emergency service agencies, triggering an immediate response.

THE 9-1-1 SYSTEM

The 9-1-1 system has created a national emergency telephone number for all emergencies. Unfortunately, lifeguard agencies may be poorly served by the system because it is generally designed to meet the needs of police, fire, and emergency medical services, not lifeguard services. Emergency calls for lifeguard services may actually be delayed or obstructed by the 9-1-1 system unless steps are taken by lifeguard agencies to correct this situation.

Prior to the advent of the 9-1-1 system, people summoning emergency assistance chose the emergency service they considered most appropriate to handle the emergency and called that agency's seven digit telephone number. Under the 9-1-1 system, people reporting emergencies no longer call directly to the responsible emergency service provider. Instead, they dial 9-1-1 and the operator becomes responsible for conveying the information to the most appropriate emergency service provider. While this generally works well for police, fire, and emergency medical providers, 9-1-1 operators are not always familiar with lifeguard services, and calls best handled by lifeguards can be misrouted to other emergency service providers, delaying the response of lifeguards.

Communication area, Hermosa Beach, California. Note clipboards with answering protocols for 9-1-1 calls.
[Photographic Credit: Rob McGowan]

Once the 9-1-1 operator receives a call describing the need for response, conveyance of the information can generally take one of three forms: call transfer, call referral, or direct dispatch. The simplest system is direct dispatch. This is utilized by smaller communities with a central dispatch center for all emergency services. Under this system, the central dispatch center receives the 9-1-1 call, gathers pertinent information, and directly dispatches the emergency service provider.

Call referral and call transfer are used in areas where various emergency services maintain separate dispatching centers. Under call referral, the initial 9-1-1 operator elicits necessary information from the caller about the emergency, then calls the appropriate emergency provider by telephone and advises of the details. This system requires expertise on the part of the 9-1-1 operator about the details needed by each emergency service provider from callers.

Call transfer is a system under which the 9-1-1 operator makes a quick initial assessment, decides which is the most appropriate emergency provider, and immediately transfers the call to that agency. A dispatcher for the responsible agency then has the opportunity to speak directly to the caller.

More advanced 9-1-1 systems include features known as automatic number identification (ANI) and automatic location identification (ALI). These features allow the 9-1-1 operator to see the location and call-back number of the caller on a computer screen. This can be particularly valuable for tourists unfamiliar with the address from which they are calling. Better 9-1-1 systems allow ANI and ALI to follow a transferred 9-1-1 call to the destination agency.

Lifeguard agencies should take strong steps to ensure that they are integrated into the 9-1-1 system to the fullest extent possible. Often monies for 9-1-1 are generated through surcharges on telephone bills and are available to assist in implementation or purchase of equipment. Under any circumstance, lifeguard agencies should ensure that 9-1-1 operators are fully knowledgeable about the lifeguard service's area of responsibility, and that these operators have ways to immediately contact lifeguard agencies about reports of emergencies in areas under the supervision of lifeguards. This is of critical importance because misrouted 9-1-1 calls can and have resulted in unnecessary injury and even death.

CHAPTER TWENTY THREE

RECORDS AND REPORTS

CHAPTER HIGHLIGHTS

Logbooks

Reports

IN THIS CHAPTER

Lifeguard logbooks are legal documents which may be publicly inspected or used in criminal or civil court cases. Lifeguards should never enter information into logbooks that is other than completely professional.

One important duty of a lifeguard is precise documentation of activities. Lifeguards, like other public safety providers, often view report writing as drudgery, but documentation helps justify continued funding, allows for future planning of staffing levels and facilities, and serves as the official record of an agency, which may be used in case of legal action. Few people can speak with certainty about the specifics of an incident that occurred in the distant past without referring to notes taken at the time.

Report forms and required records vary from agency to agency throughout the United States, based on local or regional reporting requirements and laws. As a minimum requirement, however, most lifeguard agencies report on the topics covered in this chapter. A collection of generic lifeguard reporting forms can be found in Appendix B.

LIFEGUARD LOG

All lifeguard agencies should maintain a station or tower log, indicating, among other things, the weather and water conditions of the day, beach attendance, lifeguards on duty, workouts performed, rescues, and other key activities accomplished through the workday. Some agencies utilize simple hard-bound datebooks. Others use photocopied forms. The daily log is used to document statistics for the lifeguard service's activities throughout the operating season or year. It also serves as a record of each day in case of inquiries at a later time. USLA-affiliated agencies also use lifeguard logs to collect data used to report lifeguard activity statistics throughout the United States. Categories of lifeguard activities used for USLA statistics include:

- Beach Attendance
- Rescues Performed
- Preventive Actions
- Medical Aids
- Boat Rescues
- Drownings
- Fatalities
- Missing Persons
- Public Safety Lectures

Lifeguard logbooks are legal documents which may be publicly inspected or used in criminal or civil court cases. Lifeguards should never enter information into logbooks that is other than completely professional. A sample of the statistical analysis form used for annual reporting to USLA is included in Appendix B. It includes the various categories of information which each agency should compile.

REPORTS

RESCUE REPORTS

USLA defines a water rescue of a swimmer as any case in which a lifeguard physically assists a victim in extrication from the water when the victim lacks the

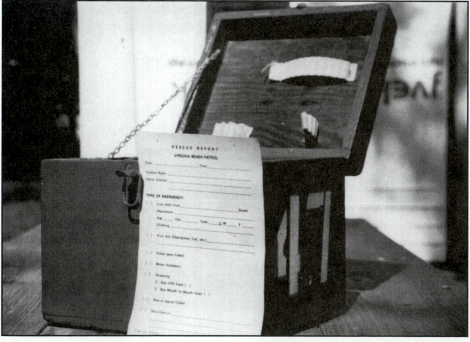

[Photographic Credit: Dave Foxwell]

apparent ability to do so alone. Even rescues considered routine by a lifeguard can represent the saving of a life which would otherwise be lost. This is a basic responsibility of lifeguards and should always be fully documented. The United States Lifesaving Association has developed a half-page Incident Report Form for use in documenting rescues, medical aids, and other activities. It is included in Appendix B and may be reproduced by any lifeguard agency.

MEDICAL AID REPORTS

Medical aids include all incidents in which medical care is rendered to a beach visitor. All medical aids should be documented. The level of documentation depends on the severity of the injury and disposition of the victim. For minor medical aids, a brief report is adequate. The example Incident Report Form in Appendix B should suffice. Major medical aids, such as those involving life-threatening injury or illness, should be documented more thoroughly. A Major Injury Report Form can be found in Appendix B.

Another form valuable in medical aid cases is the AMA form. AMA stands for "against medical advice." A person who refuses treatment that a lifeguard believes is needed, should be strongly encouraged to sign an AMA form, indicating the informed and deliberate refusal of that treatment. AMA forms can significantly reduce liability problems caused when people later accuse lifeguards of refusing to provide treatment, or of downplaying the seriousness of their injury. Attorneys should be consulted in creating an AMA form. Local emergency medical services are often good sources for language which meets local legal requirements.

BOATING ASSISTANCE REPORT

Boat rescues include all cases in which lifeguards provide physical assistance to a vessel in apparent distress. Some agencies record the rescue of boats using the same

A lifeguard prepares to take a report. [Photographic Credit: Mike Hensler]

format as for the rescue of swimmers. Other agencies require that a special form be completed. Usually, this report form indicates the number of people rescued with the craft, and the estimated dollar value of the vessel before the rescue. The Incident Report Form in Appendix B can be used for most routine boat rescues.

MISSING PERSON REPORTS

Missing person incidents include situations where people, usually children separated from their group or parents, require assistance from lifeguard staff in being reunited. Missing person incidents are common emergencies at many beach facilities. Standardized report forms remind lifeguards to ask pertinent questions, and allow ready dissemination of the information to others.

While missing person cases are often seen as routine by lifeguards, there are situations in which these people are not found for days. In these cases, full documentation of the time and circumstances surrounding the initial report is crucial to the continuing search. Since it can never be known whether the missing person will be quickly located, the initial report should be thorough. Taking a report also helps to demonstrate a sincere concern to the friends or relatives of the missing person. An example Missing Person Report can be found in Appendix B.

DROWNING AND DEATH REPORTS

Thorough reports should be completed whenever a death occurs in a beach area under the responsibility of lifeguards. In particular, a report should be completed whenever a drowning occurs at or near a protected or unprotected beach. This report is usually required as part of a formal investigation into the drowning incident and may be required by law. The Major Injury Report Form in Appendix B can be used to report deaths.

PUBLIC SAFETY PROGRAM REPORTS

Many lifeguard agencies are actively involved with programs given to the public at or away from the beach as a means of public education. Most agencies require that these programs be reported using special report forms, which usually indicate the estimated number of program participants.

LOST AND FOUND REPORTS

Most lifeguard agencies provide lost and found services for the visiting public. People who have lost personal possessions can report their loss to lifeguards at stations or towers. People who have found items can turn them in. Since lifeguard stations are often relatively accessible to beach patrons and others, valuables must be secured properly. Some lifeguard agencies utilize simple hang tags for lost and found items, allowing the receiving lifeguard to document the time the item was turned in, the place found, and the name of the lifeguard. The item is then logged in on a report form. For cash, credit cards, or other valuables, a supervising lifeguard should be required to take custody of the item and find an appropriate place to secure it.

GENERAL NARRATIVE REPORTS

At times there is a need for reports that do not fit into the standardized areas noted previously in this chapter. In other cases, there is a need to add further narrative descriptions or diagrams to detail the circumstances of a case. Appendix B includes a sample Narrative Report form and a form for creating a diagram. Use of report forms such as these can present a more professional image and ensures that important information about the author and incident are included.

CHAPTER TWENTY FOUR

PUBLIC RELATIONS

CHAPTER HIGHLIGHTS

Principles of Lifeguard Deportment

Uniforms

Cultural Diversity

IN THIS CHAPTER

Lifeguards must always remember that they are hired to protect and serve beach users. Therefore, extensive courtesy should be paid to all persons requesting assistance, even those filing a complaint.

Lifeguard operations are wide open to public view. It is often said that lifeguards work in a fishbowl, as they are constantly watched by beach visitors. On a busy day, every action of every lifeguard is probably watched by someone. Conversations are often overheard, despite belief to the contrary. With the advent of video-cameras, there is an ever increasing likelihood that lifeguard behavior will not only be seen and heard, but also memorialized on videotape. Lifeguards must conduct themselves accordingly.

Each day, lifeguards have repeated contacts with beach users for a wide variety of reasons. As a result, each day provides an opportunity to improve the standing of a lifeguard service in the eyes of the beach users who are served. There is also, of course, an opportunity to negatively impress and to tarnish not only the image of the lifeguard involved, but all lifeguards.

Lifeguards must always remember that they are hired to protect and serve beach users. Therefore, extensive courtesy should be paid to all persons requesting assistance, even those filing a complaint. The fact that a beach user may seem very rude is no license for the lifeguard to respond in kind. Lifeguards must learn to keep an even temperament and a helpful approach, regardless of how they may be treated by others. This is a major aspect of a professional demeanor.

Another important reason for concern over lifeguard image involves the public perception of lifeguard services in general. Despite the critical role lifeguards play in public safety, they are sometimes seen as less professional emergency service providers than police, firefighters, or paramedics. In fact, some people see the lifeguard's job as little more than an opportunity to socialize on the beach and impress others. This stereotype can reflect negatively on the degree of respect lifeguards are paid and can seriously affect funding decisions for lifeguard staffing, equipment, and pay. Lifeguards can help to counteract this perception by displaying a professional image *at all times,* whether on-duty or off.

PRINCIPLES OF LIFEGUARD DEPORTMENT

The word "deportment" refers to a manner of personal conduct or behavior. Lifeguard deportment is a very important aspect of ensuring a professional image and all the benefits that accrue with that image. There are two major areas of lifeguard deportment: professional conduct and public contact.

PROFESSIONAL CONDUCT

- *Lifeguard appearance should be professional*—An alert, well-groomed, physically fit lifeguard in proper uniform attire immediately conveys a feeling of security to beach visitors, particularly parents. Male lifeguards are encouraged to report to work clean-shaven or with well-groomed facial hair, depending on agency requirements.
- *Lifeguards should not keep items which create distractions in lifeguard towers*—Such articles may include musical instruments, unrelated reading materials, photographs, games, television sets, phonographs, tape players, or toys.
- *Lifeguards should not participate in beach or water games while on duty*—The only exception is authorized, organized agency workouts that are obvious as such to the viewing public.
- *Lifeguard stations and equipment should be maintained in a neat and clean condition at all times*—Vehicles should be regularly polished. Assigned lockers should be neat, clean, and dry. Emergency equipment should always be in a ready condition and located in an obvious and highly visible place. Unnecessary noise in and around the station should be minimized or eliminated to the greatest extent possible. The public should not be permitted to use lifeguard stations as dressing rooms, checkrooms for valuables, or club rooms. Only authorized personnel should be allowed in towers.
- *Lifeguards should help to keep the beach environment clean*—Although lifeguards should not be assigned to general beach maintenance, when problems can be quickly and easily rectified lifeguards should not avoid taking reasonable steps to help clean up. The beach should be regularly checked for general cleanliness and any potentially dangerous debris. If a condition can not be rectified easily, appropriate maintenance personnel should be notified through proper channels. Lifeguards should never litter.
- *Lifeguards must always be alert*—Lifeguards should attempt to position themselves so that the beach and water is always in full view and face the water.
- *Lifeguards on duty should avoid congregating in one location*—While all lifeguards need occasional breaks, when several congregate for an extensive

period of time it can create an appearance of having nothing productive to do. If time is available, routine tower straightening and cleaning are alternatives. Workouts may be appropriate and patrols of the beach can be useful.

- *Horseplay and pranks constitute unprofessional conduct.*
- *Binoculars should be used only for professional reasons*—Binoculars are an important lifeguard tool but will be noticed if they are used to view objects or people for reasons unrelated to normal duties. Gawking, whether using binoculars or not, is totally unprofessional.
- *Leering and discussion about the bodies of others have no place in lifeguarding*—Many people who come to the beach are proud of their physical fitness and appearance. They may seem to want to be viewed and appreciated. The skimpy covering provided by many bathing suits can easily attract attention. Lifeguards are not expected to ignore these things, but a glance is more than enough, and extensive discussions about the appearance of a particular beach visitor are unprofessional.
- *Lifeguards should address lifeguard supervisors by their title* (chief, captain, lieutenant, etc.) rather than by first names or nicknames, particularly when in the presence of beach visitors and other lifeguards.
- *Lifeguards should not engage in public disputes with other emergency service providers*—Problems should be worked out in a businesslike manner, with the assistance of supervisory personnel if needed.
- *Lifeguards should avoid posing for any photograph that could portray them in a less than professional manner*—In the interest of good public relations, many agencies will allow lifeguards to assist with photography or pose for pictures. Lifeguards should always present a professional image in these cases, since they are likely to end up in somebody's slide show.
- *Lifeguards should enforce all rules and regulations equally, with tact and diplomacy.*
- *Lifeguards should never use foul language in the performance of their duties.*

Public Contact

- *Lifeguards should keep social conversation with non-lifeguards to a minimum*— One stereotype of the lifeguard is of a person who uses the position to make social contacts. This appearance diminishes the public's perception of lifeguards. Therefore, social conversation with non-lifeguards should be kept to an absolute minimum, reserving social conversation for after work. Conversations with beach visitors should be polite and friendly, but brief.
- *Lifeguards should give courteous attention to the beach visitor, answering all questions asked*—When asked a question to which the lifeguard cannot supply an answer, the lifeguard should politely direct the visitor to a source where the information is available. When speaking to a beach visitor, it is usually more polite to remove sunglasses.
- *Lifeguards should be prepared to supply beach visitors with answers to commonly asked questions*—Examples are air and water temperature, times of tides (if any), forecast weather, the correct time, and conditions for swimming, surfing, diving, and other activities. If the station has a bulletin board containing this information, the board should be updated regularly and neatly.

Lifeguards should avoid writing unofficial remarks on tower bulletin or chalk boards.

- *News media inquiries should generally be referred to a supervisor* or a lifeguard designated for media contact. The media is generally very supportive of lifeguard services, but lifeguards can be unwittingly quoted in a newspaper, television, or radio report making a casual comment never intended for publication. Lifeguards should assume that anything they say to a media representative may be quoted verbatim. It is particularly important to remember this in the aftermath of a drowning or other serious accident, or in regard to a controversial issue. Many agencies have specific policies regarding news releases, interviews, and lifeguard statements.

- *Public address systems should be used only for official matters*—Lifeguards using public address systems and radios should realize that remarks made on these devices will be heard and judged by the public. Courtesy is particularly important when the message will be heard by large numbers of people.

- *Lifeguards should never reprimand an individual who has been rescued*— This person has probably already learned a lesson. If a lifeguard considers it important to say something to help the person learn about the reason that person was rescued and ways to avoid it in the future, the contact should be private and diplomatic. Often the egos of those who have been rescued are very bruised.

- *Lifeguards should avoid lecturing beach visitors*—If a point needs to be made, fully explain the rationale and request for compliance.

- *On-duty lifeguards should immediately provide their full name, position, and employer to any person requesting the information*—The lifeguard who refuses to provide such information suggests a need to hide from a complaint that may or may not be valid.

- *Lifeguards should address all people in a friendly and courteous manner*— Avoid approaches that start with a shout of "Hey you" or similar words—this will no doubt set the visitor in a defensive posture that will make understanding or compliance difficult. Whenever possible, visitors should be approached personally and spoken to individually. The use of public address systems, whistles, and signals is good for general announcements, but is often embarrassing when used to address individuals and should be avoided.

UNIFORMS

Uniforms are a very inexpensive way to establish a professional image for a lifeguard service. They are a valuable public relations tool which immediately identifies the wearer and shows authority. For example, when warning swimmers to move from one area to another due to a hazardous condition, the uniform makes people aware that the lifeguard is someone who knows about such things and is authorized to make the request. Uniforms can be especially helpful in emergencies since the public tends to defer to people in uniform. Properly designed uniforms also provide excellent protection from the elements.

The most typical lifeguard uniforms are trunks for men and tank suits for women. The latter may be permitted to wear trunks over the tank suits. The color is most often all red or orange. Usually an authorized patch including the agency name and logo is sewn on one thigh (always the same thigh) of the trunks or the lower side of the tank suit. A T-shirt of consistent color and design is also typical. The inexpensive cost of silk-screening allows easy creation of a uniform appearance.

Often lifeguards are seen from behind while watching the water or crouching over an injured victim. For this reason, some lifeguard agencies make a point of silk-screening the word "LIFEGUARD" in bold letters on the upper back of the shirt, along with the name of the agency. The large wording immediately identifies the lifeguard to the public, other emergency responders, and the media.

Other uniform items include hats, jackets, wetsuits, and so on. The neater and more uniformly attired lifeguards are, the more professional the lifeguard agency will appear. It is important to remember that most beach visitors will never actually speak to a lifeguard or observe a rescue taking place. Their image of a lifeguard will be based on what they see and hear. Uniforms are a major part of that image.

The San Diego Lifeguard River Rescue Team poses in front of their special rescue vehicle wearing "Class A" dress uniforms. [Photographic Credit: Dean Collins]

A lifeguard heads to a rescue. Note identifying patch on lower right thigh.
[Photographic Credit: William McNeely, Jr.]

To be effective, uniforms should be identical or nearly so. Lifeguard agencies should issue policies to help in this regard. Few variations or changes from year to year should be permitted so that uniformity is maintained and readily understood by the public. While lifeguards sometimes eschew uniformity in favor of comfort, this is counterproductive to maintaining a professional image. In some agencies, lifeguards of different ranks may have different colored uniforms, but within ranks they should be identical. Uniforms should always be neat and clean.

The wearing of uniform items by off-duty lifeguards is no more professional than it would be for police or firefighters, and the lifeguard image is perhaps more easily tarnished. For this reason, most agencies issue policies restricting the wearing of official uniform components during off-duty time. This policy should be strongly enforced since the design of lifeguard uniforms makes this clothing particularly attractive for casual wear by off-duty employees who are proud to be lifeguards. They should recognize that the image of the entire lifeguard service can be compromised by the indiscriminate use of lifeguard uniforms while off-duty.

CULTURAL DIVERSITY

The United States is sometimes called a melting pot, with people of many different backgrounds and cultures. People often take understandable pride in their cultural and ethnic roots. Lifeguards must take great care to treat all people with equality and respect regardless of any personal feelings. It is not the role of a lifeguard to judge others.

From time to time lifeguards are called upon to mediate disputes between beach patrons. A calm and even approach is essential in these cases. Nothing is more likely to incite anger than the appearance that the lifeguard is unfairly treating one person's opinion over another's. On the other hand, if all people are treated with a strong degree of fairness and equality, the lifeguard's decision, recommendation, or direction is much more likely to be accepted by all.

CHAPTER TWENTY FIVE

LINES AND KNOTS

CHAPTER HIGHLIGHTS

Knots

Splicing

IN THIS CHAPTER

The short list of knots described and illustrated in this chapter will meet all the ordinary lifeguarding situations. Lifeguards must learn these knots and practice them until they can be tied with speed and certainty. Supervisors should regularly test these skills.

Lifeguards need to work with rope (also referred to as line) on a continual basis. The RFD is attached to the lifeguard by means of a lanyard which is usually spliced to the rescue buoy on one end and the harness on the other. Knots must be used repeatedly aboard rescue vessels for towing and other purposes. In rescue situations, lifeguards must be able to make a line fast (tie it to a fixed point) quickly and effectively. To accomplish these tasks requires an understanding of basic knots and splicing techniques.

KNOTS

The knots described and illustrated in this chapter meet all the ordinary lifeguarding situations. Lifeguards must learn these knots and practice them until they can be tied with speed and certainty. Supervisors should regularly test these skills. It is better to know these few knots expertly than to have superficial knowledge of many.

A knot or splice is never as strong as the rope itself. The average efficiency of knots varies from 50–60% of the rope's strength. However, a well-made splice has about 85–95% of this strength. Splices are therefore preferred for heavy loads.

The strength of a rope is derived largely from the friction that exists between the individual fibers, yarn, and strands of which the rope is made. The twisting of these fibers into yarn, then into strands, and finally into cables is done in such a manner as to increase the amount and effectiveness of the friction between the rope elements.

Knot tying uses this same principle of friction. Properly tied knots create a level of friction adequate to keep the end of a line secure (fastened) when a load is placed on the line. Knots that can be tied and untied swiftly can make the difference between life and death, or the saving and destruction of property.

The square or reef knot (Figure 25-1) is perhaps the most useful knot known. It should not be used to tie together lines of different sizes, as it will slip. The square knot is used for tying light lines together, not for tying heavy hawsers. Although simple and effective, the square knot has one serious flaw — it jams and is difficult to untie after being heavily stressed.

Fig. 25-1
Square Knot

The sheet or becket bend (Figure 25-2) is used for tying two lines of different sizes together. It will not slip, even if there are great differences in the size of the lines.

Fig. 25-2
Sheet Bend

The bowline (Figure 25-3) will not slip, does not pinch or kink the rope as much as some other knots, and does not jam and become difficult to untie. This knot is the most desirable one for carrying heavy loads, and it is the most useful and important knot for lifeguarding purposes.

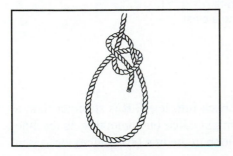

Fig. 25-3
Bowline

The clove hitch (Figure 25-4) is actually composed of two half hitches, tied in such a way that they work together. This knot is used for making the line fast temporarily to a piling or bollard.

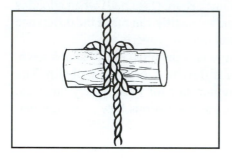

Fig. 25-4
Clove Hitch

The fisherman's bend (Figure 25-5), also called the anchor bend, is handy for making fast to a buoy or the ring of an anchor.

Fig. 25-5
Fisherman's Bend

Cleats (Figure 25-6) are found on most boat docks, on flagpoles, and in other places. They allow the free end of a line to be quickly and securely fastened, and detached with equal ease. Tying a line to a cleat involves running the line around the base of the cleat, and then tying a half hitch around one of the horns. Usually, an additional half hitch is tied to the other horn in such a way that the line falls together on the cleat.

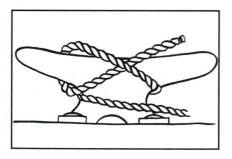

Fig. 25-6
Tying to a cleat

SPLICING

Splicing essentially involves weaving a rope back into itself. It is stronger than a knot and cleaner, without a large bulge that might catch on something as the line plays out. Splicing is usually done to create a loop in the line (eye splice), or to join the ends of two lines. The following explanations cover the splicing of twisted, not braided, line. For purposes of explaining splicing and knots, rope is said to have a *standing portion* and a *free end*. The free end is the end of the rope in which the knot is tied or the splice made. The standing portion is the remainder of the rope, away from the free end.

END SPLICE

An end splice (Figure 25-7) is used to permanently join the ends of two lines to create a single line. The splice will be much stronger than any knot and much cleaner. This enlarges the rope's diameter at the splice, but much less so than would a knot. *Step 1*—To start the end splice, the splicer first unlays the strands of both rope ends for a short distance as described for the eye splice. The six strand ends are taped to prevent unraveling. In this type of splice, it may be helpful to wind a small piece of tape or string around the standing end of each line at the junction where unlaying of the strands was started, as this will help avoid further unintended unraveling. Next, the ends are married together so that the strands of each rope lie alternately between the strands of the other.

Step 2—One of the three free strands on one line is tucked under a strand on the other line just above where the unlaying was done and past the tape or string. Then the next strand is tucked under the next adjacent strand in the standing line, and finally the third. It may be easiest to fully splice one line into the other in one direction, until the ends are fully tucked, before beginning the splice in the other direction.

Step 3—Once the splice has continued in both directions until all six strands are fully tucked, the splice is complete. For adequate strength, there should be at least five tucks per strand. After the splice is finished, it can be rolled under foot to smooth it up, then a strain put on it, and finally the excess ends are cut off.

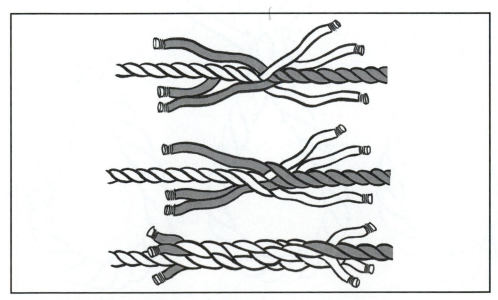

Fig. 25-7
End Splice

EYE SPLICE

The eye splice (Figure 25-8) creates a permanent loop in the end of a line. The loop can be spliced around a fixed object, such as the end of a rescue buoy, to create a permanent attachment, or simply left in the end of a line for other purposes. One end of a boat tow, for example, is an eye splice.

The eye splice is started by separating (unlaying) the twisted strands about six inches to a foot or more back from the end of the line, depending on the size of the rope being spliced. The ends should be taped using masking tape or similar, to prevent unraveling of the strands during splicing.

Next a loop is formed in the rope by laying the free end back along the standing portion of line so that the center strand lies over and directly along the standing portion. The size of the loop is determined by the point where the opened strands are first tucked back into the line.

Step 1—The splicer starts by selecting the topmost strand of the standing portion of the line and tucking B under it. It should be pulled up snugly, but not so tight as to distort the natural lay of the strands in the standing portion of the line. Note that the tuck is made from right to left, against the lay of the standing portion. Next, the left strand (A) is tucked under a different strand of the standing line, which lies to the

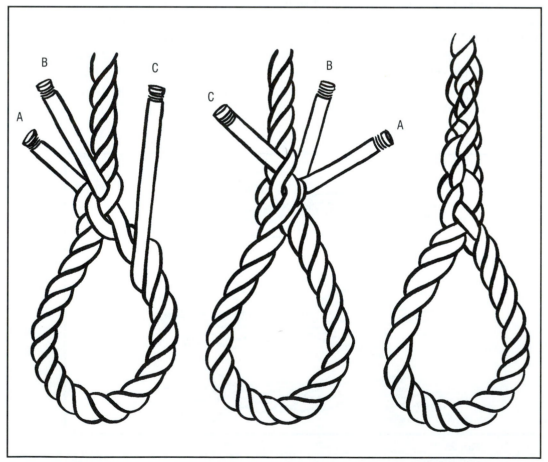

Fig. 25-8
Eye Splice

left of the strand under which B was pulled. The splicer tucks from right to left in every case.

Step 2—The loop should be turned over as has been done in Step 2 of Figure 25-8. Strand C is now pulled under the third strand of the standing portion of the line. The greatest risk of starting a splice incorrectly is in the first tuck of strand C. It should go under from right to left. If the first tuck of each of the strands A, B, and C, is correctly made, the splice at this point will look as shown in Step 2.

Step 3 — The splicer then returns to strand A, lays it over the next strand up the standing portion of the line, and then tucks it under the one after that. The same is then done with B and C in order. This process is repeated, one tuck at a time, until the ends have been woven (spliced) fully into the standing portion of the line with no significant end left. When complete, the splice should appear as in Step 3 of Figure 25-8.

CHAPTER TWENTY SIX

THE RESPONSIBLE LIFEGUARD

Chapter Highlights

Legal Considerations

Professional Responsibility

In This Chapter

There is a tendency in the United States to focus heavily on the civil liability system. Many people say that Americans are lawsuit happy. Unfortunately, the tremendous emphasis on liability tends to overshadow the real issue, which is that lifeguards, like all other public safety providers, need to live up to the tremendous trust placed in them by the public, not because the law says they must, but because it is the right thing to do.

Many new lifeguards understandably experience a great deal of pride in achieving their goal of working in the lifesaving profession. With that pride comes a tremendous responsibility. Every day, people unknown to the lifeguard entrust their lives and those of their family and friends to the skill and vigilance of the lifeguard. These people may still watch their children carefully, but they have an ultimate expectation that if need be, the lifeguard will be there for them. This creates expectations, both professional and legal, that the lifeguard must meet. One inadvertent lapse may mean the difference between a happy day at the beach and the most profound tragedy of all—untimely death.

LEGAL CONSIDERATIONS

The expectation of the public and the legal system is that lifeguards will do the job they have been trained to do within the parameters of the training given. The lifeguard who is distracted for no excusable reason when a preventable accident takes place may be successfully sued, along with the employing agency. Such a situation may also result in disciplinary action and loss of employment. In general, however, lifeguards who do their job professionally, according to the training given them, should have no inordinate fear of the civil liability system.

Discussions of legal points and case histories would fill an entire textbook on lifeguard management. The administrators of any well-organized lifeguard agency spend a considerable amount of time and effort studying the legal aspects of lifeguard services and developing appropriate protocols. These protocols are not only intended to protect and serve the public, but also to protect the lifeguard service and its employees from civil suits. The training program provided by each agency is intended to reflect the protocols that have been established.

Collectively, the protocols developed will help to establish the standard of care provided by a lifeguard service. In legal terms, a safety provider found to have acted in accordance with a reasonable and accepted standard of care is without fault.

This manual will not include extensive information on the various ways lifeguards may be held accountable for their actions. Instead, the following three generalizations are provided as yardsticks used to develop legal expectations:

- *Lifeguards must perform their duties*—Each lifeguard is given a special trust by the public as a guardian of safety at the beach. That trust requires constant vigilance during duty hours. Failure to act when actions are needed can be one of the most serious charges brought against a lifeguard, especially if that failure occurred because of distraction due to unprofessional conduct.

- *Lifeguards must perform their duties consistently*—In addition to establishing policies and procedures for lifeguard duties, each agency establishes criteria for the performance of those duties (whether formally or informally), including a routine that lifeguards should follow during the workday. It is important to enforce rules and regulations and take preventive actions consistently, without making assumptions about conditions or abilities of beach visitors. Take, for example, the case of a beach where lifeguards consistently make a public address announcement at the end of each day to warn beach users that they are leaving the beach. One day, the announcement is forgotten and a swimmer drowns soon after the lifeguard leaves. This inconsistency may cause a serious problem for the lifeguard and agency. Variations from normal protocol may be necessary in emergency work from time to time, but they should be considered carefully.

- *Lifeguards must perform their duties properly*—During training, lifeguards are taught many procedures and techniques for use in rescuing and treating people who are the victims of aquatic accidents. These procedures and techniques are not advice to be considered, but rather directions to be followed. While judgment skills are important, lifeguards are expected to perform their duties following the established and authenticated procedures provided in training. Deviation may result in charges of malfeasance.

LOCAL LAWS

Each lifeguard agency falls under the jurisdiction of local or regional laws that have been established either to define the professional responsibility of an agency or employee or to limit liability. Because these laws vary from region to region across the United States, they cannot be covered thoroughly in this manual. Generally, these laws fall into two categories:

Good Samaritan Laws

In many areas of the United States, Good Samaritan laws have been established to protect people from liability if they encounter an emergency situation and stop to render aid to injured or distressed people. These people may be protected from lawsuits as long as they act in good faith and to the best of their abilities. In most areas, these laws are limited to protecting lay people who provide assistance and professional emergency providers (physicians, paramedics, lifeguards, etc.) who stop to provide assistance during off-duty time. In other areas, Good Samaritan laws also protect on-duty emergency personnel, but only under many stipulations and conditions.

Immunity Laws

In some areas, certain governmental agencies will be exempt from specific liabilities under governmental immunity laws or special provisions of constitutions. Other areas may have laws which specifically define recreation as hazardous and thereby regulate claims which may be made as a result of injuries sustained in recreation. There can also be special tort laws which limit claims that may be made against agencies as a result of loss, damage, or injury.

LIABILITY PROTECTION

Most lifeguard services have access to the assistance of legal departments, corporate attorneys, district attorneys, city attorneys, or other legal experts in defending against lawsuits. Under some circumstances, these legal departments may also represent or defend employees who are named in lawsuits as co-defendants. Lifeguards should become aware of the level of protection that may be afforded to them in a liability case. Even in frivolous lawsuits, where there is clearly no fault on the part of the lifeguard, significant costs may be incurred in mounting a legal defense.

Ultimately, the best protection from liability is to perform all duties effectively, within the guidelines provided by the hiring agency. A lifeguard who stays alert, responds expeditiously as needed, and provides aid that meets a reasonable standard of care should have few worries. After all, the issue of liability arises only when errors are made that reasonably could have been prevented by prudent action. By avoiding those errors in the first place, civil liability itself becomes a moot issue.

PROFESSIONAL RESPONSIBILITY

There is a tendency in the United States to focus heavily on the civil liability system. Many people say that Americans are lawsuit happy. This focuses a great deal of attention on lawsuit avoidance. Unfortunately, the tremendous emphasis on liability tends to overshadow the real issue, which is that lifeguards, like all other public safety providers, need to live up to the tremendous trust placed in them by the public, not because the law says they must, but because it is the right thing to do.

When a father comes to the beach with his three children, he is not thinking about suing the lifeguard or lifeguard service. He simply wants to go home with his family at the end of the day with all of them safe and sound. He may not ever speak with a lifeguard, but even so he entrusts the safety of his family to that lifeguard. When lifeguards are tired or distracted, they would do well to remember that many people are counting on them—to protect their lives and those of their loved ones.

This manual, along with a training program that meets the minimum recommended standards of USLA, is intended to provide all lifeguards with the tools needed to ensure beach safety. All the training in the world however, will be to no avail if a lifeguard fails to maintain a vigilant and professional approach to the job at all times.

Lifeguards are given the gift of a job which can provide an extraordinarily high degree of personal satisfaction. The work environment is unmatched and hundreds of lifeguards go home every day having saved the life of another person. Those who choose to accept this gift should take the public trust that comes with it and protect that trust by doing the best job they can every day.

Many people who work as lifeguards have stayed with the profession for years. Others go on to take other jobs, but they invariably look back longingly. "I used to be a lifeguard," they will often say, "it was the best time of my life."

We think it will be the best time of yours, too. Good luck in your service.

APPENDIX A
USLA APPROVED ARM SIGNALS

All Clear (OK)

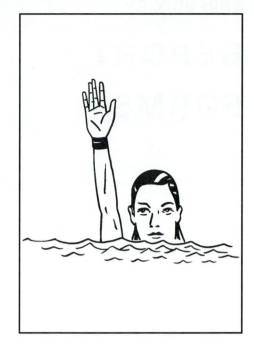

Assistance Needed

Resuscitation Case or Oxygen
Needed

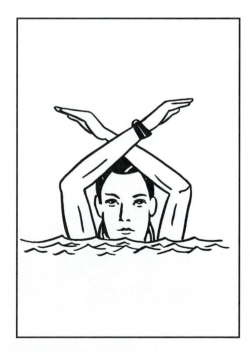

Submerged Swimmer

REPORT
FORMS

These forms are intended for photocopying.

Lifeguard Agency:
_____

Incident Location:
_____

United States Lifesaving Association
Incident Report Form

Incident Date:
_____

Time: _____ ☐ AM ☐ PM

Incident Description

☐ WATER RESCUE:
☐ Ocean
☐ Bay
☐ Lake
☐ River
☐ Other _____

☐ MEDICAL AID:
☐ Abrasion
☐ Laceration
☐ Burn
☐ Fracture
☐ Other _____

☐ LOST PERSON
☐ BOAT RESCUE
☐ CLIFF RESCUE
☐ FLOOD RESCUE
☐ ARREST
☐ OTHER _____

Victim's Activity

☐ Swimming
☐ Floating
☐ Wading
☐ Surfing
☐ Body Surfing
☐ Walking/Running

☐ Boating
☐ Skin Diving
☐ Scuba Diving
☐ Beach Activity
☐ Jumping/Diving
☐ Other _____

Disposition

☐ Released
☐ Released to parent
☐ Advised to see physician
☐ Ambulance
☐ Police
☐ Other _____

Victim Information

Name: _____ Address: _____ City: _____ State: _____ Zip: _____ Phone: _____

Age: _____ ☐ Male ☐ Female • Injury Description: _____

Details

_____
_____
_____

Lifeguards: _____

Lifeguard Agency:
_____

Incident Location:
_____

United States Lifesaving Association
Incident Report Form

Incident Date:
_____

Time: _____ ☐ AM ☐ PM

Incident Description

☐ WATER RESCUE:
☐ Ocean
☐ Bay
☐ Lake
☐ River
☐ Other _____

☐ MEDICAL AID:
☐ Abrasion
☐ Laceration
☐ Burn
☐ Fracture
☐ Other _____

☐ LOST PERSON
☐ BOAT RESCUE
☐ CLIFF RESCUE
☐ FLOOD RESCUE
☐ ARREST
☐ OTHER _____

Victim's Activity

☐ Swimming
☐ Floating
☐ Wading
☐ Surfing
☐ Body Surfing
☐ Walking/Running

☐ Boating
☐ Skin Diving
☐ Scuba Diving
☐ Beach Activity
☐ Jumping/Diving
☐ Other _____

Disposition

☐ Released
☐ Released to parent
☐ Advised to see physician
☐ Ambulance
☐ Police
☐ Other _____

Victim Information

Name: _____ Address: _____ City: _____ State: _____ Zip: _____ Phone: _____

Age: _____ ☐ Male ☐ Female • Injury Description: _____

Details

_____
_____
_____

Lifeguards: _____

Lifeguard Agency:

_____

☐ Non-Fatal

☐ Fatal

United States Lifesaving Association
Major Injury Report Form

Page 1 of _____

Report #: _____

Incident Date: _____ Time: _____ ☐ AM ☐ PM • Location (be precise): _____

VICTIM INFORMATION

Name: _____ Date of Birth: _____ Age: _____ ☐ Male ☐ Female

Street Address: _____ City: _____ State: _____ Zip: _____ Phone: _____

Description: Hair_____ Eyes _____ Weight _____ Height _____ Race/Ethnicity_____

Apparel: ☐ Bathing Suit   ☐ T-Shirt   ☐ Wetsuit   ☐ Scuba   ☐ Other (describe) _____

Evidence of: ☐ Alcohol Consumption or ☐ Drug Use • If either describe _____

Injury Description: _____

WITNESS INFORMATION

	Name	Street Address	City	State	Zip Code	Age	Telephone
1)							
2)							
3)							

INCIDENT DETAILS

☐ The area was not guarded • ☐ The area was guarded by (lifeguard names) _____

The following lifeguards responded _____

Equipment used _____

Apparent reason for injury _____

Medical aid rendered _____

Other responding agencies: ☐ Police ☐ Fire ☐ Rescue Squad ☐ Paramedic ☐ Coast Guard ☐ Park Ranger ☐ Other _____

For Water Related Cases: Water Conditions ☐ Calm or _____ foot waves • Water Temperature _____ • Water Depth _____

For Submersion Cases: Search Start Time _____ Search End Time _____ • Recovery Date _____ Time _____ ☐ None

INCIDENT NARRATIVE

☐ Report Continued

_____   _____
Report Completed By   Report Approved By

United States Lifesaving Association

Missing Person Report

Lifeguard: _____ Station: _____ Report Number: _____

Missing Person

Name: _____ Age: _____ ☐ Male ☐ Female

Physical Description	**Clothing**	**Last Seen**

Height: _____ Swimsuit: _____ Time: _____

Weight: _____ Shirt: _____ Place: _____

Hair Color: _____ Pants: _____ Activity: _____

Hair Texture: _____ Shoes: _____ Direction of Travel: _____

Eye Color: _____ Hat: _____

Race/Ethnicity: _____ Other: _____ Towel Area: _____

Local Address: _____

Local Phone: _____ Car Location/Description: _____

Other Info: _____

_____

Reporting Party (RP)

Name: _____ Relationship: _____

Street Address: _____ Home Phone: _____

City, State, Zip: _____ Local Phone: _____

Local Address: _____

Beach Location: _____

Found

Date: _____ Time: _____ Location: _____ By: _____

Lifeguard Agency:

_____

United States Lifesaving Association

Search & Recovery Checklist

Page 1 of _____

Report #: _____

Date: _____

Time

_____ Submersion victim reported by: _____

Last seen point: _____

Last seen time: _____ ☐ AM ☐ PM

Victim description: _____

_____ Preliminary search commenced

_____ Incident Commander (name): _____ declares Code X

_____ All units advised of incident via ☐ radio broadcast ☐ telephone ☐ other: _____

_____ Search and rescue team summoned

_____ Full search commenced

_____ Rescue vessel(s) requested and dispatched

_____ Emergency medical services (EMS) ambulance requested to standby at scene

_____ Availability of search helicopter checked, Incident Commander advised

_____ Helicopter requested for aerial search from (agency): _____

_____ Medical evacuation helicopter placed on standby, Incident Commander advised

_____ Crowd control assistance requested from (agency): _____

At Scene Times • who? • what unit number? • how many?

_____ _____

_____ _____

_____ _____

_____ _____

_____ Emergency medical services (EMS)

_____ Search helicopter

_____ Medical evacuation helicopter

_____ Victim recovered (or) ☐ no recovery

_____ Search terminated on order of Incident Commander

_____   _____
Report Completed By   Report Approved By

☐ NARRATIVE REPORT ONLY	United States Lifesaving Association	PAGE
☐ CONTINUED FROM	**Narrative Report**	OF
		INCIDENT DATE

AGENCY	VICTIM	INCIDENT LOCATION

I was informed by... • The type of incident was... • I observed... • The witness/victim said... • I did... • The incident was resolved by...

_____

_____

_____

_____

_____

_____

_____

_____

_____

_____

_____

_____

_____

_____

_____

_____

_____

_____

_____

_____

_____

_____

_____

☐ Report Continued

REPORTING LIFEGUARD	REPORT APPROVED BY	REPORT DATE

United States Lifesaving Association

NATIONAL LIFESAVING STATISTICS

Calendar Year _____

Agency_____ Chapter _____ Region_____

BEACH ATTENDANCE		
RESCUES - (Total)		
Primary Cause	**Rip Current**	
	Surf	
	Swiftwater	
	Scuba	
	Other	
CLIFF RESCUES		
BOAT RESCUES		
Passengers		
Vessel Value		
BOAT ASSISTS		
Passengers		
Vessel Value		
PREVENTIVE ACTIONS		
MEDICAL AIDS		

DROWNINGS - (Total)	
Unguarded Drowning	
Guarded Drowning	
FATALITIES - (other)	
ENFORCEMENT ACTIONS - (Total)	
Warnings	
Citations	
Arrests	
LOST AND FOUND PERSONS	
PUBLIC SAFETY LECTURES - (Total)	
Number of Students	

Weather **Overall** ☐ Good ☐ Fair ☐ Poor

High Season ☐ Good ☐ Fair ☐ Poor

Surf **Overall** ☐ Large ☐ Medium ☐ Small

High Season ☐ Large ☐ Medium ☐ Small

Wind **Overall** ☐ Heavy ☐ Average ☐ Light

High Season ☐ Heavy ☐ Average ☐ Light

Submitted by:_____ Date:_____

Telephone: _____

Return completed forms to:

ULSA National Statistics Coordinator
PO Box 366
Huntington Beach, CA 92648

Shark Attack Report

International Shark Attack File
American Elasmobranch Society
Florida Museum of Natural History
University of Florida
Gainesville, Florida 32611

Telephone: (904) 392-1721
Fax: (904) 846-0287

Attack Date: _____

Attack Time: _____

☐ Date/Time Known
☐ Date/Time Estimated

OUTCOME

• Fatal
• Non-Fatal

Full Name: _____ ☐ Male ☐ Female

Street Address: _____ Height: _____

City, State, Zip: _____ Weight: _____

Country: _____ Race: _____

Apparel: _____ Jewelry: _____

Major Apparel Color: _____ Diving/Surfing Gear: _____

Attack Location

City: _____ State/Province: _____ County: _____

Country: _____ Ocean: _____ Longitude/Latitude (if known): _____

Specific Location: _____

Treating Physician (Medical Examiner/Coroner for Fatalities)

Name: _____ Medical Facility: _____

Street Address: _____ Telephone: _____

City, State, Zip: _____ Country: _____

Person Completing Report

Name: _____ Agency: _____

Street Address: _____ Telephone: _____

City, State, Zip: _____ Country: _____

Victim Injury Description

Attack Site

Water Clarity: ☐ Muddy ☐ Turbid/Murky ☐ Clear — estimated feet of visibility _____

Attack Depth: ☐ Surface ☐ Underwater (depth) _____ Total Water Depth at Attack Site: _____

Number of Persons in Water within 10 Feet of Victim: _____ ☐ None   Within 10 - 50 Feet:_____ ☐ None

Were Other Persons in the Water More Than 50 Feet Away: ☐ Yes ☐ No

General Activity of Others Near Victim: _____

Fishing Activity Near Victim: _____ ☐ None

Shark Information

Appearance: ☐ Unseen ☐ Observed Appearance (describe with as much detail as possible including color,

   shape of body and fins, shape of teeth, etc.) _____

_____

Shark Behavior: ☐ Unseen ☐ As Follows (include behavior noted prior to strike, during strike, and after strike)

_____

_____

_____

_____

Shark Size: ☐ Unseen ☐ Estimated length in feet: _____ Estimated weight: _____

Victim Activity At Time of Attack and Incident Narrative
(attach additional pages as needed)

☐ Report Continued

DIVER ACCIDENT REPORT FORMS

These forms are intended for photocopying.

DIVING DECOMPRESSION ILLNESS REPORTING FORM

DATE & TIME OF ACCIDENT
MONTH/DAY/YEAR

Time _____ AM / PM

IS THIS A FATALITY REPORT?
☐ YES ☐ NO

For DAN Office Use Only
CASE
SEVERITY CODE
BMI

1. PATIENT NAME
LAST — FIRST — MI

2. OCCUPATION

3. ADDRESS
STREET — CITY — ST — ZIP

4. PATIENT PHONE (HOME)

5. PATIENT PHONE (WORK)

6. COUNTRY (IF NOT USA)

7. AGE YRS

8. SEX M or F

9. HEIGHT FT IN

10. WEIGHT LBS.

11. CERTIFYING AGENCY
A – PADI   D – YMCA
B – NAUI   E – SSI
C – NASDS   F – Other
            G – None

12. CERTIFICATION LEVEL
A – Basic   F – Commercial
B – Open Water G – Other
C – Advanced   H – None
D – Divemaster I – Student
E – Instructor

13. DAN MEMBER?
Y – Yes
N – No

14. YEARS DIVING
YEARS   MONTHS

15. NUMBER OF DIVES MADE
Total
Previous 12 months

16. PREVIOUS DIVE ACCIDENTS
A – Possible DCS
B – DCS
C – AGE
D – Pul. barotrauma
E – None

17. CURRENT MEDICATIONS
Y or N
☐ Prescription
☐ Non-prescription
List _____

18. CIGARETTE USE
A – Presently
B – In past
C – Never
☐ Packs per day
☐ Years Smoking

19. PREVIOUS MAJOR ILLNESSES/ SURGERY
(Provide up to 3 responses)

A – Chest-lung
B – Asthma
C – Chest-heart
D – Gastrointestinal/Abdomen
E – Brain
F – Spine/Back
G – Limb or joint of DCS site
H – Circulation/Blood
I – Neurologic/Nervous system
J – Muscle/Skeleton system
K – Eye
L – Mental/Emotional
M – Other _____
N – None

Past:
A – 2-6 months
B – 7-12 months
C – 1-3 years
D – 2-5 years
E – 6+ years

List and describe specific problems:

_____
_____

20. CURRENT HEALTH PROBLEMS WITHIN PREVIOUS 2 MONTH
(Provide up to 3 responses)

A – Chest-lung
B – Asthma
C – Chest-heart
D – Gastrointestinal/Abdomen
E – Brain
F – Spine/Back
G – Limb or joint of DCS site
H – Circulation/Blood
I – Neurologic/Nervous system
J – Muscle/Skeleton system
K – Eye
L – Mental/Emotional
M – Other _____
N – None

List and describe specific problems or additional current medications

_____
_____

PLEASE ATTACH SEPARATE SHEET FOR ADDITIONAL INFORMATION OR NARRATIVE.

I understand that the information in this form will be used for research purposes only, and that all personal information will be kept strictly **confidential**. I also understand that the Divers Alert Network may need to contact me in the future for clarification of information provided on this form.

_____
Patient Signature

DIVE ACCIDENT

21. PURPOSE OF DIVE
- [ ] A – Pleasure
- [ ] B – Work/Labor

22. DIVE ACTIVITY (up to 2 responses)
- [ ] A – Wreck
- [ ] B – Cave
- [ ] C – Night
- [ ] D – Photography
- [ ] E – Under Instruction
- [ ] F – Providing Instruction
- [ ] G – Spearfishing/ Game collecting
- [ ] H – Sightseeing

23. ENVIRONMENT
- [ ] A – Freshwater
- [ ] B – Saltwater

24. ALTITUDE OF DIVE
- [ ] A – Sea Level
- [ ] B – > Sea Level but <1000 ft.
- [ ] C – >1000 ft.

25. Was this dive or dive series typical of your normal type of diving?
- [ ] Y – Yes
- [ ] N – No

IF NO, Explain _____

26. DIVER'S PERCEPTION OF TEMPERATURE
- [ ] A – Cold
- [ ] B – Hot
- [ ] C – Comfortable

27. CURRENT STRENGTH
- [ ] A – Strong
- [ ] B – Moderate
- [ ] C – Mild
- [ ] D – None

28. AIR SUPPLY
- [ ] A – Scuba Air
- [ ] B – Surface Supply Air
- [ ] C – Mixed gas
- [ ] D – None/Breath-hold dive

29. AIR CONSUMPTION
- [ ] A – Ran low
- [ ] B – Out of air
- [ ] C – Not a problem
- [ ] D – Buddy breathing (not octopus)

30. BUOYANCY PROBLEM
- [ ] Y – Yes
- [ ] N – No

31. RAPID ASCENT
- [ ] Y – Yes
- [ ] N – No

32. WITHIN LIMITS–Y or N
- [ ] Tables (which table _____)
- or
- [ ] Computer (type _____)

33. TYPE OF SUIT
- [ ] A – Wet
- [ ] B – Partial Wet
- [ ] C – Dry
- [ ] D – Lycra
- [ ] E – Swim

34. EQUIPMENT USED ON DIVE: (please check all that apply)
- [ ] Depth gauge
- [ ] Timing device/watch
- [ ] Buoyancy vest
- [ ] BC Inflator hose in use
- [ ] Decompression computer

35. EQUIPMENT MALFUNCTION:
- [ ] A – None
- [ ] B – Regulator
- [ ] C – BC Vest
- [ ] D – Weight belt
- [ ] E – Dry suit
- [ ] F – DC Computer
- [ ] G – Inflator hose _____
- [ ] H – Contaminated air supply
- [ ] I – Equipment was not familiar to you.
- [ ] J – Other
- Reason: _____

36. TYPE OF DIVE
- [ ] Y – Yes
- [ ] N – No
- [ ] Single
- [ ] Repetitive

37. WOMEN, PLEASE RESPOND (up to 2 responses)
When the accident occurred, were you:
- [ ] A – Menstruating
- [ ] B – On birth control medication
- [ ] C – Pregnant
- [ ] D – None of the above

38. DIVE LOCATION:
State, Province, or Island: _____

Country or nearest country: _____

39. How long ago was your last Dive Trip/Series?
[ ]   Circle one: Days   Weeks   Months

40. STRENUOUS EXCERCISE
- Y – Yes
- N – No
- [ ] 24 hours predive
- [ ] During dive
- [ ] 6 hours postdive

41. PREDIVE HEALTH
- [ ] A – Nausea/vomiting
- [ ] B – Hangover
- [ ] C – Diarrhea
- [ ] D – Other
- [ ] E – No Problem

42. ALCOHOL
Please check:
- [ ] None
- [ ] Night Before
- [ ] Predive
- [ ] Between Dives
- [ ] Post Dive

Number of drinks, beers. or wine
- [ ]
- [ ]
- [ ]
- [ ]
- [ ]

43. RECREATIONAL DRUG USE
Prior to, between, or after dive
- [ ] Y – Yes
- [ ] N – No

44. Do you consider yourself physically fit?
- [ ] Y – Yes
- [ ] N – No
- [ ] Do you excercise on a weekly basis? (Y or N)
- [ ] # Days per week

45. FATIGUE OR LACK OF SLEEP PRIOR TO DIVE?
- [ ] Y – Yes
- [ ] N – No

46. DIVE SERIES

Please fill in all that apply up to and including your last dive If you skipped a day please leave that day blank.

	DAY 1	DAY 2	DAY 3	DAY 4	DAY 5	DAY 6	DAY 7
Total # of dives	[ ]	[ ]	[ ]	[ ]	[ ]	[ ]	[ ]
Any night dive? (How many)	[ ]	[ ]	[ ]	[ ]	[ ]	[ ]	[ ]
Any symptoms? (Y or N)	[ ]	[ ]	[ ]	[ ]	[ ]	[ ]	[ ]
A – All no stop dive(s) / B – Any safety stop / C – Any dive requiring decompression stops	[ ]	[ ]	[ ]	[ ]	[ ]	[ ]	[ ]
A – Multilevel (time divided) / B – Square	[ ]	[ ]	[ ]	[ ]	[ ]	[ ]	[ ]
Deepest Dive (ft.)	[ ][ ][ ]	[ ][ ][ ]	[ ][ ][ ]	[ ][ ][ ]	[ ][ ][ ]	[ ][ ][ ]	[ ][ ][ ]

DIVE ACCIDENT (cont.)

47. DIVE PROFILE FOR DAY OF DIVE ACCIDENT

Computer NDL For Next Dive _____ Depth / Time

1st DIVE   2nd DIVE   3rd DIVE

GROUP LETTER

SURFAC INT (MIN)

DEC STOPS (MIN)   10' 20' 30'

DEPTH (FT)

BOTTOM TIME (MIN)

Computer NDL _____ Depth / Time

4th DIVE   5th DIVE   6th DIVE

GROUP LETTER

SURFAC INT (MIN)

DEC STOPS (MIN)   10' 20' 30'

DEPTH (FT)

BOTTOM TIME (MIN)

PRE-CHAMBER INFORMATION

48. INITIAL CONTACT WAS:

- A – DAN Emergency
- B – DAN Non-emergency
- C – Hospital emergency room
- D – Emergency medical service
- E – US Coast Guard
- F – Physician
- G – Dive instructor/shop
- H – Other: _____

49. Total delay from symptom onset to contacting DAN or other medical help:

HOURS   or   DAYS

50. FLYING OR INCREASED ELEVATION AFTER DIVING AND PRIOR TO TREATMENT?

- A – Commercial airliner
- B – Unpressurized aircraft
- C – Med Evac Flight
- D – Mountain elevation
- E – Does not apply

Hours post dive (flew or went into elevation)

_____ elevation (in feet)

51. SIGNS & SYMPTONS

1st Symptom
2nd Symptom
3rd Symptom
4th Symptom
5th Symptom
6th Symptom

- A – Pain
- B – Rash
- C – Itching
- D – Weakness
- E – Numbness/Tingling
- F – Dizziness/Vertigo
- G – Semi-consciousness
- H – Unconsciousness
- I – Restlessness
- J – Extreme fatigue
- K – Visual disturbance
- L – Speech disturbance
- M – **Headache**
- N – Paralysis
- O – Difficulty breathing
- P – Nausea/Vomiting
- Q – Hemoptosis/coughing blood from lungs

- R – Muscle twitching
- S – Convulsions
- T – Hearing loss
- U – Ringing ears
- V – Decreased skin sensation
- W – Bladder problem
- X – Bowel problem
- Y – Personality change
- Z – Difficulty walking/ standing
- 1 – Reflex change
- 2 – Other: _____

52. LOCATION: Block A = location of symptom
Then please check (✔)
L = Left   R = Right   B = Bilateral/Both Sides

A   L   R   B

1st Symptom
2nd Symptom
3rd Symptom
4th Symptom
5th Symptom
6th Symptom

- A – Head
- B – Face
- C – Sinus
- D – Eyes
- E – Ears
- F – Neck
- G – Shoulder
- H – Entire arm
- I – Upper arm
- J – Elbow
- K – Forearm
- L – Wrist
- M – Hand
- N – Fingers
- O – Chest
- P – Back
- Q – Upper back
- R – Lower back

- S – Abdomen
- T – Buttock
- U – Groin
- V – Hip
- W – Entire leg
- X – Thigh
- Y – Knee
- Z – Calf
- 1 – Shin
- 2 – Ankle
- 3 – Foot
- 4 – Toes
- 5 – Trunk
- 6 – Generalized
- 7 – Other:

53. SYMPTOM ONSET:

HOURS   MINUTES   or   BEFORE SURFACING FROM DIVE

1st Symptom
2nd Symptom
3rd Symptom
4th Symptom
5th Symptom
6th Symptom

54. ANY OF THE SYMPTOMS FROM #51 PRIOR TO THE LAST DIVE?

- Y – Yes
- N – No

If yes, which symptoms?

1st   Other
2nd   Explain:
3rd _____
4th
5th
6th

55. FIRST AID ADMINISTERED BEFORE HOSPITAL OR CHAMBER HELP WAS RECEIVED?

- Y – Yes
- N – No

Oxygen

Aspirin

Oral fluids

Head down position/ Trendelenburg

If oxygen was received was delivery by:
- A – Demand valve
- B – Freeflow valve
- C – Don't know

PRE-CHAMBER INFORMATION (cont.)

56. HOSPITAL TREATMENT ADMINISTERED

(Please check all that apply):

- [ ] None
- [ ] Oral fluids
- [ ] IV fluids
- [ ] Oxygen
- [ ] Steroids
- [ ] Anticoagulant
- [ ] Aspirin
- [ ] Other medication

_____

_____

57. RELIEF BEFORE CHAMBER TREATMENT?

- [ ] A - Complete
  B - Partial
  C - Temporary
  D - None

59. PRE-CHAMBER RELIEF OCCURRED:

- [ ] A - Without first aid or medical care
  B - Following first aid
  C - Following pre-chamber hospital care
  D - No relief occurred

58. IF ANY RELIEF OCCURRED, WHICH SYMPTOMS FROM #51 ABOVE?
(Please check):

- 1st [ ]
- 2nd [ ]
- 3rd [ ]
- 4th [ ]
- 5th [ ]
- 6th [ ]

CHAMBER TREATMENT

60. CHAMBER TREATMENT FACILITY LOCATION

CITY

STATE   COUNTRY

Date & Time of Treatment

MONTH/DAY/YEAR

Time _____ AM PM

Name of hyperbaric facility:

Treating doctor

Form Completed By

_____

61. TYPE OF CHAMBER
(please check)

Initial Treatment

- [ ] Monoplace
- [ ] Dualplace
- [ ] Multiplace
- [ ] No chamber treatment given

Retreatment Chamber

- [ ] Monoplace
- [ ] Dualplace
- [ ] Multiplace

63. INITIAL TREATMENT

- [ ] A - USN TT4
  B - USN TT5
  C - USN TT6
  D - USN TT6A
  E - HART Protocol
  F - KINDWALL Protocol
  G - 45 fsw 90 min
  H - 33 fsw 120 min
  I - Other

  _____

  _____

62. TOTAL DELAY FROM SYMPTOM ONSET TO RECOMPRESSION

HOURS   or   DAYS

[|]   [|]

64. TABLE EXTENSIONS REQUIRED?

- [ ] Y - Yes
  N - No

65. RELIEF AFTER INITIAL TREATMENT OF SYMPTOMS FROM # 51?

- 1st [ ]
- 2nd [ ]
- 3rd [ ]
- 4th [ ]
- 5th [ ]
- 6th [ ]

Please indicate:
A - Complete
B - Partial
C - Temporary
D - None

66. RETREATMENT GIVEN
(Provide up to 3 responses)

TABLE | NUMBER OF TREATMENTS

[ ] [|]
[ ] [|]
[ ] [|]

A - USN TT4
B - USN TT5
C - USN TT6
D - USN TT6A
E - HART Protocol
F - KINDWALL Protocol
G - 45 fsw 90 min
H - 33 fsw 120 min
I - Other

_____

67. RELIEF AFTER HYPERBARIC THERAPY COMPLETED?

- [ ] A - Complete
  B - Partial
  C - Temporary
  D - Hyperbaric therapy not completed
  E - None

69. DURATION OF RESIDUAL SYMPTOMS

(Circle one)

[|]

DAYS

WEEKS

MONTHS

68. RESIDUAL SYMPTOMS AFTER HYPERBARIC THERAPY COMPLETED?

- [ ] A - Pain only
  B - Neurologic
  C - Hyperbaric therapy not completed
  D - None

70. FINAL DIAGNOSIS:

- [ ] A - DCS I
  B - DCS II
  C - Air Embolism
  D - Pulmonary Barotrauma
  O - Other:

  _____

  _____

  _____

I WOULD LIKE TO RECEIVE DAN INFORMATION.

- [ ] Y - Yes
  N - No

Diving Fatality Reporting Form

DAN research use only:

DAN CN _____ — _____ Source 1 _____ Source 2 _____ Source 3 _____ Source 4 _____

ME CN _____ First Contact _____

IA CN _____ Telephone _____ — (_____) — _____ — _____

Diver classification _____ Region _____

Diver Information

Date / time of accident _____

Date / time of death _____

Accident location _____

County _____ State _____ Country _____

Death location _____

County _____ State _____ Country _____

Name of deceased _____ _____ _____

        last   *first*   *middle*

Occupation _____

Date of birth _____

Age _____ **Sex** *(please circle)* Male   Female   **Race** _____

Height *(please circle)* _____ feet & inches   centimeters   **Weight** *(please circle)* _____ pounds   kilograms

Marital status _____ **Next of kin** _____ **Relationship** _____

Next of kin telephone _____ — (_____) — _____ — _____

Diver Experience

Certified *(please circle)*   Yes   No

Certifying agency *(please circle)*   BSAC   CMAS   NASDS   NAUI   PADI   PDIC   SSI   YMCA   None

Other _____

Certification level *(please circle)*   Open Water   Open Water I   Open Water II   Advanced   Rescue   Divemaster

Instructor   Assistant Instructor   Commercial   Other _____   None   Student

Number of years diving _____ years _____ months

Total lifetime dives made _____ Number of dives made in past year _____

Time since last dive series _____ days _____ months _____ years

General experience level *(please circle)*   Non-certified   Novice (0 to 5 dives)   Inexperienced (6 to 20 dives)

Intermediate (21 to 40 dives)   Advanced (41 to 60 dives)   Experienced (61+ dives)

Experience level with activity / environment *(please circle)*   Non-certified   Novice (0 to 5 dives)

Inexperienced (6 to 20 dives)   Intermediate (21 to 40 dives)   Advanced (41 to 60 dives)   Experienced (61+ dives)

Diver Health

Previous major illness _____ **When** _____ years _____ months

Current health problems _____

Undiagnosed health problems _____

Current Medications   *Prescription (please circle)*   Yes   No   *(please list)* _____

                      Nonprescription (please circle)   Yes   No   *(please list)* _____

Previous dive accidents *(please circle)* Yes   No   *(please list)* _____

Physically fit *(please circle)*   Yes   No   **Regular exercise** *(please circle)*   Yes   No

Cigarette use (*please circle*)   Have never smoked   Have smoked in past   Presently smoke

Years smoking _____   Packs per day _____

Predive health (*please circle*)   Nausea   Hangover   Diarrhea   Predive alcohol   No problem

Other _____

Influences at accident time (*please circle*)   Alcohol   Recreational drugs   None

Mental status (*please circle*)   Stressed   Anxious   Quiet   Agitated   Talkative   Depressed   No problem

Other _____

Fatigue (*please circle*)   Yes   No

Dive Conditions

Type of water entry (*please circle*)   Shore   Private boat   Charter boat   Pool

Other _____

Altitude of dive (*please circle*)   Sea level (below 1,000 feet)   Greater than 1,000 but less than 3,000 feet

Greater than 3,000 feet

Water environment (*please circle*)   Saltwater   Freshwater

Water temperature _____ °F °C   **Water depth** (*please circle*) _____ feet   metres

Seas _____   **Visibility** (*please circle*) _____ feet   metres

Surge _____   **Current** (*please circle*)   None   Mild   Moderate   Strong

Bottom type _____

Weather conditions (*describe*) _____   **Air temperature** _____ °F °C

Overhead environment (*please circle*)   Yes   No

(*if yes, please circle*)   Cavern   Cave   Ice   Wreck penetration

Other _____

Diver's first time at location (*please circle*)   Yes   No   **Surface observer** (*please circle*)   Yes   No

Surface tender (*please circle*)   Yes   No

Dive Profile

Dive activity (*please circle*)

Primary	*Secondary*
Wreck (no penetration)	Wreck (no penetration)
Wreck (penetration)	Wreck (penetration)
Cave	Cave
Cavern	Cavern
Night	Night
Ice	Ice
Photography	Photography
Under instruction	Under instruction
Providing instruction	Providing instruction
Spearfishing / game collection	Spearfishing / game collection
Pleasure / sightseeing	Pleasure / sightseeing
Work / task; commercial; deep dive	Work / task; commercial; deep dive
Other _____	Other _____

Specialty dive (*please circle*)   Yes   No   **Specialty certified** (*please circle*)   Yes   No

Buddy (*please circle*)   Yes   No   **Buddy separation** (*please circle*)   Yes   No

Number in buddy team _____   **Number in dive party** _____

Single dive (*please circle*)   Yes   No   **Decompression dive** (*please circle*)   Yes   No

Nitrogen narcosis (*please circle*)   Yes   No   **Lost** (*please circle*)   Yes   No

Trapped (*please circle*)   Yes   No   **Entangled** (*please circle*)   Yes   No

Dive profile	Dive 1	Dive 2	Dive 3
Depth (feet)	_____	_____	_____
Bottom time (min)	_____	_____	_____
Surface interval (hours / min)	_____:_____	_____:_____	_____:_____
	hours : min	hours : min	hours : min

Dive Equipment & Problems

Familiar with equipment *(please circle)*   Yes   No

Equipment source *(please circle)*   Borrowed   Rented   Owned

Dive computer *(please circle)*   Yes   No

Computer	Model		Computer	Model
Beuchat	_____		Scubapro	_____
Dacor	_____		Sherwood	_____
Mares	_____		Suunto	_____
Oceanic	_____		Tekna	_____
Orca	_____		U.S. Divers	_____
Parkway	_____		Other	_____
			Unknown	_____

Air supply *(please circle)*   Scuba   Surface-supplied   Mixed-gas scuba   Mixed-gas surface   Breathhold diving
Rebreather   Bad air supply

Air tested *(please circle)*   Yes   No   Agency _____

Air consumption *(please circle)*   Not a problem   Low on air   Out of air   Buddy breathing / sharing air

Exposure suit *(please circle)*   Wet   Partial wet   Dry   Lycra   Swim   None   Other _____

Weight belt *(please circle)* _____ lbs kgs   **Weight belt dropped** *(please circle)*   Yes   No

Buoyancy problem *(please circle)*   Yes   No   **Rapid ascent** *(please circle)*   Yes   No

Infrequent diver *(please circle)*   Yes   No   **Equipment problems** *(please circle)*   Yes   No

List problems (1) _____ (2) _____ (3) _____

Recovery & First Aid

Was event witnessed *(please circle)*   Yes   No   **By whom** _____

How long into the dive did the problem occur _____ *(minutes)*   _____ *(feet)*

When problem occurred *(please circle)*   Surface pre-dive   Immediately   Early dive   Mid-dive   Late dive   Post-dive
Unobserved

Where problem occurred *(please circle)* Surface pre-dive   Descent   Bottom   Ascent   Surface post-dive   Unobserved

Signs of diver in distress *(please circle)*   Yes   No   **Panic** *(please circle)*   Yes   No

Immediate search *(please circle)*   Yes   No

If no, after _____ *(days)*   _____ *(hours)*   _____ *(minutes)*

Body recovered *(please circle)*   Yes   No

If yes, after _____ *(days)*   _____ *(hours)*   _____ *(minutes)*

CPR done *(please circle)*   Yes   No   Not applicable

Oxygen available *(please circle)*   Yes   No   **Oxygen administered** *(please circle)*   Yes   No   Not applicable

USCG *(please circle)*   Yes   No   **Medevac** *(please circle)*   Yes   No

Emergency Treatment

Hospital _____

Location *(city, state, country)* _____

Contact _____

Telephone _____ — (_____) — _____ — _____

Hyperbaric treatment *(please circle)*   Yes   No

Type of chamber *(please circle)*   Monoplace   Dualplace   Multiplace

Attending physician _____

Hospital treatment including hyperbaric treatment

_____
_____
_____
_____
_____

Investigative Report

Agency *(please circle)*   Police   Sheriff   USCG   Other

Investigator / Contact _____

Telephone _____ — (_____) — _____ — _____

Accident scenario _____

_____

_____

_____

_____

Medical Examiner Report

Medical Examiner's name _____   **Coroner's name** _____

Address *(street, city, state, zip, country)*

_____

_____

Place death was registered _____

DAN research use only:

Probable cause of death _____   ICD-9-CM _____

Due to or as a result of 1 _____   ICD-9-CM _____

Due to or as a result of 2 _____   ICD-9-CM _____

Due to or as a result of 3 _____   ICD-9-CM _____

Due to or as a result of 4 _____   ICD-9-CM _____

Due to or as a result of 5 _____   ICD-9-CM _____

Contributing condition(s)

1 _____   ICD-9-CM _____

2 _____   ICD-9-CM _____

3 _____   ICD-9-CM _____

4 _____   ICD-9-CM _____

Manner of death *(please circle)*   Natural   Accident   Homicide   Suicide   Pending

Autopsy done *(please circle)*   Yes   No

Organ donor *(please circle)*   Yes   No

Organs harvested *(please list)*

_____

_____

Individual Submitting This Report

Name _____   **Daytime Telephone Number** _____ — (_____) — _____ — _____

Address *(street, city, state, zip, country)*

_____

_____

I understand that the information in this form will be used for research purposes only and that all personal information will be kept strictly confidential. I also understand that Divers Alert Network may need to contact me in the future for clarification of information provided on this form.

Signature _____

Diving Emergencies (919) 684-8111 • **Medical/Safety Information** (919) 684-2948 • **FAX** (919) 493-3040

ROWING TECHNIQUES

To operate a rowed rescue boat, the lifeguard takes a position in the exact center of the seat (or thwart) and places feet on the foot rest (or stretcher). The legs are bent slightly in a comfortable position. The back is kept straight, and the shoulders square. Oars are gripped as close to the ends as possible, fingers over the top and thumbs underneath. Thumbs should never be placed over the ends of the handles, where injury is possible. The oars are held with the wrists straight, and the blade of each oar perpendicular to the surface of the water. Hold the oars firmly but with ease.

In starting the stroke, the body is bent forward at the hips with the arms extending straight ahead. The blades are nearly vertical but with the lower edges slightly forward. This is done by raising the wrists slightly and rotating the knuckles partially down. Raise the arms and dip the blades gently into the water, straightening the wrists so that the blades are perpendicular and begin to pull. The arms serve chiefly as connecting rods between the shoulders and the oars, having no part in the actual heaving of the oars. This pulling is done with back and shoulders, bending at the hips and the arms fully stretched. The stroke is finished by bending the elbows and pulling with the arms, thus bringing the body upright again. The arms come into play on the final third of the stroke and serve to pull the body erect and ready for the next stroke.

The stroke should be steady, firm, and even. As the arms pull against the oars at the finish, bringing the body upright, the natural spring of the oars adds a final "kick" to the stroke which increases propelling power and aids in the recovery. Do not reach too far foward at the beginning of the stroke, or carry it too far at the end. Such movements increase the length of the stroke, but at these extremes the stroke has little propelling force and, consequently, nothing is gained.

At the end of the stroke, the body will be upright and the elbows close to the sides. When the stroke is finished and the oars are still in the water, drop the wrists a little and turn the upper edges of the blades slightly forward. Then slip them out of the water easily. When the blades are clear of the water, drop the wrists farther and bring the blades to a horizontal position parallel to the water. Straighten arms by pushing them forward and, at the same time, bend the body forward at the hips. The rower is then in a position to start the stroke again. As the blades come forward they will be flat and parallel to the water. Bringing the blades forward on their edges is called "feathering." In this position the blades offer a minimum of resistance to the air, and in case a blade touches the water or nicks the top of a wave, the rhythm of the movement is affected only slightly. Feathering is essential in good rowing and should receive careful attention.

When launching a rowed rescue boat in heavy surf one must be sure that all required equipment is in the boat. Spare oars are necessary in case of breakage or loss. With the bow toward the sea, run the boat out by pushing at the stern. Judge the waves for the best time to launch, vault into the boat and start rowing at once. Keep the bow toward the weather until the boat is past the breakers. A quick shifting of the rower's weight sternward just prior to impact of a wave will provide additional lift that will facilitate clearing the wave. Do not allow the boat to swing broadside to the breakers as it may be swamped, or get out of control. The rower must judge the proper point of balance between the force of the wind and that of the waves. In the event that control is lost and the boat must be abandoned, enter the water on the off-shore or weather side to avoid injury as the boat washes toward the shore or the lee.

The backwater stroke is used to reach shore in heavy surf so as to keep the bow of the boat facing the waves. Ship oars in shallow water, vault over the weather side, grasp the boat and run to shore.

BIBLIOGRAPHY

Research and publications relating to water safety, lifesaving, and lifeguarding span several decades and disciplines. The following list of references represent many of the books, periodicals, papers, and publications that were consulted in the development of this textbook. Some of these publications are no longer in print.

1992 Report on Diving Accidents and Facilities, ed. J.A. Dovenbarger, Durham, NC: Divers Alert Network, 1992.

American Academy of Sports and Medicine, *Exercise Prescription and Standards Manual,* American Academy of Sports and Medicine, 1991.

American Red Cross, *Emergency Response,* St. Louis, MO: Mosby-Year Book, Inc., 1993.

American Red Cross, *Lifeguarding,* Washington, D.C: American Red Cross, 1990.

Austin Parks & Recreation Department, *Lifeguarding Policies and Procedures Manual,* Austin, TX: Austin Parks & Recreation Department, 1992.

Baker, Susan P., *The Injury Fact Book,* (2nd ed.), New York: Oxford University Press,1992.

Barnett, J.P., *The Lifesaving Guns of David Lyle,* Plymouth, IN: Town and Country Press, 1974.

Bascom, Willard, *Waves and Beaches,* New York: Doubleday, 1980.

Burgess, G. H., "Shark Aggression in Nearshore Waters: A Florida Perspective," *Proceedings of Sea Symposium 89*, ed. J. Fletemeyer, Florida Sea Grant Press, 1989.

Burnett, Joseph, "Sunburning, Sun Damage and Sun Protection," *American Lifeguard,* Summer 1988.

Chicago Park District, *Lifeguard Academy Instructor's Manual,* Chicago, IL: Chicago Park District Beach and Pool Unit, 1987.

Chicago Park District, *Lifeguard Manual,* Chicago, IL: Chicago Park District, 1983.

East Bay Regional Park District, *Lifeguard Service Manual,* Oakland, CA: East Bay Regional Park District, 1993.

Grant, and others, *Emergency Care* (5th ed.), Bowie, MD: Brady Publishing, 1990.

Hall, Timothy, *Lifeguard Services Manual,* Hamilton, Bermuda: Bermuda Department of Agriculture, Fisheries and Parks, 1988.

Halstead, B. W., *Poisonous and Venomous Marine Animals of the World,* Pennington, NJ: Darwin Press, Inc., 1978.

Incident Command System, The (NFA-ICS-SM), Emmitsburg, MD: National Emergency Training Center, FEMA, 1992.

Iversen, I. and R., Skinner, *How to Cope with Dangerous Sea Life*, Miami, FL: Windward Publishing Co., 1989.

Johnson, Robert Erwin *Guardians of the Sea, History of the United States Coast Guard,* Annapolis, MD: Naval Institue Press, 1987.

Linton, Steven J. and others, *The Dive Rescue Specialist Training Manual,* Fort Collins, CO: Dive Rescue Inc., 1986.

Lippman, John, "Dive Rescue: Some Considerations and Uncertainties, 1994," *The Undersea Journal,* First Quarter Edition, 1994.

Long Beach Patrol, *Training and Operations Manual*, Long Beach, NY: 1994.

Los Angeles County, *Ocean Lifeguard Training Manual,* Los Angeles, CA: County of Los Angeles Department of Beaches and Harbors, 1993.

McCloy, James M., and James A. Dodson, *Guidelines for Establishing Open Water Recreational Beach Standards: Conference Proceedings*, Galveston, TX: A&M University, 1980.

McDaniel, David, "What's New in Dermatology," *American Lifeguard,* January 1986.

McNeely, Jr., William, *St. Lucie County Marine Safety Operations Manual*, St. Lucie County, FL: 1993.

Model, Jerome H., *The Pathophysiology and Treatment of Drowning and Near Drowning,* Springfield, IL: Charles C. Thomas, 1971.

Occupational Safety and Health Administration (OSHA), *Occupational Exposure to Bloodborne Pathogens,* 29 CFR Part 1910.1030, 1991.

Ocean Grove Beaches, *Ocean Grove Lifeguard Manual*, Ocean Grove, NJ: Ocean Grove Beaches, 1994.

Orlowski, James P., "Adolescent Drownings: Swimming, Boating, Diving and SCUBA Accidents," *American Lifeguard,* Autumn 1988.

Quinn, William P., *Shipwrecks Around Cape Cod*, Farmington, ME: Knowlton and McLeary, 1973.

Royal Lifesaving Society of Canada, The, *Alert Lifeguarding in Action,* Ottawa, Ontario: The Royal Lifesaving Society of Canada, 1993.

Ryder, Richard G., *Old Harbor Station,* Norwich, CT: Ram Island Press, 1990.

San Diego Lifeguard Service, *Lifeguard Manual,* San Diego, CA: San Diego Lifeguard Service, 1994.

Sandy Hook Beach Patrol, *Lifeguard Manual*, Sandy Hook, NJ: Sandy Hook Beach Patrol, 1994.

Silvia, Charles E., *Lifesaving and Water Safety Today*, New York: Association Press, 1965.

United States Coast Guard, *Boating Statistics 1992,* Washington, DC: United States Coast Guard, 1993.

United States Lifesaving Association, *Guidelines for Open Water Lifeguard Training & Standards,* Huntington Beach, CA: United States Lifesaving Association, 1993.

United States Lifesaving Association, *Lifesaving and Marine Safety,* Huntington Beach, CA: United States Lifesaving Association, 1981.

Volusia County Beach Patrol, *Standard Operating Procedure Manual,* Volusia County, FL: Volusia County Beach Patrol, 1993.

Williams, Jack, *The Weather Book,* New York: Random House, 1992.

YMCA of the USA, *On the Guard: The YMCA Lifeguard Manual,* Champaign, IL: Human Kinetics Publishers, Inc., 1986.

GLOSSARY

abaft   aft of, to the rear of

abeam   on the side of the vessel, amidships, at right angles to

about   to go on the opposite tack, change directions

abyss   an extraordinarily deep area of the ocean

accretion   gradual build-up of sand or shoreline due to current or tidal action

adrift   floating at the mercy of wind or current

aft   toward the stern of a vessel

aground   a vessel which has struck bottom; also known as grounded, beached

air embolism   in scuba diving, a serious disorder caused by rapid expansion of air in the lungs during a fast ascent—as air pressure increases, the air goes through the walls of the alveoli, causing bubbles to form in the bloodstream, and can then travel throughout the circulatory system, resulting in blockages and related complications

all terrain vehicle (ATV)   a small three or four wheel vehicle with oversized tires or treads designed for use on rough terrain

alveoli   small sacs in the lungs where exchange of carbon dioxide and oxygen takes place

amidships   middle point of a vessel between bow and stern

anoxia (also anoxemia)   absence of oxygen

antifouling paint   a substance applied to the hull of a vessel which is intended to chemically resist the attachment of marine organisms

antimicrobial   a substance that is capable of destroying or inhibiting growth of microorganisms

Aqualung (TM)   see scuba

artificial respiration   inflating the lungs of a person by mechanical means or by blowing into the airway of the victim

ash breeze   absence of wind; calm

aspirate   to inhale a substance into the lungs; a typical finding in a near drowning incident is *water aspiration* (NOTE: Statistics suggest that for every drowning, there are well over 10 cases of water aspiration. All victims of a near-drowning should be checked carefully for water aspiration and treated appropriately. Because of the potential for secondary drowning, transportation to a medical facility may be necessary.)

aspirator   tool used to clear fluid or food regurgitation from the air passages of an asphyxiated or non-breathing patient

astern   behind a vessel

atmosphere   (physics) a unit of pressure equal to the air pressure at sea level; pressure at sea level (one atmosphere) is 14.7 pounds per square inch (psi), but it doubles at 33 feet in water depth (two atmospheres), triples at 66 feet in depth (three atmospheres), quadruples at 99 feet in depth (four atmospheres), and so on

awash   covered by water; usually the state of a vessel overcome by waves or tide

backboard   see spineboard

backrush   see backwash

backup   safety personnel who respond in order to assist or stand by at a rescue operation

backwash   seaward return of water following the uprush of a wave on the beach

backwater   (1) water turned back by an obstruction, opposing the current, or the like; (2) to propel a rowboat or dory in a stern first direction using a reverse rowing or boating stroke

bag valve mask resuscitator (BVM)   a hand-held ventilation device used for artificial respiration consisting of a self inflating bag, a one-way valve, and a face mask; used with or without oxygen

ballast   broken stone, gravel, or other heavy material used in a vessel to improve stability or control the draft

bar   a submerged or emerged embankment of sand, gravel, or mud built on the sea floor in shallow water by waves and currents

barometer   an instrument for measuring atmospheric pressure and generally used for predicting changes in the weather

bar port   a harbor that can be entered only when the tide rises sufficiently to permit passage of vessels over a bar

bather   (dated term) a swimmer or wader

bathymetric chart   a map delineating the form of the bottom of a body of water, usually by means of depth contours

BC, BCD   see buoyancy compensator

beach break   waves breaking in long lines on a sharply sloping sand beach

beach erosion   the carrying away of beach material by wave action, tidal currents, littoral currents, or wind

beam   (1) a vessel's maximum width; (2) the side of a vessel

beam sea   wind at right angles to a vessel's keel

bearing   the direction of an object from an observer or from another object *becalm*   a sailing vessel is becalmed when there is no wind adequate to propel the vessel forward; also known as being "in irons"

belly board   a small surfboard or similar inflexible object ridden in the surf in a prone position; also known as a paipo board, Boogie Board®, or bodyboard

bends   see decompression sickness

berm   a narrow shelf, path, or ledge created by wave action on the sand

bilge   lower internal part of a vessel's hull

billow   usually a great wave or surge of water; any wave

bitt   a vertical post (usually one of a pair) fitted into a vessel's deck for securing lines for towing, mooring, or other purposes

blind rollers   long, high swells that have increased in height almost to the breaking point as they pass over shoals or run in shoaling water

bloodborne pathogen   an agent carried in the blood, particularly a living microorganism, capable of causing disease

blown out   the state of waves which have been knocked down by wind

board surfing   any activity that involves riding waves with the use of a surfboard, or being carried along or propelled by the action of waves with the use or aid of a surfboard; also known as surfing, riding

boating   the standing, forward facing rowing position used by the stern rower of a dory

boat tow   a short length of line with a fastener at each end that enables a swimming lifeguard to tow a boat in distress; one end is secured to the end of a rescue buoy and the other clipped to the bow eye of the vessel in distress

bodyboard   see belly board

body skimming   sliding along the beach on thin water in a prone position after gaining momentum from running and leaping forward; also known as body whomping

body surfing   riding a wave without the aid of a floating device; also known as body whomping, wave riding

boil   up-welling of water caused by a swell riding or striking shallow water or rock formations, causing a visual disturbance on the water surface; also known as up-swelling, swirls

Boogie Board®   see belly board

bosun's chair   a seat in which a person hangs while being moved from one vessel to another or to shore

bow   the forward part of a vessel

breaker   a wave breaking on the shore, over shoal water or reef; a wave which makes an audible noise as it spills over; also known as a crasher

breakwater   a structure protecting a shore area, harbor, anchorage, or basin from waves or current; also known as seawall, jetty

broach   to veer sideways to the wind or swell; a vessel which broaches in the surf is in great danger

buddy system   two persons, usually divers, swimming together for mutual support and safety

bulkhead   (1) any upright partition separating compartments on a vessel; (2) a wall or embankment for holding back earth and protecting a shoreline from erosion due to wave action

buoy line   (1) a line supported by buoys, used to delineate a boundary in the water; (2) separated buoys placed in a line to delineate a water boundary

buoyancy compensator (BC)   an inflatable vest-like device used by divers to compensate for changing buoyancy when descending and ascending; most can be filled by breathing into a mouthpiece or directly from a scuba tank by opening a valve; often attached to a CO_2 cartridge which will fully inflate the vest instantly in an emergency by pulling a cord; also known as a buoyancy compensator device (BCD)

Burnside, Bob   the Los Angeles County lifeguard credited with bringing the modern plastic rescue buoy to use, still known to some as the *Burnside Buoy*

calm   the state or condition of the water surface when there is no wind, wave action, or surface disturbance

can rack   storage rack for rescue buoys

cataract   a clouding of the lens of the eye, associated with long-term exposure to sunlight

cat's paw   a puff of wind; a light breeze affecting a small area, one that causes patches of ripples on the surface of a water area

certification officer   (USLA) person appointed by the USLA; primarily responsible for evaluating whether an applying agency adheres to the recommended USLA open water lifeguard training guidelines

chafe   to rub or damage by rubbing

chafing gear   anything used to prevent chafing

channel   (1) a natural or artificial waterway that periodically or continuously contains moving water, or that forms a connecting link between two bodies of water; (2) the part of a body of water deep enough to be used for navigation through an area otherwise too shallow for navigation; (3) the deepest portion of a stream, bay, or rip current through which the main volume or current of water flows

chock   a heavy casting of metal or wood with two short horn-shaped arms curving inward between which ropes or a hawser may pass for towing, mooring, etc.

chop   disturbed surface of water usually caused by strong wind or after-effects of waves; white caps

cleat   a metal fitting with two horns pointing in opposite directions and used for temporarily fastening line; usually attached to a dock, pier, or vessel

close hauled   setting a sail such that the boom roughly parallels the length of a vessel, when sailing in the direction of the wind; also known as reefing

coast   the general region of indefinite width that extends from the sea inland to the first major change in terrain features

coastal current   a relatively uniform drift usually flowing parallel to the shore in the deep water adjacent to the surf line; may be related to tides, winds, or distribution of mass; also known as offshore current

Code III   the code in many states for an expedited emergency response; requires emergency lights and siren for an emergency vehicle

Code X   (1) the USLA approved code word which signifies a missing (submerged) swimmer and causes implementation of an emergency plan for locating and retrieving a missing swimmer; (2) the USLA approved signal for a missing (submerged) swimmer formed by crossing the arms overhead in the form of an X

comber   a deep water wave whose crest is pushed forward by strong wind

coral   (1) a rocklike structure or reef formed of the hard calcareous skeleton of various anthozoans; (2) a polyp of the family Anthozoa

coral head   a mushroom or pillar-shaped coral growth

countercurrent   a current flowing adjacent to the main current but in an opposing direction

crasher   a wave breaking hard from top to bottom; also known as pounder, coming over, heavy, sand buster, cruncher

crest   the highest part of a wave

crest width   the length of a wave along its crest

curl   curved portion of a wave which tumbles forward

current   a stream of flowing water

daily information board   a sign displayed by lifeguards advising the public of ambient weather and surf conditions, as well as other topical information

davit   a small crane-like device on a vessel used for launching a small boat over the side or hoisting cargo; usually used in tandem with one holding the bow and the other the stern of the small boat

dead reckoning   a method of navigation utilizing only the speed and heading of the craft, without reference to astronomical observations or mechanical positioning devices

decompression illness a scuba diving affliction which occrs when compressed gases in the body produce bubbles which form in the cells or circulatory system as the diver ascends or at some point after the dive; generally associated with rapid ascent; the two types are decompression sickness (the bends) and arterial gas embolism, also known as air embolism

decompression sickness scuba diving disease which occurs when the diver ascends too rapidly and nitrogen trapped in the body cells forms air bubbles

defibrillator a device that sends an electric shock through the body in an attempt to change the rhythm of an ineffectively beating heart to a productive rhythm

degree (1) a unit of temperature; (2) a unit of angular distance; 1/360 part of a circle

demand valve a valve attached to a face mask that delivers oxygen to a breathing person on demand

diver's flag a flag, generally flown on a floating device, intended to warn boaters of submerged scuba divers; standard appearance of the diver's flag is either square red with a white diagonal bar or the alpha flag (burgee) with inner half blue, outer half white

dive tables chart of rules for scuba divers to use to avoid decompression sickness; also known as decompression tables

documented vessel vessel registered with the U.S. Bureau of Customs or the U.S. Coast Guard

dorsal fin the main fin located along the back of many fish and marine mammals

dory (lifeguard) boat with narrow flat bottom and high flaring sides propelled by rowing and designed for use in surf

draft the depth of a vessel below the water line

drowning asphyxiation by submersion in water or other liquid

dry suit diver's suit designed to protect and retain body heat without allowing water to permeate

ebb current outgoing tidal current associated with a decrease in the height of a tide

ebb tide outgoing tide

eddy a circular movement of water usually formed where currents pass obstructions, between two adjacent currents flowing counter to each other, or along the edge of a permanent current

Eight Plate® descent device shaped like the number 8 which, when properly used, exerts friction on a line passing through it and allows control of the line with a load placed on it; used in cliff rescue; also known as figure eight

electrolysis (nautical) chemical decomposition of metals or alloys caused by an electrical current and the marine environment

embayment an indentation in a shore line forming an open bay

Emergency Medical System (EMS) network of community resources and medical personnel to provide emergency care to victims of sudden illness or injury

emergency operation plan (EOP) a plan for efficient response to an anticipated emergency situation

equalize to bring air pressure in the sinuses to a point equal to ambient air pressure; necessary primarily in scuba diving and flying; also known as clearing

equatorial tides tides occurring approximately every two weeks when the moon is over the equator

erosion a natural process by which sand, soil, or rock is broken up and transported, usually by wind or water

estuary the area where a river meets a tidal bay; also known as drowned river mouth, branching bay, firth, forth

exostosis an abnormal bony growth on the surface of a bone or tooth (sometimes a complication in the ear canal of swimmers due to long term exposure to cold water)

fake (n) one coil of a rope; (v) to lay out line in such a way that it will easily play out when one end is thrown or otherwise pulled

fathom a six foot measure of water depth

fathometer device used to measure the depth of the water; also known as depth gauge, depth finder, depth sounder

feathering (1) a wave just beginning to break, blowing white water on the peak of a wave caused by wind or momentum; also known as knifer, hanging up; (2) rowing technique involving dropping the wrists to cause the oar blades to be parallel to the water on the return stroke

feeder channels channels parallel to the shore along which feeder currents flow before converging to form the neck of a rip current

feeder current of water moving along the shore providing water to a rip current; usually created by wave action and gravity

feeling bottom the action of a deep water wave on running into shallow water and beginning to be influenced by the bottom

fender cushion to protect a boat from bumping against a dock or another boat; also known as bumper

fetch (1) an area of the sea surface over which seas are generated by a wind having constant direction and speed; (2) the length of the fetch area, measured in the direction of the wind in which the seas are generated

first responder a medical aid provider who is first at the scene of a medical emergency

flag system consistently colored flags used to designate certain water activity or surf conditions

floatation device any device that a person uses for support on the water surface

flood   the incoming tide

flotsam   floating debris, driftwood, etc.

flow   the combination of tidal and nontidal current that represents the actual water movement

free ascent   an emergency ascent by a scuba diver attempting to reach the surface when air supply is unexpectedly unavailable; a free ascent is likely to result in decompression illness

free diver   a diver operating without the benefit of scuba equipment; also known as a skin diver

freeboard   the vertical distance from the water to the gunwale of a vessel

full-time lifeguard   lifeguard appointed to a full-time, year round position as a lifeguard at an open water beach

fully developed sea   the maximum height to which ocean waves can be generated by a given wind force

gang grapnel   a series of hooks set in a parallel pattern and used in the same fashion as a grappling hook

glassy   smooth, unrippled sea surface caused by the absence of wind

grappling hook   a device with four, five, or more flukes or claws used to drag on the bottom to snag corpses or other objects

groin   a small jetty, extending at roughly right angles to the shore, usually designed to trap lateral drift and/or retard erosion of the shoreline

ground swell   a long, high ocean swell

guarded area   water recreational area with lifeguards on duty; also known as a guarded beach

guide lines   lines secured to an object to prevent it from being damaged; lines attached to aid in control of a floating or suspended object

guidelines   the USLA Guidelines for Open Water Lifeguard Training & Standards promulgated by the USLA for use in the national Lifeguard Agency Certification Program

gully   a relatively narrow ravine in the ocean bed

gunwale (gun-el)   the upper edge of the side of a vessel; also known as the rail

gutter rip   a short, powerful, fast-moving rip current found on a scalloped, steep, sloping beachfront; gutter rips can sweep people off their feet by surprise and into the next wave; the sweeping underwater current action is often confused with the misnomer "undertow"

harbor   an area of water affording natural or manufactued protection for vessels

hawser   a heavy line used to moor or tow a vessel

head of a rip   area where the neck of a rip widens and disperses and the power of the rip ends

heavy sea   severe water disturbance caused by winds or swell; also known as rough sea

heavy surf   large breaking waves; also known as heavies, surf's up, crashers, blue birds on the horizon

helm   wheel or tiller by which a vessel is steered

helmsman   one who steers a vessel; also known as driver, operator, pilot

high siding   leaning body weight toward that side of a boat that is broadside and being pushed by a wave in an effort to avoid capsizing

high water mark   the highest point that water reaches during a tidal phase; it varies daily with the changing lunar phases and meteorological conditions; also known as high water line, beach line, tide line

hurricane wave   a sudden rise in the level of the sea associated with a hurricane; also known as hurricane surge, hurricane tide

hydrofoil   a vessel equipped with planes that provide lift when the vessel is propelled forward

hyperventilation   excessive breathing in and out; skin divers hyperventilate when preparing to hold their breath; hyperventilation purges the breathing stimulant, carbon dioxide, out of the respiratory system and to a minor degree increases the percentage of oxygen in the lungs; hyperventilation can cause unconsciousness and drowning

incident command system (ICS)   a system used to control and direct resources at the scene of an emergency; commonly used by emergency providers

incident commander (IC)   the person in charge of an emergency incident; most often used when the incident command system has been formally implemented

inshore rescue boat (IRB)   an inflatable soft hulled boat powered by an outboard engine capable of carrying several lifeguards and rescue equipment; also known as an inflatable rescue boat

inflatable rescue boat (IRB)   see inshore rescue boat

inhalator   machine used to administer a fresh flow of oxygen or air on demand to a breathing patient

in irons   a condition that prevents a sailing vessel from moving forward; the operator of a sailing vessel that is in irons is unable to change the position of the vessel to allow the sails to fill

inlet   a short, narrow waterway connecting a bay or lagoon with the sea

inside   area between the breaking waves and the shoreline; usage: "he was caught inside by large surf" *intersecting waves*   one of the component waves that, when superimposed on others, produces cross-swells; also known as sugarloaf sea, pyramidal sea

intertidal zone   that portion of the shoreline lying between the high and low tide marks

intramuscular   within a muscle (e.g., an intramuscular injection involves first inserting a needle into the muscle)

intravenous   within a vein or administered into a vein (e.g., intravenous fluids are administered by first inserting a needle into a blood vein)

inversion layer   a layer of water in which temperature increases with depth

invertebrate   an organism that lacks a spine, such as a sea urchin or mollusk

isthmus   a narrow strip of land, bordered on both sides by water, that connects two larger bodies of land

jettison   to throw objects overboard, especially to lighten a craft in distress; to remove articles from a person to allow more buoyancy, such as the weight belt from a scuba diver

jetty   a structure, usually of rock, extending into a body of water to protect a harbor or shoreline from erosion and storm activity; also knowns as a groin

junior lifeguard   adolescent or younger person involved in a program taught by professional lifeguards to learn lifeguarding techniques; also known as nipper, J.G., junior guard

keel   a longitudinal structure extending along the center of the bottom of a vessel that gives main support to the vessel's hull bottom; the keel often projects below the bottom; also known as center line, skeg

kelp   the general name for large species of seaweeds; kelp forests are common along the West Coast with single plants extending 60 or more feet from the bottom; also known as seaweed

Kimball, Sumner Increase   first and only leader of the U.S. Lifesaving Service during its existence from 1878 to 1915; formerly chief of the Revenue Marine Division, which included lifesaving services from 1871 to 1878

knee board   a type of belly board designed and used to surf in a kneeling position

knot   one nautical mile per hour (a nautical mile is 1.15 times a statute mile)

lagoon   a shallow sound, pond, or lake generally separated from the open ocean

landline   line swum out to a victim or victims caught in a rip or other current and used to pull them to shore; also known as a reel, line, or lifeline

landmarks   conspicuous objects on land or sea that mark a locality; a visual line-up of two or more fixed objects on the beach to obtain a precise location on the water surface; also known as marks

lead line   (1) a line, wire, or cord used in sounding; (2) a light line which is thrown, shot, or swum to make a connection between two points and to then pull a larger line, such as a hawser, between them (usually for towing purposes)

leash   a short line used to secure a surfboard, belly board, bodyboard, or similar floatation device to the user's wrist or ankle; also known as a tether, surf leash

leeward   the side (usually of a vessel) away from the wind

life car   a device used by the first lifesavers in conjunction with the breeches buoy apparatus to evacuate several victims at a time from a distressed ship

lifeguard boat   vessel used by lifeguards to save lives and property or to patrol an assigned area; also known as rescue boat, patrol boat, surf boat

lifeguard stand   a primitive elevated observation post used by lifeguards, lacking first aid or storage facilities; usually staffed only in the busy season; also known as seasonal tower, bird cage, supplementary tower, perch, bench

lifeguard vehicle   vehicle used to transport backup lifeguards and lifesaving equipment to needed areas and to patrol an assigned area; also known as a jeep, rescue vehicle, four-wheel drive vehicle, mobile unit, area unit, lifeguard truck

life ring   a floating ring which can be thrown to a person in distress, often including rope around the edges

littoral transport   the movements of material along the shore in the littoral zone by waves and currents

littoral zone   the nearshore zone

log book   book kept at main stations, on rescue boats, and in emergency vehicles listing pertinent daily activities and times; used as a record of lifeguard activity

low water   the lowest limit of the surface water level reached by the lowering or outgoing tide

lull   period of lower waves between sets of unusually large waves

lunar tide   that part of the tide caused solely by the tide-producing forces of the moon as distinguished from that part caused by the forces of the sun

Lyle, David   originator of the Lyle gun used by early lifesavers to deploy the breeches buoy apparatus

macular degeneration   loss of central vision, associated with long-term exposure to sunlight

main tower   a lifeguard station, usually staffed all year, that supplies assistance to other lifeguard facilities in a given area; also known as tower zero, mother station, central vantage tower, control tower

make fast   to secure the end of a line by tying it to a fixed point

mass rescue   a rescue involving multiple victims, usually more than two or three; also known as multiple victim rescue

mat surf   surfing waves with the aid of an air-filled, semi-flexible object; also known as air mattress, rubber raft, float

mean high water   the average height of high tides

mean low water the average height of low tides

mechanical resuscitation resuscitation done with the aid of a mechanical device, as opposed to mouth-to-mouth

mooring an anchored buoy to which a boat is secured when not in use

mouth-to-mouth resuscitation of a non-breathing victim by blowing air from the mouth of the rescuer into the victim's airway; also known as rescue breathing

mouthpiece the breathing end of a snorkel

mud flat a muddy or sandy coastal strip usually submerged by high tide

narcosis (nitrogen narcosis) a sense of stupor or drunkenness felt by deep sea divers due to increased levels of dissolved nitrogen in the blood; also known as rapture of the deep

neck portion of a rip where most drownings and rescues take place

nematocyst stingers, found in jellyfish and Portuguese man-of-war, which are intended to paralyze prey and ward off attackers

nontidal current any current that is caused by other than tidal forces

notice to mariners a periodic notice containing information affecting the safety of navigation

observer a person in a vessel delegated to watch a person or object being towed by the vessel

offshore wind a wind blowing seaward from the land in a coastal area; also known as land breeze, opposing wind

one-feeder rip rip current fed by a current coming from only one direction

onshore wind a wind blowing landward from the sea in a coastal area; also known as a sea breeze

open water any sizable natural body of water such as a lake, river, ocean, or bay

OSHA acronym for the Occupational Safety and Health Administration of the U.S. Department of Labor, charged with ensuring that workplaces are safe

outflow the flow of water from a river or its estuary to the sea

outside anything on the offshore side of the surfline; also known as back side, out back

over the falls object or person falling without control from wave peak to the wave bottom; also known as a wipeout

painter a short line attached to the bow of a small boat primarily for purposes of fastening to a dock or towing

parenteral brought into the body other than through the digestive tract, such as by intravenous or intramuscular injection

passage a narrow navigable pass or channel between two land masses or shoals

pathogen an agent, particularly a living microorganism, which causes disease

patrol walking or driving in an emergency vehicle or rescue boat, with ready rescue gear, to observe and inspect a beach and water area; also known as a beach check, beach run, down to the line

peak the top of a wave at the maximum point before breaking

permanent lifeguard (see full-time lifeguard)

personal floatation device (PFD) a buoyant device designed to be held or worn to keep a person afloat; also known as a life jacket

Peterson, Pete the Santa Monica lifeguard who designed the first rescue tube, still known to some as the *Peterson Tube*

photokeratitis damage to the cornea of the eye from exposure to intense light

plunging wave wave that tends to curl over and break with a crash; also known as crasher, heavy, breaker

pod a school of marine mammals, such as seals or whales

porpoise (lifeguarding) an action taken by a lifeguard to move through water, particularly incoming surf, during the transition from high stepping through shallow water to swimming; the arcing motion of repeatedly diving forward in a surface dive, grabbing the sand, crouching, and then diving forward again

port side of a vessel to left when aboard the vessel and facing the bow

posted area area that has signs, flags, or signals regulating water and beach activities; also known as designated area, signed area

pothole a hole in the ocean floor in the surf line a few feet or yards in diameter; also known as hole, inshore hole

prevailing current the flow most frequently observed during a given period, usually a month, season, or year; also known as prevailing drag

preventive action providing verbal commands or advice to people to help them avoid or extricate themselves from a dangerous area; note: a preventive action is not a rescue; see rescue

primary zone a lifeguard's assigned water zone of responsibility

protocol standardized method

psi acronym for pounds per square inch

pterygium a callous-like growth that can spread over the white of the eye, caused by exposure to sunlight, wind, and dust or blowing sand; requires surgery to remove

race a very fast current flowing through a relatively narrow channel

radio code numbers used in place of often-used words or phrases for the purpose of abbreviating radio conversations and masking their meaning; also known as code list, codes, code

rail   the edge of a rescue board or surfboard running lengthwise

ready about   warning by the operator of a sailing vessel to the crew to prepare for a change of tack and swing of the boom

recompression   the treatment of decompression sickness or an air embolism, in a recompression chamber, which simulates returning the injured diver to an underwater depth

recurring training   training conducted cyclically to maintain proficiency in rescue, physical, and EMS skills

red tide   rust-coloring in the ocean caused by a natural dinoflagellate plankton bloom, usually in the spring and summer

reef   any hard geographical structure that is underwater at high tide

reef break   isolated waves breaking over shallow waters of a reef; also known as peak break

reflected wave   a wave that is returned seaward when it impinges upon a very steep beach, barrier, or other reflecting surface; also known as back wash

refraction of water waves   a phenomenon by which wave trains approaching a beach from an acute angle tend to wrap to a direct, perpendicular angle prior to striking the shoreline

regulator   a mechanical device for adjusting the high pressure flow of air from a compressed air cylinder to the current atmospheric pressure so that it can be comfortably breathed

repetitive dive   more than one saturation dive over 33 feet using scuba gear; also known as repeat

rescue   any case in which a lifeguard physically assists a victim in extrication from the water when the victim lacks apparent ability to do so alone; also known as a run, save, pull out, jump, job (see preventive action)

rescue board   a large, wide surfboard over ten feet long, usually with handles, used to make rescues; also known as a paddle board

rescue boat   a boat used in the observation and rescue of swimmers, surfers, or boats; may be motorized or manually powered; some rescue boats are used in firefighting and related functions; also known as a patrol boat or lifeguard boat

rescue breathing   resuscitation of a non-breathing victim by blowing air from the mouth of the rescuer into a non-breathing victim's airway; also known as mouth-to-mouth

rescue buoy   cylindrical floatation device with handles, which can be towed by a lifeguard using an attached line and harness, used to effect a swimming rescue; modern rescue buoys are made of hard plastic; also known as a torpedo buoy, torp, can, or can buoy

rescue floatation device (RFD)   elongated floatation device, which can be towed by a lifeguard using an attached line and harness, used to effect a swimming rescue; the two major types of RFDs are the rescue buoy and rescue tube

rescue tube   a flexible, foam rubber RFD which can be wrapped around a victim's chest, fastened, and used by a lifeguard to tow the victim to safety

resting stroke   swimming stroke used to rest the body without losing buoyancy or forward motion; may indicate fatigue; common resting strokes are sidestroke, breaststroke

resurgence   the continued rising and falling of a bay or semi-enclosed water body many hours after the passage of a severe storm

resuscitation   process of rhythmically inflating the lungs of an asphyxiated victim with oxygen or air

resuscitator   machine used to rhythmically inflate the lungs of an asphyxiated victim with oxygen from a tank

retardation   the amount of time by which corresponding tidal phases grow later day by day

RFD   acronym for "rescue floatation device"

rhumb line   the path of a vessel that maintains a fixed course without variation

rip current   current of water traveling away from shore generated by wave action; also known as a rip, hole, seaward current, run, runout; note: the rip current is commonly misnamed a "rip tide," although tides have only a peripheral impact on the formation of rip currents

roller   (1) one of a series of waves, usually a long-crested wave that rolls up a beach; (2) a cylinder used to facilitate moving small boats on the land

rowboat   a small boat designed to be propelled with oars

rudder   the device used for steering and maneuvering a boat, particularly a sailboat or a large motorized boat

run   lifeguard or equipment enroute to a rescue or assist; assist or rescue in progress; also known as a rescue assist, emergency, Code III

sand bar   a ridge of sand submerged or exposed in the surfline; also known as a bar, shoal

scuba   self-contained underwater breathing apparatus which involves the use of a tank of compressed air and a regulator to reduce the pressure of the air to a breathable pressure

scull   (1) an oar positioned at the stern of a boat and used to propel it forward through a back and forth motion; (2) either of two oars at the side of a light boat used by a single rower; (3) a light racing boat propelled by rowing; (4) to propel a boat using a scull or sculls

sea anchor   device attached to a vessel by a line which traps water, thus creating a drag; used to retard the drift of a vessel, usually in the open ocean where depths do not allow anchoring

seaboard   a general term for an extensive expanse of coastal region bordering the sea; e.g., the Eastern Seaboard refers to the East Coast of the United States *sea level*   the height of the surface of the sea at a given point in time; also known as water level

sea wall   a manufactured structure of rock, concrete, or wood built along a portion of coast to prevent wave erosion of the beach

search pattern   a preplanned course for covering an area in an effort to locate a missing person or object; also known as a search line

seasonal current   a current that changes with seasonal winds or swell direction

seasonal lifeguard   lifeguard employed during the summer months, vacations, weekends, and holidays, usually an hourly employee; also known as a recurrent guard, weekend guard, part-time guard, guard as needed, temporary guard, summer guard

seaward   the direction away from shore and toward the sea

seaweed   any macroscopic marine algae, such as seagrass or kelp

sediment   any natural material carried in suspension by water that causes underwater visibility obstruction

seiche   an occasional and sudden oscillation of the water of a lake, bay, or estuary resulting in dramatic changes in the water level caused by wind or change in barometric pressure; may result in sudden shoreline flooding

senior guard   a lifeguard who by virtue of experience, knowledge, and/or maturity has been assigned to a key station, tower, area, or special departmental function that carries with it added responsibility and/or supervisory duties

set   series of waves larger than the norm

shallow water blackout   loss of consciousness of a free diver while underwater due to lack of oxygen or an imbalance of carbon dioxide; normally occurs when a free diver attemps to stay submerged too long on a single breath of air

shelf   a rock ledge, reef, or sandbank in the sea

shoal   a submerged ridge, bank, or bar usually consisting of or covered by mud, sand, or gravel that is at or near the water surface and constitutes a danger to navigation; if composed of rock or coral, it is called a reef

shoaling effect   the alteration of a wave as it passes over a shoal

shorebreak   waves which quickly peak and break onshore to a sharply sloping beach; also known as inside break, insiders

side current   body of water traveling parallel to shore, generated by wave action, wind, or tide; also known as drag, parallel drag, feeder, trough, lateral drift, long shore current

skeg   the fin on the bottom of a surfboard or bodyboard which helps provide stability in the water; a timber that connects the keel and sternpost of a ship; also known as a keel

skim board   a flat, thin board, usually round, ridden after being thrown into very shallow water over a flat sand beach

skin diver see free diver

slack water the interval when the speed of the tidal current is very weak or zero; usually refers to the period of reversal between ebb and flood currents; also known as slack tide

slider wave breaking with its white water sliding in an even motion down its face; also known as a feathering wave

slough a marshy or reedy pool, pond, inlet, backwater, etc.

small craft warning storm signal warning pleasure craft vessels of dangerous water surface conditions caused by strong wind

snorkel a J-shaped tube held in the mouth and used in conjunction with a mask that permits breathing when a person's face is just at water level or just under the surface

snub to quickly secure a rope by wrapping it around a cleat, post, etc.; also known as make fast, secure

solar tide the tide caused solely by the tide-producing forces of the sun

sounding the measurement of the depth of water beneath a ship

spilling wave wave breaking gradually over a considerable distance; also known as a slider

spineboard a rigid board used to immobilize and transport victims suspected of having suffered spinal injury; also known as a backboard

stand-by a state of readiness during which a lifeguard prepares for an imminent emergency response; a stand-by may proceed to an emergency response or be canceled if the emergency is resolved

starboard side of vessel to the right when standing on the vessel and facing the bow

stern the rear end of a vessel; also known as the transom, aft

Stokes Basket® a contour stretcher constructed of tubular frame woven with wire mesh; also known as a litter, litter basket, Stokes stretcher

storm surge increased water level due to storm activity and resultant surf

stretcher portable platform or body contour platform used to transport any injured or deceased person in a lying position; also known as a gurney, litter

surf (n) breaking waves; (v) to be propelled or gain momentum using the forward motion of a swell or wave with or without the aid of a floating device; to board surf; to body surf

surface dive the act of submerging underwater in a forward motion, usually a forward rolling motion

surface wave a wave on the surface of the water; most often formed by wind, but may be formed by seismic activity or the gravitational pull of the moon and sun

surfboard   any rigid, inflexible device upon which, or with the use or aid which a person can ride waves, or be carried along or propelled by the action of waves; also known as a board, stick

surfing   riding or being propelled by the action of a wave with the aid of a surfboard; also known as board surfing, surfboarding

surfing area   area open to surfboarding only, no swimming unless incidental to surfboarding

surfline   the offshore point along a beach where waves are breaking at a given time, bordered on the outside by the most offshore break and on the inside by the most shoreward break; the distance of the surfline from shore varies with the size of the waves since larger waves break farther offshore than smaller waves

surf zone   area between the furthest outside waves that are just beginning to break and the edge of the water on the beach

surf's down   waves breaking smaller than normal; no surf at all

surf's up   waves breaking larger than normal

surge   a swelling or sweeping rush of water, a violent rising and falling of water

swell   a surface wave in open water before it strikes a beach

swim fins   flat, webbed rubber footwear used by swimmers to increase the power and speed of their kick by artificially enlarging the surface area of the feet; also known as fins, flippers

swimming area   water area open to swimming only

tertiary zone   area of responsibility checked by a lifeguard in less frequent pattern than primary and secondary zones

tether   a short line used to secure a surfboard, belly board or similar floatation device to the user; also known as a leash, surf leash

thermocline   a layer of water in a lake or similar body of water that is of distinctly different temperature than the layer above or below; most often used to refer to a sudden and dramatic lowering in temperature when descending in a lake; most likely in still water, since current tends to adversely affect formation

three points of a rescue   the three components of every water rescue as identified by USLA: (1) recognize and respond; (2) contact and control; and (3) signal and save

thwart   a seat that runs across the beam of a boat or vessel

tide   alternating horizontal movement of water associated with the rise and fall of the tide caused by the astronomical tide producing forces; tidal current

tidal delta   sand bars or shoals formed in the entrance of inlets by reversing tidal currents

tidal flat a marsh or sandy or muddy coastal flatland covered and uncovered by the rise and fall of the tide; a mud flat

tidal wave a very large wave caused by an underwater earthquake; tidal waves generally have extraordinarily long periods which make them almost invisible in the open ocean, but deadly when they arrive onshore and break; also known as a tsunami, seismic wave

tideland land that is under water at high tide and uncovered at low tide

tide mark (1) a high water mark left by tidal water; (2) the highest point reached by a high tide; (3) a visual mark indicating any specified state of tide

tide pool a pool of water remaining in the intertidal area after recession of the tide

tide race a very rapid tidal current in a narrow channel or passage

tide tables tables that give daily predictions of the times and heights of the tide

tideway a channel through which a tidal current flows

tiller bar or handle for turning a vessel's rudder

topside upon the upper deck of a vessel; also known as above deck

trainee a lifeguard in training; (USLA: A lifeguard trainee may work only under the direct and immediate supervision of an Open Water Lifeguard with 1,000 hours of experience or a Full Time Open Water Lifeguard, with a ratio of one trainee to one experienced lifeguard)

transverse bars slightly submerged sand ridges that extend at right angles to the shoreline

treading water maintaining a stationary position on the surface of the water by using the legs and arms

trough parallel inshore channel in the ocean floor running a few to many yards in length, which may help to foster development of a rip current; also known as a hole, feeder, trench, drop-off, channel

tsunami see tidal wave

two-feeder rip rip current generated by two currents which merge, feeding the neck of the rip current

undertow a misnomer which suggests a current pattern (not known to exist) that drags a person under the water; this word is not used by knowledgeable lifeguards except to correct others; usage note: this term may have been coined to refer to a combination of phenomena involving a person being knocked down by a wave, pulled offshore by a backrush or rip current, and submerged due to lack of swimming ability

underway vessel in motion

uplifted reef a coral reef exposed above the water

up rush the rush of water up onto the beach following the breaking of a wave

up-welling bottom water reaching the surface because of disturbance caused by swells, waves, or current

victim any person who is imperiled or injured and (usually) requires the assistance of a lifeguard; a person caught in a rip current is considered to be a victim; depending on circumstances, a victim may also be known as a casualty, accident victim, or patient

wake path of disturbed water left behind a moving vessel or moving object in water

warning verbal contact by voice or electronic equipment explaining an existing danger

water ability personal performance and endurance in all types of water conditions, such as surfing, diving, swimming, paddling, etc.

waterspout a tornado occurring over water

wave a ridge or swell, representing a force of energy, moving through water; surface waves are most often caused by wind on the water

wave crest the highest part of a wave

wave generation the creation of waves by natural or mechanical means

wave train a continual series of water waves moving in the same direction and generated by the same source

wave trough the lowest part of a wave; the area between two ocean swells

weight belt belt containing varying weights worn by a diver to compensate for surface buoyancy

wetsuit foam neoprene rubber suit that fits snugly to the body and helps insulate a swimmer, surfer, or diver from cold water

white cap wind-blown surface chop that has white froth or foam appearance

whitewater in the surf zone, water that is mixed with air causing it to turn white; also known as soup, surge, slop, fizz, foam

wind-driven current current fed by wind

wind-mixing mechanical stirring of water due to motion induced by the surface wind

windward the direction from which the wind is blowing

wind wave a wave formed by wind

INDEX